A Shri___

*Learn_*

to Whistle

To Jesus,

with best wishes

Sarah Hurst

Sarah Hurst

Elephant Publishing

33 Elvendon Road, Goring-on-Thames, Near Reading, RG8 ODP
Tel/fax: (01491) 873227   e-mail: rivervalley@easynet.co.uk

First published in 1997

Some of the interviews in this book first appeared in *The St Petersburg Press* between 1995 and 1996.

ISBN 0 9530172 0 6

Elephant Publishing
33 Elvendon Road
Goring-on-Thames
Reading
RG8 0DP
ENGLAND
Tel: 01491 873227

Typeset by Elephant Publishing
Printed in England by Antony Rowe Ltd, Chippenham

To the people who inspired, encouraged, financed,
fed, nurtured, loved, chauffeured,
housed, educated and created me...

...Mum and Dad

CONTENTS

Introduction

St Petersburg sunbathers stand on a city-centre beach, their pale flesh a shiver away from the wall which surrounds the Peter-and-Paul Fortress. The Neva river is still frozen solid and mist rises eerily over the Winter Palace on the opposite embankment. Getting a tan is a struggle in these conditions. In Russia the whole of life is a struggle, as people there will remind you at every opportunity.

'I'm going to die soon,' my 30-year-old landlady informed me, flinging hundred dollar bills out of her handbag in a desperate search for the doorkey. 'Our life is so hard. I can't understand why you came here. You foreigners are so naive. It's so stressful, all I want is to go to Australia.'

The landlady, Lena, had been poor and miserable under communism and had become rich and miserable under capitalism. Her permanent condition of gloom and despair blew away shards of good news as carelessly as she lost her US currency and exaggerated every misfortune to the point of an impending apocalypse. If a young, single, wealthy businesswoman has that many problems, I thought, what hope is there for the average Olga or Alexander on the street? All Russians are having trouble adjusting to their titanic change in circumstances; the burden of deep pessimism which so many of them carry around doesn't make things any easier.

Up until August 1991 the Struggle had not only a capital letter, but also a purpose: Soviet citizens were building their bright socialist future. Then, overnight, the country which is geographically the largest in the world had democracy and freedom thrust upon it. 'They gave me freedom yesterday, what am I going to do with it?' the poet Vladimir Vysotsky asked more than two decades ago, dying of drink long before his less contemplative compatriots began to pose themselves the same question.

In the Soviet Union the state guaranteed a salary or a student grant or a pension and the state made sure people could get life's basic necessities - slowly. Independent thinking was not a

1

prerequisite of existence, and indeed those who attempted to practise it as a regular pastime found it a distinct hindrance.

Now that decadent Western capitalism has hit Russia in the form of Blue Pepsi, Snickers bars and Wrigley's Spearmint (sugar-free!), it can be a struggle just to pronounce the foreign brand names and make a realistic guess at what exactly lies within the attractive but enigmatic packaging. For those who are old enough to have survived mass terror and a war in which 27 million Soviet citizens died, who are used to being told nothing and are afraid to ask, this is an unexpected and meaningless struggle which makes the last years of life almost as frightening as the early years when Stalin and Hitler were around.

A joke I heard expresses this problem succinctly. A babushka (an old woman) comes to buy something at a typical street kiosk where a range of imported goods are on display behind glass. She inspects them curiously for a few moments and then says to the vendor, 'I'll have Snickers, please.'

'Sorry, there aren't any left,' replies the vendor.

'Oh dear,' says the babushka. 'Well, in that case, I'll have Tampax.'

Of course, getting the names right isn't as important as getting enough money together to buy one of these delicacies. That really is a struggle in the new, every-man-for-himself Russia, for pensioners who can hardly afford bread and for university lecturers, doctors and newspaper editors who save a few thousand roubles by persuading a friendly student to buy them a reduced-price pass for public transport.

Even if it were possible to achieve the 'transition to a market economy' from a disastrously stagnating centrally planned system painlessly and swiftly, there would have been a fair share of psychological trauma. 150 million people were told to discard all the values they had been indoctrinated with since birth and embrace the philosophy of their mortal enemy. There is no reason to think this was any easier for President Boris Yeltsin, aged 60 in 1991, than for the rest of the country.

In his autobiography, *Against the Grain*, Yeltsin emphasised the rebellious aspects of his character, proudly recounting the story of how he narrowly evaded being expelled from school by arguing his case at a tribunal. But Yeltsin was no dissident: he went on to become a career politician, forging his way up the ranks of the Communist Party during the Brezhnev era. In 1976 he was named Communist Party first secretary of his home town of Sverdlovsk (now Ekaterinburg) in the Urals. For nine years his orders were obeyed without question. 'Everything that one did was expressed in terms of pressure, threats, and coercion,' he later recalled. Yeltsin's services were rewarded in 1985, when the new Soviet general secretary appointed him Moscow Party boss.

In the 1991 coup the image of Yeltsin standing on a tank outside the Moscow White House fixed itself in the minds of Western observers, establishing him as a steely fighter against communism. In fact the newly-elected President of the Russian Soviet Federated Socialist Republic was saving his own skin. Why he wasn't arrested immediately by the coup leaders is a mystery to this day. Possibly they hoped he would take their side; or perhaps they were simply too busy dealing with an unexpectedly defiant Gorbachev. Whatever the reason, Yeltsin was free to act - he could even send out messages to the Western press unhindered - but he had to act quickly. He knew that if the coup succeeded he would either follow Gorbachev to the firing squad, or perhaps just live out the rest of his natural life as an exile in Irkutsk, so when he stood on the tank he had nothing to lose and everything to gain.

Once his victory had been secured, Yeltsin accumulated more and more power in his own hands. And why not? For centuries Russia had known only autocracy and dictatorship. Throughout history it was brute force which dragged most of the population away from the vodka bottle for a few hours in the day so that some kind of vaguely purposeful activity could take place. Subservience was consistently rewarded and individual initiative was crushed. So it was by force that Yeltsin resolved his dispute in October 1993 with the Communist-dominated parliament and by force that he attempted to subdue the unhappy republic of Chechnya.

Yeltsin gave himself more power than Tsar Nicholas II ever had, and the latter, by the way, was overthrown by revolutionaries who considered him too despotic. The success of Vladimir Zhirinovsky's ultranationalists and Gennady Zyuganov's

Communists in the parliamentary elections of 1993 and 1995 had no serious impact on the business of government because the Russian president could personally appoint ministers and was authorised to make laws by decree, bypassing the Duma (parliament) altogether. This according to the new constitution proposed by Yeltsin and approved by the people in a 1993 referendum.

Democracy by decree sounds like a contradiction in terms. It is. A measure of authoritarianism to keep extremist political groups at bay might be justifiable, but Yeltsin's decrees also plunged Russia into a catastrophic civil war. Russian soldiers were sent to kill Chechen soldiers and civilians (tens of thousands of whom conveniently all turned out to be 'armed bandit groups'), with the aim of persuading those same murderous Chechens to joyfully re-integrate into the Russian Federation and live in peace happily ever after.

The war cost untold billions of roubles, draining the coffers of every government department. Health, education, housing, public transport, state-owned industry, social security - penniless. Meanwhile a handful of people had become dollar millionaires importing consumer goods and exporting raw materials or setting up pyramid share schemes, and these so-called New Russians made everyone else feel more sorry for themselves by shamelessly flaunting their BMWs and cellular telephones.

New Russians are probably just as confused as old Russians by the pace of events, but it's hard to sympathise with them as much. Confusion is the single noun which sums up the situation in Russia today and the state of mind of the Russian people. Other books on current affairs set out to offer explanations, to find rationality and logic, to analyse and predict. I subscribe to the cock-up theory of history - I think that mistakes and accidents have more of an influence on events than cunning and planning. If you want to know what's going on in Russia and why, read no further, because I'm as clueless as you are. In the seven years I have been visiting Russia I have found only one truth about the country: it can't be tamed.

Nostalgia: How Russians see their Past

There was one phrase that tended to crop up in conversation with Russians more often as the Soviet Union receded into the past - 'It was better before.' *It,* meaning life, *before,* meaning before the collapse of communism. This is not a phrase used by grizzled old Party members. They expressed their opinions rather more directly, composing catchy slogans for the 1990s such as, 'Remember, blackguard, Stalingrad', 'Down with Yeltsin and his mafia who have robbed and sold Russia, making the labouring people beggars' (on placards at a pro-Communist demonstration), or simply made loud toasts to their great commander-in-chief, Joseph Vissarionovich Stalin, as four veterans did in a café I was in on Victory Day, 1996.

These lifelong Communists were some of the most enthusiastic political activists in Russian society. The people who sat at home moaning, 'it was better before', and 'there's no point voting, it doesn't make any difference', were usually aged between 18 and 25. Stalin had been mouldering in the grave for a long time before they were born; they were too young to serve in Afghanistan but reached conscription age just in time to be landed with the democrats' war in Chechnya.

For this generation the worst memories they had of communism were ignorant teachers who offered a reward for any pupil who persuaded their parents not to paint an Easter egg, as a postgraduate friend of mine recounted. She and her classmates were brought up to think that their future consisted of free higher education, guaranteed employment and a financially secure retirement. Then, suddenly, the state withdrew its hard line on Easter egg-painting, but such abstract freedoms came at the price of all those rather attractive material benefits.

Russian students looked to the past because the present didn't give them any opportunity to flourish. If their family lived in a big city with a university or institute, they usually studied there and stayed at home with their parents. Students who went somewhere far from home lived in hostels which made British halls of residence look like the Hilton. Four people of the same sex may have been assigned to a room with two single beds in it for the duration of their course. If a fifth person was sent along then the room really was overcrowded and he might have had to get hold of an old door to sleep on.

In some hostels every two rooms had their own kitchen space; in others, like the one where I lived in Minsk,[1] there was one kitchen with several cookers for the whole corridor to share. I had a large number of rich Jordanian and Syrian neighbours who insisted on eating in the style to which they were accustomed at home. I had an unnerving experience one day when some of them slaughtered a sheep and left the skin and bloody neck draped over the hob.

There wasn't much in the way of nightlife for students. They didn't have money to spend in bars or restaurants, and although tickets to the Minsk Theatre of Opera and Ballet cost about the same as a loaf of bread when I was there in 1994, there was a psychological limit to the number of operas and ballets you could sit through in a week, especially when the ballets were accompanied by a record player instead of an orchestra and the operas were sung half in Belorussian and half in Italian. Two other English students bought tickets in advance for every performance of their three-month stay, loyally attending *Tosca, La Traviata* and *Swan Lake* twice and even three times, while the rest of the hostel indulged in the marginally less masochistic pursuit of sitting in their rooms drinking.

A popular activity which temporarily relieved boredom amongst Russian students was to get married and have a child (most found that one was enough). Some felt pressured to get married young because their parents did it; others discovered they were about to have a child and got married on its behalf. A few years later the boredom returned and parents whose student life was anything but wild made up for it by divorcing or having affairs - I'll delve into that more deeply in the next chapter.

I found that the social life of students in St Petersburg in 1996 wasn't much of an improvement on Minsk two years earlier. The population of Minsk was 1.5 million and the population of St

---

[1] Minsk is the capital of Belarus, which I have included in this book because it is virtually indistinguishable from a Russian province. There are no customs controls between the two countries.

6

Petersburg was 5 million, so I expected the city which is supposed to be the most liberal and enlightened in the former Soviet Union to be considerably livelier.

One of the first friends I made in St Petersburg that year was 20-year-old Rozanna, who was studying in two institutes simultaneously and working part-time as a journalist at the local radio station, earning £1.50 for a 2-minute report - enough for 20 journeys on public transport. She lived with her parents and sister in a two-bedroom flat with no telephone. One of the pieces she did for radio was about a student café with live music, and she invited me to go there with her.

From everything I'd read and heard about the Soviet Union I felt instantly that I'd stepped into a time warp. The café was an immense hall in an institute of design, full of tables and chairs (almost every one of which was taken), with a stage at the far end. The young women were in their smartest dresses, faces painted like matryoshka dolls, and the men were in dark trousers with waistcoats or dinner jackets, with neatly-trimmed moustaches, slicked-back hair or both.

The compère on the stage was a balding man in his mid-fifties who had let his moustache grow a little out of control, probably in compensation. I recognised his type because he looked exactly like the man who was the compère at the St Petersburg Jazz Philharmonic Hall. I was with a group of seven people when I went to listen to the jazz and the compère insisted that only six people could sit around one table and that the seventh had to sit on their own. We had borrowed a chair from another table, as there were plenty of spare ones, and when we refused to give it back, the compère tried to drag it physically out from under the person who was sitting on it. That's why I had bad vibes when I saw the man on the stage of the café, and my instinct was spot on.

This latest incarnation of a Stalinist entertainer would certainly have enjoyed making a gruff-voiced demand for absolute silence, but the students didn't give him that pleasure because they already were absolutely silent. So he moved right on to the business of the evening, announcing the first act: himself playing the acoustic guitar and singing melancholic Russian pop songs of the 1970s.

Rozanna and I thought we'd sample the café cuisine. There was no food. Incredibly, there was no alcohol. Here were 300 students having a night on the town, and they were all drinking tea. That was the only substance on offer for consumption, and from the general demeanour of the clientele I deduced that no one had yet overdosed on the caffeine. When I rowdily asked Rozanna a question, students on all the surrounding tables turned round and glared at me with fingers to their lips.

Surveying our quiet companions, it soon became evident that a large percentage of them had brought acoustic guitars. An ominous shadow began to creep over my vision of the immediate future. Rozanna had to interview the compère, and he had told her that he couldn't speak until the end of the evening. It wasn't even possible to nip in and out, because the doors were bolted shut and guarded by fiercely dedicated bouncers with neatly-trimmed moustaches who reluctantly unbolted the doors only under duress in the 30-second breaks between songs.

As the students queued up to emulate their host's talent at playing the guitar and singing hits which were old before the artistes were born, I resigned myself to my suffering - a very Russian thing to do. We were trapped in St Petersburg's answer to the Eurovision Song Contest for four hours and there was no alternative but to lean back and think of Cliff Richard.

The Russian psyche is beautifully described in a variation of a joke about an Englishman, a Scotsman and an Irishman on a desert island. In the original they find a bottle, rub it, and a genie pops out. It grants them three wishes. The Englishman and the Scotsman ask for a huge mansion, the sexiest woman in the world, and instant transportation off the island. The Irishman asks for a bottle of whisky that eternally refills itself. When he's taken a few swigs and found that it works, he is so delighted that he asks for two more.

In the variation, an Englishman, a Scotsman and a Russian are stranded on a desert island. The Englishman and the Scotsman ask for the same things as in the previous joke. The Russian asks for a bottle of vodka that eternally refills itself, a similarly endless supply of sausages, and for his third wish he says - 'Bring the other two guys back!'

You recognise the truth of that story if you've spent long Russian nights sitting at the kitchen table with two drinking companions, a few bottles of vodka and a string of sausages. Those marathon sessions used to be the staple diet of Russian social life, lasting until at least 5.30 am, when the first metro trains start running and guests can stagger home. Sleep wasn't usually an option, as in most flats there was barely room for the occupants to sleep, let alone their friends.

Since the dawn of the market economy the tradition had become more scarce, I suspect because it was no longer acceptable to turn up to work with the mental alertness of a zombie. I have sat at kitchen tables enough times, though, to know my fair share of rambling Russian toasts and anecdotes with mystifyingly abrupt punchlines. As is natural in the wee small hours under the influence of throat-shaving spirits, people reminisce about their younger days, liberally coating every tale in black or white paint.

The nostalgia which some of my hosts wallowed in didn't convince me. Even my fleeting glimpse of the Soviet Union, a five-day Intourist trip to Moscow and Leningrad in 1990 with a group from college, left me with a few unshakeable memories. The empire was cracking up. In January at least 100 anti-Communist demonstrators in Baku had been killed by Soviet troops. Two months later Mikhail Gorbachev chose to have himself elected President of the USSR by the Supreme Soviet, rather than face a popular vote. Meanwhile, Lithuania declared itself independent and Gorbachev imposed an economic blockade on the republic. This was the background when our group arrived in April, five years after the most radical reforms in Soviet history had begun.

On arrival at our Moscow hotel we were treated to a slap-up dinner of shrivelled cucumber and cold sliced tongue. This was followed by our first participatory experience of glasnost, a chance to take a democratic vote on whether to have tea or coffee. When the group had chosen, we exercised our rights yet again by voting on whether or not to have sugar. For some reason milk went into the pot automatically, presumably in deference to our country of origin, as Russians drink their tea and coffee black.

On the bedroom wall there was a gigantic radio with no buttons, just a dial for adjusting the volume. I fiddled with it for a while but no sound came out at all, so I assumed the radio was broken. It was already dark when we landed in Moscow and I fell asleep wondering what my first impression of the Soviet Union outside the hotel restaurant would be. The Red Army parading past Lenin's Tomb? A herd of downtrodden proletarians looking lustfully at our jeans? Gorbachev on a spontaneous walkabout outside McDonalds? No. In fact it was the Soviet national anthem blasting through my skull.

I flung the bedclothes off and scrambled to the window, imagining a military band was out there giving the country's newest foreign visitors an official pre-dawn welcome. These communists really are sticklers for discipline, I thought, before my room-mate turned off the radio. It had been on all the time, but the only station it received was national state radio, which stopped broadcasting for a few hours every night and returned to the airwaves with a patriotic fanfare.

Concerning radio I can say categorically that things improved in the post-Soviet years. It used to be illegal to listen to the Beatles. Lola, a journalist in her mid-forties from St Petersburg, said that when she was at school someone in her class brought a Beatles record in and wanted his friends to hear it, but she and the others ran out of the room in fright because they'd been told the Beatles were subversive. Western pop and jazz records were themselves hard to come by. Fans made illicit copies on old X-rays, so you could watch a real pelvis gyrate as you listened to Elvis.

In the nineties there were a host of new stations which played an awful lot of those Beatles numbers that Russians missed out on in the sixties. Personally, I wasn't too bothered that rave and techno hadn't quite taken off yet. In St Petersburg I was happy choosing between Radio Baltika, Radio Modern, Radio Roks, Radio Rekord, Radio Rossii Nostalgie, Europa Plus and Eldoradio. The latter was owned by an American billionaire and had an interactive studio in a hamburger restaurant where diners could select a track by touching a computer screen.

On top of a stately building on Nevsky Prospekt, overlooking the beautiful Anichkov Bridge with its rearing copper horses, RADIO MODERN was spelt out in giant letters.

'That used to say, THE COMMUNIST PARTY IS THE DRIVING FORCE OF THE COUNTRY,' a Russian friend said to me. 'It's the same thing, isn't it? It's all propaganda.'

'In a way,' I agreed. 'But you've got a choice of radio stations. You didn't have a choice of parties.'

The range of newspapers was also fairly limited in Soviet times. The official organ of the driving force of the country was *Pravda*, and on my 1990 trip I arranged an interview with the newspaper's chief editor in his office, assisted by two interpreters called Sasha. The editor, Ivan Frolov, was an academic personally appointed to the post by Gorbachev in 1989. He boasted about *Pravda*'s new openness, showing me letters he had published which criticised the government, so I couldn't resist the temptation to ask him about the fleet of black Volgas parked outside the building. They took up one side of an entire street (Pravda Street) and were more than a touch classier than the muddy Ladas driven by those citizens who could afford a car at all.

The two Sashas cut in before Frolov could answer. 'You should be glad of these 'privileged cars',' one of them said. 'We will be using one to take you back to your hotel in just a few minutes.' Thus Frolov was able to duck the question, steering the conversation to Yeltsin's big car which he was apparently using even though he'd sworn to spurn Party perks. To his credit he ignored the two Sashas and let me stay for another 90 minutes, presenting me with a choice of autographed photos at the end of the interview - 'Do you want serious, happy, suave...?'

Frolov was keen to emphasise that the Soviet Union was undergoing 'a renaissance of humanistic ideals.' When the two Sashas showed me their office downstairs, I saw that these new ideals had not yet been joined by new equipment. Their desks were strangely empty.

'Don't you have computers?' I asked. The Sashas laughed. 'Typewriters?'

'No,' one of the Sashas replied. 'At *Pravda* we work the old-fashioned way - with pen and paper.'

One material blessing Muscovites did have in 1990 was an outdoor swimming pool. Our guide stopped the tour bus for just long enough to tell us that it was once a cathedral, and then we drove on. If I'm ever in that vicinity again I'll take pleasure in explaining to bemused tourists that the city's newest cathedral was once an outdoor swimming pool, and before that it was a cathedral. Never mind that people who remember the original cathedral say it was an eyesore. After communism, Mayor Yuri Luzhkov of Moscow ordered the new one to be rebuilt in the exact image of the old one, at a cost to the state of £219 million, evidently reckoning that it was more important for Russians to cleanse their souls than their bodies.

Resurrecting a cathedral was part of a mania for restoring pre-Bolshevik glory, obliterating names given during the Soviet era regardless of aesthetics or ideology. It was logical to replace Communist-inspired city names such as Leningrad, Gorky, Frunze and Ordzhonikidze, but 19th-century poet Pushkin and 18th-century scientist Lomonosov were also dropped in favour of the previous names Tsarskoye Selo (The Tsar's Village) and Oranienbaum. At the same time thousands of stone Lenins still pointed the way to the bus stop in provincial town squares, although the pigeon droppings weren't scrubbed from their caps as often as they used to be.

The founder of the secret police organisation which became the KGB, Felix Dzherzhinsky, was hoisted from his podium outside the Lubyanka prison in Moscow as soon as the democrats had triumphed in August 1991. Dzherzhinsky was described by a contemporary as a grey kind of chap who spent his days sipping cups of tea and signing death warrants. I thought his bust in Minsk was being taken down when it was cordoned off by the city council in 1994, but as it happened they were giving him another coat of grey paint. He's also on display half a kilometre from the St Petersburg Mayor's Office.

Real live Stalinists are thin on the ground nowadays, or at least don't admit their allegiances. Someone who once called Uncle Joe his 'beloved teacher and leader' was 83-year-old Mikhail Botvinnik, whom I interviewed in 1994, a few months before his death. Botvinnik's ability to stare expressionlessly through his thick glasses for hours on end destroyed his opponents psychologically and helped him keep hold of the world chess title for thirteen years. 'I am a true communist,' he told me. 'Stalin was not a true communist, he was a poor, uneducated person who could only come to power through revolution. I am a communist in the tradition of the first communist on earth, Jesus Christ. I am also an atheist, my parents were atheist. I am Jewish by race but Russian by culture.'

The status of Jews in the Soviet Union was always ambiguous. On their passports their nationality was listed as 'Jewish', so they were made to feel separate. An Autonomous Region was created for them, but few people wanted to uproot themselves and travel thousands of miles to live there. Thousands who wanted to emigrate to Israel were denied permission and called themselves refuseniks. But the rest of the Soviet population had no alternative country to welcome them, and they weren't allowed out either. Soviet Jews were extremely successful in academia, the professions, and the arts. Because of this the number of Jewish university entrants was restricted to give priority to other nationalities, such as Central Asians. This was a controversial policy, but not necessarily a malicious one. The issue of quotas for women and ethnic minorities is still hotly debated in the West today.

Botvinnik said there were only a few instances in his life when he was insulted because of his race. 'The first time I felt anti-Semitism was at school. I liked the sister of my friend a lot, but he came up to me and said, 'Misha, she won't kiss you.'

'Why not?' I asked him.

'Because you're a Jew.' Later I knew that anti-Semitism was around, but people weren't outwardly chauvinistic towards me, they were afraid to say anything because of who I was. Such people are idiots, and you should feel sorry for idiots. Anti-Semitism never had a serious effect on me and my work.'

Benjamin Yakubovsky was another Russian Jew who was born about a year after Botvinnik. He ran the Intourist bureau of Leningrad's prestigious Astoria Hotel immediately before and after World War II. He believes that opportunities for promotion were limited because he was Jewish and said, 'the Bolsheviks are the most evil people in the world.'

Nevertheless, Yakubovsky was given a rare freedom to travel and make money during the Soviet Union's darkest hours. He was the only Russian to serve in the war on a British Arctic convoy, interpreting signals from Soviet vessels for the captain of his ship, HMS *Britomart*. After the war he was sent to Allied-occupied Hamburg to interpret at the conference which divided up the German fleet amongst the victorious powers - he witnessed the names of ships being drawn out of a hat. Yakubovsky's unusually high Soviet salary earned him a reprimand from an officer who said his habit of giving a waiter large tips was embarrassing the less wealthy British.

In the late 1940s Yakubovsky was offered a job in the far east of Russia, on the island of Sakhalin, organising a ferry company to repatriate Japanese prisoners-of-war. He returned to Leningrad in 1955 having missed Stalin's last round of purges and earned what he called 'an enormous sum of money' which enabled him to build the rickety wooden house where I visited him, in the countryside near St Petersburg. Recently he had been writing his memoirs and teaching English. Every day at noon he had his 'admiral's hour', downing a glass of vodka, or, if he could get hold of it, the Jamaica rum which he developed a taste for on the *Britomart*. 'It might sound strange, but the war was the best time of my life,' he told me.

When the Soviet Union existed its nationalities were seen from outside as a homogenous mass, the country was often referred to simply as 'Russia', and because Soviet Jews were the most vocal and politicised ethnic group, their plight received the most international attention. Jews certainly did suffer discrimination, but since 1991 it has become obvious that other nationalities are also the target of hostility and violence.

Lola, the journalist who ran away from the Beatles, had typically Central Asian broad cheekbones and slanting eyes because her mother was a Tatar. She had never lived in Tatarstan - which in any case is part of the Russian Federation - she was brought up in Kazakhstan and moved to Moscow to go to university. After communism she worked in St Petersburg and said she'd never leave because it was the only place in Russia where she wasn't asked by nosy passers-by, 'What nationality are you?'

'I live in Russia and I speak Russian, but I don't look Russian, so I will always arouse suspicion,' Lola told me. 'In St Petersburg the problem isn't ordinary people, it's the OMON [special interior ministry police force created by Yeltsin's government]. I used to stand in a very long queue at one particular kiosk which sold excellent fresh bread. One day I had waited for ages and was the next in line to be served, when an OMON man told me to leave the queue to show him my passport. I missed my turn and I don't go to that kiosk any more.'

The police routinely arrested people if they couldn't provide documentary evidence of their address. Lola said she was lucky to have a press card which got her off the hook instantly. She had a friend with Asian features who couldn't even drive in St Petersburg because he was stopped so frequently by the traffic police. Those who had the most trouble were people from the Caucasus republics, recognisable by their darker skin and known derogatorily as 'blacks'. Five or six years ago they were all suspected of being in mafia gangs; since the Chechen war the police thought they were all terrorists.

For Lola the Soviet Union had its advantages. When her parents moved from Russia to Kazakhstan they were travelling to a different region of a single country. Now they are separated from their daughter by a national border and prohibitively high train and air fares. Police harassment was a problem in the 1970s, when Lola was a student, but everyone was subject to it equally.

Soviet leader Leonid Brezhnev (who continued to make public appearances after his doctors had secretly declared him brain-dead) once had the bright idea of 'instilling discipline during the working day'. He sent the police into shops to find out who was truanting when they were supposed to be toiling on the production line or behind a desk. Lola was caught in a raid: the doors of the shop were locked and those who didn't have a passport with them were detained. Lola's passport was in her student hostel across the road. She wanted to go and get it but the police wouldn't let her - they drove her and the other miscreants to the other side of Moscow. There they were held in a police station which was so full of illegal shoppers that they had to sit on the floor.

Conscription of all young men into the army during peacetime was one of the methods used in the Soviet Union to wipe out undesirable manifestations of individuality. In 1988, when Gorbachev promised to reduce it by 10%, there were 5 million men in the armed forces. Like the internal passports system, conscription continued for years after Yeltsin's reformers came to power. (Desperate to restore his credibility as a liberal, Yeltsin hit on the idea of abolishing conscription a few weeks before the presidential election of June 1996.)

Alexander, a St Petersburg scientist in his late thirties, saw his army service as a challenge. His ability to laugh in the face of adversity and keenness to fling himself out of aeroplanes were the sort of qualities which made him the right person to lead a year-long expedition to the North Pole some time afterwards. These came naturally to him anyway; dishonesty was the one additional talent which he learnt in the army, Alexander told me.

'I became a great liar in the army. I had to lie to get my discharge, but I was so convincing that I almost got rid of something more than my uniform.' With a glint in his eye and a cheeky grin Alexander related the story of his struggle with Red Army bureaucracy. Just as he was due to return to civilian life, he found that an administrative mix-up had added an extra month to his period of service.

'I had a word with a friend of mine who knew something about medicine and he described the symptoms of appendicitis to me. One night in the barracks I put my plan into action, writhing around on the floor in agony, clutching my side. I was taken straight to a doctor, who did a test and said I had to have my appendix out immediately. He woke up the head surgeon, who didn't want to operate until the next morning. I had a tough few hours, expecting to be slit open for no good reason except that the consequences of admitting what I'd done would probably be worse.

'In the end I was lucky. The head surgeon did another test and decided my appendix was healthy enough to stay inside my body - and I got my discharge as well, on grounds of questionable fitness. Mental or physical, I don't know.'

So Alexander left the army unscathed. Dima, the same age as Alexander and also from St Petersburg, lost a tiny fragment of his nose during his service in the icy wastes of Lapland. I asked him what the soldiers there were supposed to be doing. 'We were guarding a supply base.' Who from, Finnish fishermen? 'I don't know, we were just told to guard it. Nothing was ever explained to us, we had our orders and that was that.'

The only real enemy on the northernmost border of the Soviet Union was the cold. Dima got his permanent reminder of Lapland, frostbite, by standing on duty outside for hours in a thin jumper. 'You weren't allowed to put another shirt or jumper on. The funny thing was, when the temperature rose from minus 30 to minus 20, you actually cheered up and began to feel warmer.'

When they could get hold of it, Dima and his comrades warded off the cold by drinking Eau de Cologne. One man was caught doing this, or committing some other minor disciplinary offence, and his punishment was an extra 40 hours in the snow. The prospect of such an ordeal was too much for him, and he shot himself. 'I've asked myself what the point of serving in the army was, and I can think of only one thing - you get to tell lots of stories about it afterwards,' said Dima, who went on to tell stories for a living as a radio journalist.

In the summer of 1995 I witnessed the unveiling of St Petersburg's monument to the Afghan war dead, a plaster sculpture of five men looking pathetically vulnerable with bare chests, their shirts draped over their shoulders. The Soviet government was ashamed of the failure in Afghanistan and never did anything to honour the soldiers it sent to fight there. Veterans had to fight again, and again, to get financial and medical help. The new monument's honesty contrasted sharply with the tasteless Soviet memorials to the glorious heroes of World War II - black, thrusting obelisks, or a muscular goddess in flowing robes pointing a sword to the heavens, or a troop of soldiers in full combat gear charging to their deaths - but this was more likely due to one particular sculptor's sensitivity than a shift in the official attitude towards war.

Earlier that year a piece of land in Moscow was levelled to make way for a park to commemorate the 50th anniversary of VE Day, or the day of victory in the Great Patriotic War, as so many Russians still referred to it. The Poklonnaya Gora park was appropriately situated at the end of a highway named after the army commander who repelled Napoleon's invasion, Kutuzov.

The park sloped upwards gradually, each level separated from the previous one by three steps. You ascended past a series of black granite plinths, one for each year of the war (from 1941). A constant stream of betrothed couples took their wedding vows in a brand new Orthodox church complete with gold cupolas and replica medieval icons. This was a development of the Soviet tradition of visiting a war memorial after the wedding ceremony: now the whole event took place at a war memorial. For me it was rather disturbing that young people who should be celebrating the present, looking forward to the future and maybe the imminent birth of new human beings went on that day to a place dedicated to the mistakes of the past and the violent deaths of millions of people.

At the top of the slope was a towering black obelisk with St George (the patron saint of Moscow) at its foot, seated on a rearing horse and somehow managing to slice the dragon like a sausage using the point of a spear. Soldiers, weapons, aeroplanes and the names of Soviet cities where battles took place were piled on top of each other in a jumbled engraving reaching to the pinnacle of the obelisk, from which the ubiquitous goddess with a laurel wreath jumped out, flanked by two angels tooting on trumpets. This monstrosity precisely emulated the style of its Stalinist predecessors and deserved to be considered seriously by God as a possible venue for the dead souls to gather on Judgement Day.

A semicircular, white building on concrete stilts formed a protective barricade behind the obelisk. It was a war museum, and only by going inside did the visitor see the first evidence that countries other than the Soviet Union fought in the war. Here, at least, some effort had been made to interpret the past more objectively. But having put the brutalities of war on display in a museum, the Russian government was simultaneously re-enacting them in Chechnya.

I had a copy of *The Moscow Times* with me as I wandered around the victory park. Its front cover was dominated by a picture of a 21-year-old veteran who had just had artificial arms fitted at the expense of a foreign journalist. Others, less lucky, sat in the tunnels of the metro showing off their stumps, waiting for donations.

Vladimir, 19, returned from Chechnya in one piece and started to work as a carpenter's apprentice in St Petersburg. I met him when he was putting up a wardrobe in Rozanna's flat. His hair was still cropped short, so recently had he been at the front. He was very shy but did say a few words about his experiences. 'We were occupying a village. Before we went to Chechnya, no one explained to us what the war was all about, we had no idea. We were friendly with some of the Chechens and exchanged cigarettes and vodka with them. Other Chechens we fought with. About one soldier each week tried to desert from our unit, but they were all caught and sentenced to five years in prison.'

The St Petersburg Afghan monument stood in a military cemetery, right in the midst of new graves, shiny marble slabs with fresh flowers on them. These were the final homes of soldiers killed in Chechnya. They too might get a memorial in a decade or so, if any space is left in the cemetery by that time. The surviving veterans of Chechnya, Afghanistan and World War II need much more than a block of carved stone, though. While they are waiting for something to alleviate their physical, psychological and financial hardship, the next war breaks out and pushes them further down the list for assistance. The story of the Russian military is stuck in a loop that no political leader has yet had the courage to cut.

I was used to people's emotions being stirred up by the various wars since 1941 - considering their devastating effect on the country, it was to be expected - but I was very surprised at how fierce the passions were in the debate about the remains of Tsar Nicholas II and his family. A commission of scientists announced in 1995 that the remains found in a shallow grave three years earlier, in a forest near the town of Ekaterinburg, were those of Nicholas II, his wife Alexandra and three of their five children. The last tsar and his family were executed in 1918 by the Bolsheviks, who doused the bodies with acid to make them unrecognisable. The remains were identified by exhaustive DNA tests and by matching the skulls with a photograph of the children taken after their heads had been shaved due to an illness. A genetic sample from Britain's Prince Philip, a relative of the Russian dynasty, was also used for comparison.

The mayor of St Petersburg, Anatoly Sobchak, said the remains should be given a ceremonial burial in the Peter-and-Paul Fortress, where the tombs of previous tsars are located. When I contacted a St Petersburg monarchist to ask for his reaction to the decision, I thought he'd be overjoyed that the imperial family was to be honoured at last. Far from it. 'My name is Nick Nick,' said the nervous little man as he greeted me in a café of his own choosing. He was in his mid-sixties, had a lean face and full grey beard distinctly reminiscent of Nicholas II's. 'Nick Nick, heh heh heh. That sounds English, doesn't it? It's short for Nicholas Nikolayevich Braun.' I offered to buy him a coffee but he wouldn't hear of it. With his impeccable manners and obvious disdain for far-flung Western notions of sexual equality, he insisted on paying and serving me himself.

The tsar was already a footnote in the communist history books when Nick Nick was born, but it was the tsar to whom he turned for comfort when he was chopping logs in a Siberian labour camp. After his release he rose through the ranks of Russian monarchists until he'd reached the lofty position of official representative in St Petersburg of the alternative commission for identifying the imperial remains. He had the documents with him to prove it, legitimised by the stately signature of Pyotr Koltynin-Vallovsky, president of the US-based commission of Russian émigrés.

Koltynin-Vallovsky had been quoted by Reuters as saying, 'The Russian specialists based their findings on biological evidence; however, this is not enough.' Nick Nick's task was to justify this bold statement to sceptical journalists. He had a detailed critique of the scientific evidence, several typed A4 pages which he could let me read but couldn't give me because he hadn't made any photocopies. The financial resources of the Russian nobility had depleted considerably since Nicholas II's reign, it seemed.

The report by the monarchists said the quantity of acid poured on the bodies after they were shot was unlikely to have left any traces at all. It accused one laboratory of confirming results from another without doing any testing and pointed out that the imperial family's medical and dental records had not been found.

This was all highly circumstantial, and I wondered what had really made Nick Nick and his colleagues so determined to do battle with the massed forces of late 20th-century science. The answer was that they believe in a myth that Nicholas II's head was taken to Moscow straight after the execution and put on display in the Kremlin.

'We are not just talking about a family, we are talking about saints,' Nick Nick told me. 'If the true remains have been found then they should be canonised. But I regret that there has been no investigation into whether the tsar's head was temporarily separated from his body.' Soon after my chat with Nick Nick, the governing synod of the Russian Orthodox Church also expressed doubts that the remains were genuine. The director of the Peter-and-Paul Fortress told me she was unsure whether the remains would ever be buried there. For the moment, rumour and religion had triumphed over rationality. The ghosts of Russia's past showed no signs of resting in peace.

Personal Lives

Close friendships can be formed extraordinarily quickly in Russia. Socialising is much more intimate than it is in Britain; it takes place in the confines of a one-bedroom flat, or a sauna, or the compartment of a train on an overnight journey. This chapter is a series of sketches of people who have shown a slice of their lives to me in a country where the word 'privacy' doesn't exist.

The lecherous policeman and his moody mother

Alexei probably wouldn't be tall enough to be a policeman in Britain, but that's what he was in Voronezh, his home town in south-western Russia. The birthplace of a couple of dead poets, Voronezh has very little in the way of fun to offer its 860,000 residents, apart from a puppet theatre and a few cinemas. Its greatest claim to fame is that Peter I chose it as the location to build the first ships of the Russian fleet. But that was a long time ago. When I was there, the council didn't even have the technology to provide running water 24 hours a day - the supply was turned off during the afternoons.

I never saw Alexei in his uniform - he usually wore jeans and a denim jacket with the words 'US Army' sewn over the breast pocket. At the age of 29 his sleek, black hair was receding from his shiny forehead, his moustache was in full bloom and he chain-smoked. He and his mother, Svetlana, were earning some extra money by giving room and board to myself and another student in 1992.

Vitaly, Svetlana's second husband, was so meek that the family's pet dog had more influence in the household. It was certainly given a bigger share of the food. The image of Vitaly that has stuck with me is him cringing as Svetlana threw a glass of water at him during one of her frequent temper tantrums. Alexei and Svetlana had one major hereditary characteristic: their personalities drove people as far away as possible. Svetlana's first husband had gone to live in Siberia and Alexei's wife was somewhere in Azerbaijan with their son, or 'the grandson', as Svetlana lovingly referred to him. She hadn't seen the grandson for 18 months, but she was convinced that her daughter-in-law would bring him back in the next few days. She put the jar of marmalade and box of chocolates I'd brought her from England in the fridge and didn't touch them for the entire month I stayed with her, as she was saving them for the grandson. The chocolates were turning white when I left and the grandson was still mysteriously absent.

In the evenings after dinner Svetlana sat with me and the other student and reminded us with an angelic smile that we knew nothing about England and nothing about Russia. Her knowledge of England came from Jerome K Jerome's novel, *Three Men in a Boat*, which was written in 1889 and was required reading for Soviet schoolchildren. Anything we said that contradicted her idyllic portrait of upper-class country life she sternly rebuffed.

One way of keeping Svetlana in a good mood was to admire her soap collection. She had a modest number of bars with drab wrappers and obscure East European brand names, and I was right in thinking that one of my bright green bars of Palmolive would cheer her up. She went into raptures when she saw it, fingering it, kissing it, sniffing it, stroking it, and rewarding me with an exclusive viewing of her newly-purchased lipsticks.

Svetlana was a presenter at the local television station. The one thing that excited her more than soap was the video she'd made of her interview with Emma, a Cambridge University student who'd stayed with her the year before. Svetlana made it abundantly clear to us that we were inferior to Emma in every way. Our worst fault was that we couldn't speak Russian (we'd been learning for nine months) - Emma spoke perfect Russian. Emma went to Cambridge; why didn't we go to Cambridge? Emma wrote long letters to Svetlana; would we be as considerate when we were back in England? In the interview Emma said how wonderful it was to be in Voronezh and how wonderful it was to be living with Svetlana. She sounded spookily like one of the hostages used as a human shield by Saddam Hussein during the Gulf War.

On television Svetlana's long hair was piled into a neat bun, her face was made-up to look vaguely feminine, and she wore an attractive blouse and skirt. Her viewers could relax in blissful ignorance of what Svetlana was like at home in the mornings on a bad day. She was a witch. We discovered her true nature when we

24

decided to have a lie-in instead of going on our group's designated excursion to a stud farm.

At about 8 am Svetlana stood outside our room in tight, black leather trousers with her arms folded and hair spiking out aggressively in all directions. She was waiting for us to get up. She didn't wake us, she just waited there until we opened our eyes, sensing her domineering presence. She said she'd made our breakfast and wouldn't go to work until we'd eaten it and left for the stud farm.

On a good day, Svetlana would fry us pieces of meat for breakfast, seasoned with strands of her hair which fell into the pan. This was a bad day, so she served us green pieces of rock. I mean rock in the geological sense, not the confectionery. We chomped agonisingly through the breakfast under her steely gaze, listening to her extol the virtues of sitting on a bus for two hours in the pouring rain, getting out in a muddy field, watching some horses humping and then sitting on the bus for another two hours. By the end of her tirade even she was unconvinced and she stomped off to the television station. We went back to bed.

Svetlana always assured us that Alexei was a hard worker and that they divided the domestic chores between them equally (Vitaly was never mentioned in conversation). In fact, Alexei never cooked a meal and came home early every afternoon to watch videos and drink tea. His views on men and women would have been prejudiced in Fred Flintstone's day. 'Women here have to get married before the age of 20, otherwise no one will look at them,' he told us. 'If a wife doesn't cook the dinner, then she's only good for sex, and it's easier to go out and buy sex.'

Alexei couldn't cook, but he could make cocktails. He was a dab hand at pouring vodka down the blade of a knife into a glass of orange juice so that they didn't mix. He showed us his technique one night when Svetlana and her husband were staying at their dacha (a wooden shack in the countryside where they grew vegetables). Svetlana left a big meal for us because we'd told her we wanted to have a friend round for a party. Alexei had his own ideas about how to celebrate, and thoughtfully invited two male friends.

At midnight Alexei was still on his own with three drunk girls - he rang his friends again but their parents said they weren't in. Alexei made toasts along the lines of, 'Let's suppose all the leaves on the trees are virgins, and let's drink to all the trees being bare.' We were in no condition to give him a lecture in Russian on political correctness, so we spent the night dancing with him, accompanied by his Pink Floyd and Queen videos. We fell asleep somewhere near the climax of the Ken Russell film *Whore*, also from Alexei's collection. When our guest woke up in the morning she found a red rose on her pillow.

Letters from a friend

From Voronezh I went to an international workcamp in Czechoslovakia, where I met Natasha. She added her own imaginative embellishments to Russian fairy tales, telling them in excellent English to our group as we raked and hoed in the bright sunshine. Her home city is Kaluga, about 250 km southwest of Moscow, and she was studying Hungarian and German at Moscow State University. I visited Natasha a few times in Moscow, but we really got to know each other through letters. After finishing university she was a bilingual secretary for a while, before getting a job interpreting from Russian into English for the correspondents of a Japanese newspaper.

In these excerpts from Natasha's letters I have noted which language she was writing in, English or Russian.

4.12.92

ENGLISH

...I must say that Russian is the only language I write letters/and - I hope - speak perfectly without thinking over what tence to use or to put here a coma or not. Anyway you study Russian and are going to come to Russia - so - I shall taunt you a little: my letter will be in Russian.

RUSSIAN

...We say: 'All women are stinkers, all men are dirty scum.' It isn't very joyful, but then it is a truly expressed thought. I think that you would get on very well in our company - 7 girls, all scum in the best sense of this word, all single, pretty, all terribly ironic,

26

don't have boyfriends, but on the other hand have a circle of admirers who periodically come to drink tea with us, sit with red ears, poor things, over their cups and curse themselves for always poking their noses in here, for we - 7 such nice, fine, merciless girls, train them in eloquence. I must say that very few of them stand it - they leave (after 2-3 weeks), but those who remain become our friends - there are very few of them, 5 boys in all - but then such boys!!! Proven, hardened, with such a sharpened sense of humour that it's pleasant to talk to them.

ENGLISH

...oh, dear, you can't even imagin: there is snow here from the 13th of October; three days ago it was -17 -20°C in day-time, and -25 - 27°C at night! Of course, we have already forgotten how does sun look like, and what does the word 'summer' mean! And the word 'autumn' as well. Only winter, only snow, only darkness and white bears walking along Moscow streets. In fact it's very dangerous to walk after 17 o'clock (this time it becomes dark in Moscow) - very dangerous, because of that notorious bears, which is Russia so famous for. The matter is that they are always hungry - 'cause their salary is too small - even smaller than our scholarship (our scholarship is 1400 roubles [per month], their - 1200 roubles) - now it's nothing - you know - it's only 3 kg of meat - so they're hungry and are scouring the city trying to get man's meat without payment. Of course it's marauding but it's a shame - but in our Criminal code there is no such an article about the punishment of the bears - so they are still free - what can we do? Just not to go out after 5 pm or to learn bears language and try to find the points of understanding with them - but one more foreighn language after my Hungarian, German and English it's too much!!! So I try not to go out - or to go so fastly than they prefer to give up as lost to reach me.

...In two week our session [of exams] starts. It continues one month (20/XII - 20/I) and promise to be so hard that I now - beforehand - feel a toothacke thinking about it: your Christmas, New Year, our Ortodox Christmas we're supposed to meet with books in our hands and linguistics in our heads - what a brilliant perspective!!! But you're student too - you understand me perfectly.

...I like to receive and to write letters - it's some kind of avoiding of the cruel reality, this damned snow and hungry Polar bears.

2.3.93
RUSSIAN
...not so long ago I had a proposal. But as this presented itself to me I decided: 'No!' It's certainly better to entertain oneself alone in this abnormal country. And I turned down the marriage proposal of this young man. But we meet all the same. And he brings flowers. And he invites me to drink expensive Danish liqueurs, wonderful beer, and to eat fried potatoes. And moral torments trouble me: both wanting and stinging: I sort of refused the man, but to refuse the beer!!! That is beyond my strength! And I drink the beer and pangs of conscience torment me, understanding perfectly that this gives the man hope that I'll change my final decision. And, you know, I haven't changed it. This is what I think: if I'm really getting married - it has to be for love. Or with such despair, that it's already all the same, 'either marriage, or to the grave!' It's boring to be without love but a marriage of convenience is wretched.

3.2.94 [Natasha had just returned to Moscow after living in Hungary for 3 months]
ENGLISH
...it's a very strange feeling of coming home. I'm in my room now, sitting at my table and listening to my favourite music, which - by the way - I used to miss very much in Hungary - and it seems to me that I haven't moved from this place, that it was just a dream, and I start to hate my country and to hate this horrible winter and snow. And my University. I have to pass some exams and to defend my diploma (which is not written yet, by the way). I have so many very serious things to do! But I'm absolutely out now. Out of this life. I cann't under-stand very simple, every-day things and what's the most important - I don't want to understand them. OK. I know it'll be over in several weeks, I'll get back to the norms of this life. I don't want, but I can't help this. Tomorrow I'll have my first exams already, I still cann't remember, how is the subject called. I've not seen the teacher. I know nothing. I don't care - or I

pass it or I don't. Tomorrow evening I'll go home to mark my birthday with my family. On the 7th of Febr. I'll be 22. I have no emotions on this score. I don't think it changes anything neither in this world, nor in my personal life.

What about my life in Budapest? Oh, it was great: new country, new people, everything new and exciting. I had a lover too - he is married and what's more has two small daughters but his family lives in this country so, though I feel pity about this fact, I've never met with his wife. She doesn't even know about me... She's still happy with her husband and consider him to be the [best] husband, father and a lawer [lawyer?] in the world. I can add: the best lover as well.

6.4.94
RUSSIAN
...Now I'm actively engaged in the writing of my dissertation, as the defence of it is relentlessly getting closer - the 25th of May. I'm writing it round the clock, but the end is still not in sight. I haven't yet decided whether to do a postgraduate course or not: I'm already fed up of studying, but on the other hand they give you a room in the hostel for another 3 years, which is very important, as renting a flat has become terribly expensive: from 150 dollars [£100 a month] for a one-bedroom flat without a telephone in a distant suburb, that is, 40 minutes by bus from the last metro stop, which itself is another 40 minutes from the centre. In other words, it's not practical. Well, we'll see.

1.6.94
RUSSIAN
...I finished university. Last Wednesday. It was all pleasant enough, but exhausting: they asked us a huge number of questions on topics which had nothing to do with our dissertations, everyone had to show how clever they were, as the Hungarian literature questions are a secret from the students and the lecturers at our university until they're printed, and they asked very general questions - supposedly about Hungarian literature but also about French literature, or English literature, or about anything. The questions were all phrased in a very vague manner,

but, as they say, all's well that ends well - we got an 'excellent' [the top mark] and were extremely happy.

The next day I went out to work. An ordinary secretarial post in a solid company - well, solid enough. In theory I'm supposed to be the director's personal secretary for management and sales, he's English and doesn't speak Russian but today he's in London and he isn't coming to work until tomorrow. So at the moment I just answer the telephone, send faxes and type documents. There's absolutely nothing interesting and to do this getting a university degree was completely unnecessary. But I suppose this is only the beginning and it will be interesting later. A little bit, I hope.

10.9.94
RUSSIAN
...My Canadian acquaintance has been and gone already. Or rather, I persuaded him to go. He was planning to stay in Russia and look for a job. But I said that this country is not for him - he's spent 4 months here but hasn't made any real friends or learnt the language and doesn't have any chance of getting a job. It's all an illusion. He thought that Russia is a magic country where everything is very simple, you don't have to do anything and everything will be yours. And this wouldn't be so bad if he thought that at home in America, without having seen the country. But he lived there for all that time and understood NOTHING. So why all this? He simply doesn't like Russia or Russians, and only Russians or people who really like all this can survive here. Like, probably, you. He left offended but I hope that he'll understand very soon that I was right.

8.12.96
RUSSIAN
...As I'm learning French, I'm trying to socialise with French people. You'll probably despise me for this. But they're nice, although their sense of humour doesn't always work... I'm still an admirer of the British, but the French speak French. There aren't too many French-speakers in Moscow. Generally, expatriates living in Russia have a lot in common, whether they're from Britain, Australia or France. They even hang out together. They

30

buy food in supermarkets, try to be discriminating in their choice of restaurants, and convince themselves that $30 per head for dinner isn't that expensive. Yes, it's more expensive than in Paris, but then they earn more here. Again, their company pays for a flat in the city centre, and a car, petrol, a housekeeper... No, they're nice, different to us, and don't assimilate, however long they live in Russia and however they perfect their Russian language. They can swear in Russian, use slang expressions... but to hear slang with an accent is still strange, even funny. They're always going to be different, NOT LIKE US, as we say, 'not of this world'.

The Arctic volcano

Alexander is the polar explorer mentioned in the previous chapter who lied about appendicitis to get out of the army. In 1987 he spent a year on an ice floe in the Arctic: when his group of Soviet scientists arrived, they spent three sleepless days and nights building their base camp. Strong vodka kept them going. Their supplies were dropped from a helicopter. When some tins of tomatoes smashed open, they didn't go to waste - the men scraped up the tomatoes together with the ice they'd landed on and put them in vodka to make Bloody Marys. Expeditions such as Alexander's took place every year until the collapse of the Soviet Union. Then the funding disappeared and a host of Russian ships, including the icebreaker *Akademik Fyodorov*, which took Alexander to the Arctic, were impounded in foreign ports for non-payment of taxes and other fees.

After his expedition, Alexander was chosen to head a Soviet-Norwegian joint venture scientific research company. Whilst nothing could ever replace the exhilaration and danger of the North Pole, women and money gave Alexander's life its edge. His other favourite pastimes were playing with his pet rotweiler, Fram (named after Arctic explorer Nansen's ship), and going for hair-raisingly fast drives in his Japanese car with dozens of scraps of paper blowing about in the back - his unpaid speeding fines.

Sitting at a desk in the Arctic and Antarctic Research Institute in St Petersburg, smoking heavily, Alexander in middle age began to develop a noticeable paunch. The broad chest and sturdy legs, proudly displayed in a photograph behind his desk in which he was standing on the ice in a pair of swimming trunks, were sagging a little. He may no longer have been at his physical peak, but in all other respects, he was still on the boil. 'I am a volcano,' Alexander told me.

I've given you the impression that Alexander veers towards the egotistical side, and the fact that his son was also called Alexander might just confirm that. 'He's named after his grandfather,' Alexander senior protested, holding his sincere look for long enough to be half-convincing, and then his devilish wink let me know I'd been fooled. 'My children look up to their father,' he continued. 'To them he's a big hero.'

Like a politician building up a fantasy image of his harmonious family life, Alexander took me to his home for the day and showed me his loving wife, Elena, and perfectly-behaved 10-year-old daughter, Natasha. His teenage son was on an exchange visit to England. I had come to work for Alexander's company in the summer of 1993, teaching English and translating bizarre scientific texts about lever-loading anti-polar bear rifles and sea creatures whose names could best be rendered as *leatherneedles* and *stomachlegs*.

When a female friend of mine from England arrived on the scene to assist me with Russian marine terminology, Alexander's family suddenly exited. First he treated us both to a three-course meal in a restaurant, washed down with vodka, champagne and cognac; then he took us on an overnight excursion to the former Finnish town of Vyborg, where we sweated together in a sauna, drank more vodka and ate salted fish. The charming, funny, handsome man with the dark beard seduced my friend and provided a conniving friend of his own (a deep-sea diver, what else?) to keep me occupied.

On another occasion Alexander came to my flat (where his new mistress was staying) in the evening with a bottle of vodka in his briefcase. The three of us sat at the kitchen table drinking until the small hours. My friend asked him if he was planning to drive home and he said no, he had already cleared things with his wife. Alexander's rule was, 'A good lie must always have an element of truth in it.'

His cover story was that an employee of his company had to get to the airport urgently with half a million roubles (£300) cash in a briefcase (because cheques are not used in Russia) to pay for a plane to be refuelled in Murmansk. This would leave Alexander stranded late at night on the wrong side of the river because St Petersburg's bridges open for several hours to let ships through, so he had ostensibly arranged to sleep in the flat of another employee who lived in that district. The half million roubles and the plane in Murmansk were real enough, but Alexander had really delegated someone else to drive to the airport so that his schedule would be free for a night of debauchery.

Alexander's mind was positively humming with creativity that week, as he had also conceived an excuse for taking me and my friend to Vyborg again and leaving his family behind. Alexander had some English guests and the two of us were to come with him to interpret: the work would be far too strenuous for one of us alone. This time the itinerary would include a boat trip, and sadly the boat wasn't big enough for Alexander's dog, and the dog couldn't stay home on its own, so his wife had to look after it. His daughter couldn't come with us either, because she suffered from car-sickness.

As it happened, we opted out of Vyborg Part II, to Alexander's chagrin, but we saw the photographs afterwards. One thing we noticed straight away was that the boat was *very* big. It could have comfortably transported a camel. This was a reminder of how Alexander had gradually excluded Elena from the fun things in life. The highlight of their 16-year marriage was probably their honeymoon, when they stayed in bed for three days, subsisting solely on eggs and champagne. Now she had her own car, washing machine, dishwasher and microwave, and he thought this was adequate compensation for making her give up her career as an engineer - he was earning enough money, so why should she work?

'I'm sure my wife would rather live with a volcano than with a 'quieter-than-water' type, like an Englishman,' said Alexander confidently. Unfortunately, he must have been more like a burnt-out volcano on the rare occasions when he came home after his extracurricular exertions. Since his marriage Alexander had had 'between eight and ten' affairs. Elena knew nothing about them. She was still unaware of his volcanic past when she opened a letter to Alexander from my friend, drank a bottle of cognac, demanded a divorce and spent the rest of the night being sick. That was how he described her reaction when his careful deceptions were obliterated in a split second of forgetfulness. He had phoned her from the office because he needed her to read him a document from his briefcase, but the letter was in there, too. My friend by then was safely back in England and I had to take the rap.

Alexander pulled off another successful lie, averting a divorce by persuading Elena that he'd been led astray for the first time in his life by two amoral English girls. Elena demanded a meeting with me and I braced myself for an interrogation. But she had only one question: 'Has your friend got AIDS?'

'No,' I said. I'd never actually tested her for HIV, but reckoned she was considerably less likely to be infected than Alexander himself. I didn't think he was, though. He had a habit of getting away with things.

My name is Konstantin, and I'm an alcoholic

Those weren't the exact words he used as he kissed my hand on first acquaintance at a St Petersburg café, where I was taking some time out from Alexander's misadventures to indulge in some of my own. The slim, hairy man in a leather jacket and Italian suede shoes said, 'My name is Konstantin. Where are you from?'

'Birmingham,' I told him, and his instant reply was, 'Aston Villa!' So the theme of our first conversation was the English football league. I didn't have to bother pretending to know anything about it as Konstantin - Kostya - could easily have been a football trivia striker for Liverpool.

Later on that hot afternoon the conversation turned to Queen Elizabeth II, who was equalled in Kostya's league table of greatness only by Gary Lineker, and the one person who outscored them both was God. 'I'm 33, the age of Christ,' Kostya told me with a wry smile. 'An Orthodox priest told me to grow a beard a few years ago, so I did, and I can never shave it off.' Kostya was from the tiny republic of Ossetia in the North

Caucasus, a Christian enclave surrounded by Muslim neighbours such as Chechnya and Ingushetia. His real name was Kazbek, but he thought it would be simpler to tell me the Russified version of his name, so he was always Kostya to me.

I was on my way to hear a choir singing in the Smolny Cathedral. I had a spare ticket with me and after our intriguing chat I invited Kostya to accompany me. Apart from his swarthy good looks, I liked him because I could understand everything he said. His native language was Ossetian, and although he spoke Russian fluently, he didn't use much of the slang which Russians pepper their conversation with. So we had our first date in the heavenly surroundings of the cathedral. It was full of American tourists plastered in make-up. Kostya thought they looked like children because they were so well-preserved.

After he became my boyfriend, Kostya began to reveal the rather less saintly side of his nature. He did give money to beggars and cross himself whenever he passed a church, it was true. He also drank beer for breakfast and vodka throughout the rest of the day. I didn't know about this for the first few weeks because I'd only see him when he arrived at my flat at midnight with a bottle of champagne and a bunch of flowers. I did notice that he was rather drunk already, but he usually had a plausible excuse, such as commemorating the anniversary of his father's death.

Three years later I found out more about why Kostya had become an alcoholic. He was born in the Ossetian capital, Ordzhonikidze (Grigory Ordzhonikidze was the Bolshevik responsible for forcing the Caucasian republics into the Soviet Union), which after 1991 reverted to its original name of Vladikavkaz. A small city in the mountains with a population of about 300,000, it offers few career choices to its inhabitants.

Ossetian women have a very important role - in the kitchen. Bella, an artist friend of mine from Vladikavkaz, told me that in the republic married women were not permitted to speak to their fathers-in-law except via a small child, if there was one around. If a patriarch wanted to order his daughter-in-law to do something (the only possible reason for addressing her), he 'let his desires be known to the air' and she was supposed to work out who has to fulfil them. Ossetian men had two obsessions in life, football and vodka. The former paid off: as I write, the city's team are the Russian champions. The number of people whose lives have been wrecked by the latter would fill more than a mere football stadium.

Kostya had two younger brothers, but one died of leukaemia as a child. Their mother was driven mad by recurring nightmares that her dead son was freezing cold and calling for help from the grave, and she drowned herself. As a teenager Kostya was a hooligan who smoked and drank (like his father) and stole cars to joyride in. Later he earned US dollars doing business illegally. A policeman found out, blackmailed him, and Kostya beat him up. For that he got eight years in prison and labour camps. 'I would have been in for longer,' he said, 'but my father sold his car and bribed the judge.'

Just before his arrest Kostya got married and had a son, David. He thought it would be humiliating if his wife had lovers while he was in prison - it would harm her reputation too much - so he decided to divorce her. Under Soviet law, prisoners could get a divorce just by requesting one in a letter. 'The shock of my arrest followed by a divorce straight away would have been too upsetting for her, so I waited a while before I wrote the letter,' he said.

In prison Kostya almost died of tuberculosis. After his release a kidney stone (caused by alcoholism) killed his father. His aunt, Svetlana, decided that Leningrad was a healthier environment than Ordzhonikidze, so she moved into a flat there with him and his brother, Alan. To get a Leningrad residence permit, Kostya paid a woman he didn't know to marry him 'fictitiously'. As soon as the coast was clear, they divorced.

Alan was remarkably conventional: when Yeltsin came to power he started his own insurance company and even came to Scotland with some of his employees for a week's training. At home he still had his meals cooked and clothes washed by Svetlana. She still waited outside the flat at night for Kostya to come home. Sometimes he disappeared for weeks and didn't ring. After each drinking binge he swore to give up for a year, ten years, or the rest of his life, but even a kidney stone which the doctor smashed with a hammer didn't frighten him enough to keep his promise.

When Kostya was drunk he would talk to anyone he met on the street. Sometimes he challenged them to a boxing match, and other times he became their best mate for the night and the new friend would buy the next bottle of vodka. He didn't have a job - 'I'm an adventurer,' he said - he just had schemes. One was to emigrate to California with his hippy artist friend, Oleg, and live off the proceeds of the paintings; another was to become a radio sports commentator. In reality he only earned money when a friend involved him in a dodgy business deal. Usually he got money from his aunt, who worked in a shop, giving him an allowance from her apron pocket.

My brief times with Kostya were wild times. One evening we visited Oleg in his girlfriend's flat. Oleg had a wife and kids but didn't live with them when he could help it. He seemed to have gone out of the frying pan into the fire, as his girlfriend was about 20 years older than him and had a highly irritating habit of screeching 'Hello!' in a sarcastic tone of voice when she wanted to indicate that she disagreed with something. She knew how to do a decent spread of pickled cucumbers and beetroot salad, though. For several hours we drank, stuffed ourselves, and danced to Oleg's satirical rendition of 'We All Live in a Red Submarine, a Soviet Submarine' on the guitar. At 1.30 am Kostya said, 'Let's go and watch the bridges opening.'

Oleg's girlfriend's flat was on the top floor, in a building which was attached to the Hermitage, or Winter Palace. We climbed up to attic and I tripped over some pipes before making my way after the others to the roof. This wasn't the roof of a modern block of flats, it was the roof of an 18th-century mansion, and it sloped. I was rooted to the spot but Kostya took my hand and helpfully advised me to look out for the wires which were strung out in between the chimney pots. Soon the four of us were stepping from roof to roof like Dick van Dyke. It was quite a trek, which came to a spectacular end when we were directly above the Neva embankment, looking out over the river. We were standing on the roof of the Hermitage.

With some of the finest art treasures in the world beneath our feet, we opened a bottle of wine and toasted one of the most beautiful scenes I have ever looked upon. 'It's a pity we didn't come here earlier in the summer, during the White Nights,' said Kostya. Then, it would have been almost as bright as day. But this was August, and it was dark, but that meant that the bridges which stretch down the Neva as far as the eye can see were illuminated in a blaze of twinkling coloured beads. Down below, pygmy people had gathered to watch the nightly spectacle, and queues of drivers waited in cars with their engines off, there for the less romantic purpose of getting to the other side.

One of the constellations to our left began, imperceptibly at first, to shift. Then so did another, to our right. The bridges opened majestically, like honour guards forming a diamond-shaped roof over the passing ships. The dark vessels, brutish cargo ships by daylight, mystery monsters by night, glided across the water without a sound, while up on the roof Oleg gave a heartfelt rendition of the Soviet national anthem in his operatic bass voice. (Not that he loved the Soviet Union, but he didn't know the words to the new Russian anthem.) The sailors heard him and saluted. We laughed and waved at them. We were on top of the world.

Other experiences with Kostya were more fraught. When I first met him he wanted to go to Moscow for a week or so to sell televisions with a couple of mafioso types. He told me he needed $1000 to do some business and that he'd double his money. I'd never had that much money in my life, but by coincidence someone from work had introduced me to her Polish friend who had lived in Russia since childhood and was just about to emigrate back to Poland. She had about $1000 in cash and was afraid that the money would be taken from her by customs officers on the train. She was desperate for anyone, even a complete stranger, to take the money on the plane to England and send it by bank transfer to her account in Poland. 'Dollars are the only notes which don't have a magnetic strip in them, so you can put them in your back pocket when you go through the metal detector,' she advised me.

I had no intention of doing anything with the money in the single week which remained before my flight to England. The one distraction from that idealistic aim was that I did want to go to Moscow and I couldn't afford a train ticket. My conscience was knocked out in the first round of the moral wrestling match I had with myself - if a woman who'd known me for three hours could entrust me with her life savings, I could entrust them to a man I'd known for three weeks. So Kostya and I bought ourselves first-class tickets and he took the rest of the money to do his deals.

We were supposed to stay in the same flat for two days and then go back to St Petersburg together, but Kostya said it was better if I didn't live with his mafioso types, and then he said he couldn't go back with me because the business hadn't been sewn up. He phoned me every night from Moscow, promising to come back as soon as he could, but my time was running out and it looked as if I'd lost the entire $1000. I felt like picking up my Large Oxford Russian-English Dictionary and bashing myself on the head a few times. I was a textbook case of the naive foreign student who falls for a cunning older man, gives him every cent she has and gets a postcard afterwards from him on the shores of the Black Sea, where he's holidaying with his wife and children.

Not quite. Mentally, I was already wearing my McDonalds uniform, paying off my debt in the evenings and falling asleep in lectures during the day, when Kostya greeted me at the airport clutching a bunch of flowers in one hand and an envelope in the other. 'I'm sorry, it's only $700,' he said. 'I did get the $1000 back but I had to give $300 of it to a friend from Vladikavkaz who's a drug addict.'

Following instructions, I passed calmly through the metal detector and the money eventually made its way to Poland. Either the recipient didn't know how much she'd lost, because the money had been converted into pounds and then into zloty, or perhaps she did know but counted herself lucky to have got any of it back. At any rate, she was gushingly grateful and wanted to be my penfriend. I'm sure the drug addict would have, too, if he'd known my address.

How the rich live

Ruslan was the big cheese in a small town called Sestroretsk to the north of St Petersburg, on the Gulf of Finland. In summer it's a popular place for city holidaymakers to pass through on the way to the beach. The town's place in Soviet history was secured when Lenin found his ideal haystack there and hid in it while he plotted the downfall of Imperialism. At some point he must have craved a taste of the proletarian good life - he moved into a shack.

After Lenin's death the haystack showed a careless disregard for its national significance by falling down repeatedly, even after the Communist Party itself had rebuilt it, and in the end it had to be represented symbolically in stone. The shack was more durable, especially after it was encased in glass. This mini Lenin theme park was to be Ruslan's insurance policy if the Communists were ever returned to power: 'I'll just show them how well I looked after Lenin,' he joked.

In truth Ruslan stood to lose badly if wealth creation once again became a sign of degeneracy. In the forest amongst the beautiful dachas of temporarily favoured Soviet writers such as Anna Akhmatova and Mikhail Zoshchenko, Ruslan built his own magnificent abode. In England it would be no more than an average detached two-storey house; in Russia it was the luxury residence of a millionaire, protected by a 10-foot fence and a salivating Hound of the Baskervilles on a chain outside the front door. Inside, the house had varnished pine walls, a Western-style fitted kitchen and an incubator for the eggs laid by Ruslan's chickens. He was thinking of adding a sauna, but his wife forbade that, as it would mean their endless stream of guests would never leave.

Ruslan was an Ossetian friend of Kostya's, a few years older than him. Kostya said that the only way national minorities such as the Ossetians could study at the best Russian universities in Soviet times was to be excellent at sport. Ruslan got his place at Leningrad State University by virtue of his Greco-Roman wrestling. He had to stay at the top to finish the course, and was champion of Leningrad several times.

Ruslan's natural aggression was an equally valuable asset in Yeltsin's Russia. Officially, he ran a number of shashlick cafés. Unofficially, he had 'other business', as Kostya explained. He had turned his hand to something which was very popular amongst ex-wrestlers: a protection racket. While Ruslan barbecued the kebabs, occasionally clouting his nephew round the ear for chopping onion too slowly or pouring over-generous measures of cognac, his men were out barbecuing businesses which hadn't paid their dues on time. And Ruslan's wife, English teacher turned housewife, would tell their six-year-old son Borya to drink his milk so that he'd grow up big and strong like his daddy.

*   *   *

Vadik was also a daddy's boy. He was only 12, but as his father Eric (another of Kostya's friends) so proudly pointed out, he was already growing a moustache. He was in a class at school with 16-year-olds because of his prodigious academic talent; his tennis ability made Martina Hingis seem like a late developer; and if he played in a concert hall as he did at home on the grand piano, he'd have won the Tchaikovsky Prize. Or so his daddy said.

If Eric was to be believed, Vadik's only dilemma in life was choosing which brilliant career to stick with. By the way, Eric had a wife (20 years younger than him) and a new baby daughter, but they were to be seen and not heard - what else do women do? Eric even did the cooking because he knew so much about food. He ought to have done, the way his belly hung over the frying pan. 'As you can see, we don't live badly,' said Eric, grinning and licking his thick lips in case I'd missed the irony of the comment. Subtlety wasn't Eric's strong point.

'Here's our waterbed,' he said as he prodded the conjugal blancmange. 'And look at this!' He flicked a switch in the hallway, illuminating an alcove above the door where a garishly-painted statue of the Virgin Mary stood, blessing our path to the kitchen. The religious theme continued there: Eric had filled all the available spaces between the Zanussi, the Kenwood Chef and other gadgets with his collection of medieval icons.

Eric was thrilled that I was his neighbour - we lived in the same street. 'You will teach Vadik English!' he announced. 'Vadik gets top marks in English but if he is going to be a diplomat then he'll have to be perfect. You can start next week. Vadik, which evenings are you free? You have piano lessons on Tuesdays? OK, great, that means Sarah can come on Wednesdays, Thursdays, Fridays, Saturdays, Sundays and Mondays. Marvellous. We'll be expecting you, Sarah.' Somehow my street didn't seem to be quite the right place for me to live in after that and I moved further away from Eric - to England.

The intelligentsia

Rozanna, the student journalist who invited me to the Soviet-style café, was from an Armenian family which moved to St Petersburg in the early seventies, before she was born. Her parents made sure she spoke Armenian by alternating between it and Russian in conversation. Rozanna was studying sociology in one institute and journalism in another; her younger sister Lilia was studying dentistry.

The two of them shared a bedroom which doubled as the living room. Most of the time one or the other of them had exams, which meant the whole family got to hear them reading out their textbooks, as they had to memorise chapters by heart. No one (except possibly Lilia herself) was looking forward to the day when she would start revising for practical exams.

Thanks to her English language ability and knowledge of her home city, Rozanna was employed as a tour guide during the 1994 Goodwill Games. It wasn't a profession she wanted to go into (too repetitive), but afterwards she enjoyed recreating the tours for her foreign friends. She had a story for practically every building, monument and park, such as the one haunted by the ghost of the murdered tsar Paul. She introduced me to St Petersburg's second-smallest statue, Chizhik-Pizhik, a duck from a fairytale which nestles unobtrusively on the inner wall of a bridge. It was put there by the city's humour society and if you can toss a coin onto the ledge where it stands, you will have eternal luck. The smallest statue, by the way, was the humour society's newest joke: a nose to honour Gogol's *Nose*. On Rozanna's tour I also heard her theory about why most of St Petersburg's buildings are yellow - because the city is so dark in winter, they are supposed to brighten it up.

Rozanna's mother was a mathematics lecturer and her father, Gurgen, was a space scientist. He narrowly missed becoming a cosmonaut twice. The first time was in 1971 when the three-man crew of *Soyuz 11* suffocated on their return to Earth. It was the flight before the one Gurgen was supposed to be on. The men died because when a valve malfunctioned there wasn't enough room in the capsule for them to put spacesuits on. The second time was under Gorbachev, when Gurgen won a place in a competition for space journalists, but lost it when the government sold it to the

Japanese. When I met him in 1996 American astronaut Shannon Lucid was twiddling her thumbs on the *Mir* space station, waiting for him and his colleagues to finish working on a piece of equipment for her.

In Rozanna's parents' bedroom Gurgen kept his newspapers. The room has the dimensions of a fair-sized wardrobe, but nevertheless he had found a space for every newspaper he had ever bought since he moved to St Petersburg. They were stacked together in yellowing piles, in no particular order, and it took him a week to find a copy of *Pravda* for April 1986 when someone wanted it for research on the 10th anniversary of the Chernobyl catastrophe - but it was there.

The intelligentsia in Russia have been completely impoverished since the collapse of state funding since 1991. Despite national and personal economic disaster, there were traditions of hospitality to uphold in Rozanna's household. 'You are only a guest the first time you visit us,' said Rozanna's mother. 'After that, you're one of the family.' Every visitor, however unexpected, was served with a mouth-watering spread of homemade salads, fresh bread and Armenian *Ararat* cognac. The bottle had a picture of the mountain where Noah's Ark was grounded and which is the dominant feature of the Armenian capital, Yerevan, even though it is now an unattainable Mecca for Armenians, located on Turkish territory. The Turkish genocide of Armenians in 1915 was an inspiration for Hitler, who asked, 'Who now remembers it?' Armenians do, the lost mountain makes sure of that.

Although the future didn't seem to hold much promise for Rozanna's parents, she and her sister had great hopes for themselves. Rozanna had travelled already - to Paris when her French boyfriend paid for her to visit him for three weeks - and to Finland on an exchange trip financed by one of her institutes. There would be no guaranteed job for Rozanna and Lilia when they graduated, as there was for their parents, but on the other hand they would have a choice of jobs and maybe a choice of countries as well. For bright young people in Russia there may at last be a bright future.

The journalist who lost his scruples

Dima, whose nose was frostbitten in the army, once had high moral principles. Under communism he limited his own options in life by refusing to work for a state company. Amongst the odd jobs he did in Leningrad for 15 years, he was a nightwatchman, an artist's model, and a laboratory assistant. He couldn't afford the few roubles it cost to get into the Hermitage, so he mingled in with large groups of tourists. And he expected to live like this for the rest of his life.

When Mikhail Gorbachev ordered a blockade of Lithuania in 1990, Dima found a new career: journalism. He and his wife lived in a communal flat - where several families share a kitchen and bathroom - and they put their typewriter on a pillow so that the neighbours wouldn't hear as they typed reports on the activities of Lithuanian nationalists to send out to Western news agencies.

Six years later, when there was a strong chance that the Communist Party would be returned to power in the forthcoming presidential election, Dima was preparing to hoist a red flag on his desk at Radio Russia, the state radio station. 'I'll say, hello comrades, welcome back,' he told me. 'I won't protest like I did in 1990. No one needs that kind of heroism any more.' Dima's hatred of the Communists was as virulent as ever, but he'd lost faith in the people of Russia, finding it incredible that millions of them could vote of their own free will for a system which reduced them to tiny cogs in a megalithic machine.

When I asked Dima who he voted for in the 1995 parliamentary election, which the Communist Party won, he wouldn't name a party, saying, 'That's a rather intimate question.' What he really wanted for the country was 'a liberal dictatorship.' What he wanted for himself was 'complete personal freedom.' I knew his personal life was as screwed up as his views on politics because he was having an affair with me.

We met at a press conference in the Mariinsky Palace, home of the city council, and had our first date in a restaurant I was reviewing for *The St Petersburg Press*. Tall, slim, with blonde hair and endearingly crooked glasses, I had assumed he was nearer to 32 than his actual age of 39. He had a habit of deceiving me semi- or three-quarters-consciously. As he walked me to my flat that evening he asked me about my family and then casually enumerated his own - 'My father and brother are in St Petersburg too - and I live with my wife.' That was the first time he'd mentioned her. In six months he never said if he still had a mother or not, and I could hardly ask about her if he thought voting was too intimate to talk about.

Not wishing to cause anyone else's wife to worry about AIDS, I said goodnight to Dima on my doorstep. But by an amazing coincidence someone had given him a bottle of cognac that day and he'd taken it with him to the restaurant in his bag. He showed it to me and asked me if I'd invite him in to try some. I justified my acceptance by imagining his wife was paralysed from the neck down, or was a manic depressive, or had recently discovered her true lesbian sexuality. Even if she was a physically and mentally flawless heterosexual, I thought, the two of them were probably on the verge of divorce but were stuck in a room together because there was nowhere else to go. Don't laugh, it does happen in Russia.

At 3 am, with half the bottle of cognac gone, I summoned the courage to ask about the wife situation. 'We live in parallel,' said Dima. In my blurred and susceptible condition, that was the explanation I'd been waiting to hear - it precisely confirmed that they were on the verge of divorce but were stuck in a room together because there was nowhere else to go. What more could I possibly need to ask? Weeks later, when Dima had got into the habit of leaving my flat by 12:30 am to catch the last metro so that his wife wouldn't suspect anything, it struck me that 'in parallel' was a rather conceptual term which could mean whatever anyone wanted it to mean. Dima clarified it: 'We live in parallel but together.'

Dima said his wife also had a lover, but he'd found out accidentally and hadn't confronted her about it. So they were living in one room, both pretending that everything was fine, except on the occasions when they let their guard down and threw plates at each other. 'The problem with this country is that people live too close together,' Dima said. 'They're crushed together in public on buses and trains and they're crushed together at home in communal flats. Do you know that in a communal flat you have a rota for doing the cleaning? Your turn might come before a real swine of a babushka who'll take you by the arm and inspect the flat with you to make sure you haven't missed anything and made more work for her.'

For the past five years of his ten-year marriage, Dima had been trying to escape from domestic oppression by having affairs. I think what he liked best about having a girlfriend was finding someone new to listen to his stories on long walks in St Petersburg's bright white nights of summer and dark, white nights of winter. We took swigs of whisky in the woods, gazed dreamily at the canals and pelted each other with snowballs in a raging blizzard. There was no romance or passion left in Dima's marriage, but he always made it clear that his wife was the one who really mattered. He said he never went for walks with his wife because there was nothing to talk about. 'We've become too similar. But what keeps us together is the memory of 1990, when we risked our lives for freedom.'

Entertainment and the Arts

A naked Australian slapping himself on the head with a raw fish made a refreshing change from the buttoned-up world of opera, ballet, classical music and fine arts in St Petersburg. I could hardly complain about having unlimited access to the gilt balconies of the Mariinsky (formerly Kirov) Theatre or chandelier-lit hall of the Philharmonia. In 1996, when you could eat in a restaurant only if you struck lucky in a casino first, tickets to St Petersburg's most prestigious venues could be had for between 75p and £1.50. But sometimes I longed for the Barber of Seville to rip off his apron and let his hair down. For an alternative event the place to go was No. 10, Pushkinskaya Street.

Each Russian street number signifies a collection of blocks of flats loosely grouped around a central courtyard. Pushkinskaya 10 was a derelict set of 19th-century buildings two minutes from the city's main thoroughfare, Nevsky Prospekt. To see the full Pushkinskaya 10 ensemble you had to go through a crumbling archway into the courtyard, but the two front wings also gave a good indication of the place's ambience. Handmade posters plastered on top of each other announced, 'Come and hear Two Planes - music until the metro closes with live men's ice-hockey on the dancefloor', and, 'Somebody Has Eaten My Hat - a retrospective in unvarnished brick. Gallery 21.'

Inside the front entrances were a nightclub called Fish Fabrique, a Dianetics Testing Centre, a gallery devoted to electronic multimedia, a nightshelter for the homeless (more about that in the next chapter), a CD and tape shop and the headquarters of the Free Culture Foundation, which had a lease on the buildings. All these places were crammed awkwardly into flats which were inhabited until 1991, when Pushkinskaya 10 was declared too dangerous to live in and the mayor ordered it to be evacuated for repairs. In the meantime, the Free Culture Foundation was given permission to use it for artists' studios and the kinds of establishments mentioned above.

Only at Pushkinskaya 10 could the Australian performance artist Pete Moss be described as typical. He had channelled all his life's energies into being bizarre, so it must have been rather disappointing when his act was greeted in St Petersburg by sage nods and refined applause from an audience who had either no hair or too much hair, but nothing in between. Some even had more body piercing than he did.

We didn't know about the piercing at first: Pete looked like an ordinary bloke in white Hindu prayer garb and tights, justifiably irritated that the floor he was sitting on was covered in empty cigarette packets. He was irritated most because they were empty, and in his frustration he threw them around the room. In the background, colour slides of cars and mushrooms were projected onto a sepia photograph of a large Victorian family.

Then things got weird. Pete was really angry now. He picked up a microphone and addressed the audience. 'You can't understand a fucking thing I'm saying so I can say whatever I like,' he shouted. Having summarised the story so far, he put on some furry wellies and a yellow plastic raincoat, switched on an electric fan and splashed water over himself. This needed no explanation - it was obviously an abridged rendition of *The Tempest*. The storm washed away all Pete's clothes (well, he took them off, but with heavy symbolism), and that was when we were treated to a close-up of his ring, worn in a place which nature would surely have made less sensitive if she had intended it to be spliced by a piece of metal. No wonder Pete had such a short temper.

In the homosexual fetishist section of the show, Pete posed in a camp manner next to a purple bust of a bald man, tied a string of raw fish around his waist, smashed half a watermelon over his head and smeared the juice all over himself alluringly. Bored of having fish in his groin, he replaced them with a bunch of flowers and wrapped himself in clingfilm, ensuring the fish didn't go to waste by slapping himself on the head with them. As a grand finale he introduced the theme of sado-masochism. 'Let's play with nails!' said Pete, and banged some in between his toes, screaming with pain as if they were going through his feet.

I hardly needed to go back to Pushkinskaya 10 again, having seen the mother of all performance artists, but the place was too intriguing to stay away from for long. Not to be outdone by their neighbour down under, a New Zealand couple also ended up spouting their stuff there. I mean that literally, because they were university music lecturers whose experiments on the beach had resulted in the discovery of a new form of sound, emitted when the man stuck his penis down a tube and peed onto a selection of bongo drums. As there was no beach at Pushkinskaya 10 they couldn't give a live performance, so we had to be content with slides and a recording.

On the Russian side of strangeness there was no shortage of candidates. Somewhere in the courtyard or under the archway there was always a man with a dark beard and dark glasses who would stand stoically staring into the distance, pretending to be lost in thought. Whenever anyone attempted to walk past him, he offered to take them to his studio and show them his paintings. Apart from him there was Artur, a skinny artist with a goatee who would only speak English to me. I met him when the hot water wasn't working in my flat and I had to have a shower at Bella's (the artist from Ossetia).

Bella had a studio at Pushkinskaya 10 which she lived in illegally because her registered address was in Vladikavkaz. In the winter her friend (my hassled landlady, Lena) gave her a room in a flat for free because there was no central heating or hot water at Pushkinskaya 10. To get to her studio on the ninth floor Bella had to walk up a pitch-dark staircase, and to heat it she had to buy logs in the yard and chop them up to go into the furnace.

I went for my shower first thing in the morning and found Bella and Artur sharing a bottle of cognac. 'Just have one glup,' Artur implored me. 'Just one glup. Please.' I had a glup and Artur invited me to the opening of his exhibition. The exhibition was in a single room at Pushkinskaya 10, freezing cold because it was the middle of winter. A huddle of people inspected the paintings politely and then formed a semi-circle around Artur, who was standing at an easel. There were no meaningless formalities, such as, 'Welcome to my exhibition.' Artur said nothing.

A friend of Artur's in jeans and a t-shirt sat down on a chair in the middle of the room and Artur handed him a bottle of champagne to drink from. The rest of us watched thirstily as Artur painted him. The paintbrush was flying so quickly across the canvas that it seemed he would soon produce something for us to see, and we shoved our hands deeper into our pockets to keep warm. It wasn't even possible to look over his shoulder, as he'd placed the easel in the corner of the room facing away from us.

Ten minutes passed and a dissenter murmured to me that perhaps this was a crowd of people who couldn't think of anything to do on a Saturday afternoon. Ten more minutes passed and a saxophonist got up and started playing free jazz. From time to time Artur paused, stepped back from his masterpiece, and momentarily created an atmosphere of hushed suspense - had he finished? No. On the half-hour God intervened, or the Pushkinskaya 10 wiring system, plunging us into darkness. Artur's brush didn't miss a stroke, and the hard core of loyalists in the audience didn't budge from their places, but I took the opportunity to make my exit, reckoning I could happily approximate the pleasure of that experience in my own flat by counting the number of dead flies squashed on my walls.

The rock of Pushkinskaya 10 was grizzled old peace guru Kolya Vasyn. He was also its rock 'n' roll. To be honest, he wasn't that old - he celebrated his 50th birthday in 1996 - he'd just been around for a long time. For decades before he could take any of it out of the closet, Kolya was collecting John Lennon, Beatles and Elvis memorabilia. After communism he opened a two-room John Lennon Museum at Pushkinskaya 10 from which he plotted the realisation of his dreams, a floating Temple of Peace and Love on the Neva.

'If only Russians had worshipped Lennon instead of Lenin, life would be wonderful,' said Kolya, handing me a heart-shaped mug with the words, 'All you need is love' carved on it in English and Russian. 'The Beatles prevented a third world war. Once you've listened to their music you are incapable of shooting anyone.' The museum, made glorious by Beatles music, was stuffed full of Kolya's treasures. He was proud of his gold disc, but his real favourite was a red-and-white football shirt which was actually worn by John Lennon - and he had the photograph to prove it.

When I first visited the museum I joined a party in its 24th hour, commemorating the anniversary of The King's death. Although Kolya liked Elvis, it was John who lived. 'John was one of the greatest jokers of the 20th century and I believe that he faked his own death,' Kolya told me. 'A British newspaper took photographs of him in an Italian monastery a few years ago.'

If Kolya was obsessed with the past, he was also mad about the future. The second room of the museum, 'my office', was dominated by a plan, an artist's impression, and a scale model of the Temple of Peace and Love. It looked like a giant, illuminated globe perched on top of a bandstand. It was to be a concert hall and a place for chilling out and imagining all the people living for today. Kolya had the belief and the blueprints; all he needed, as he said cheerfully, was not love but twelve million dollars.

Kolya was such an essential fixture in St Petersburg that I took my parents to meet him when they came to visit me. 'Why is that wooden spoon hanging from the ceiling?' Dad asked, foolishly. Kolya saw instantly that he was ripe for initiation into his Spiritual Society of Peace and Love. 'Assume the rock 'n' roll position,' commanded Kolya. 'What?! You don't know the rock 'n' roll position? Point your feet inwards and try to form an idiotic expression on your face.' Dad tried his best and was brilliant, having been practising for several years beforehand.

'Repeat after me, I promise to faithfully uphold the principles of peace and love and to give spiritual succour to the society I have now joined wherever I may be in the world for the remainder of my natural life,' Kolya instructed Dad.

'Er - one question -,' said Dad. 'What is spiritual succour?'

'Money, of course!' Kolya replied, illustrating what he meant by holding out a basket for Dad to drop a five-dollar bill into. Dad's fate was sealed.

We then found out why the wooden spoon was hanging from the ceiling. Dad especially found out. Kolya softened him up by pouring a shot of Kolya Vasyn vodka into the spoon and feeding him with it. While Dad was still reeling from the shock of that, Kolya raised the spoon and wacked him on the forehead. The effect was lasting. For the next few weeks, everyone thought Dad was Gorbachev's twin brother. 'Doesn't peace mean the same thing as non-violence?' he asked Kolya as he swayed out of the door.

As it happened, Kolya and the other occupants of Pushkinskaya 10 were engaged in a non-violent struggle against eviction. In 1991

51

the Mayor's Office committee for management of city property gave the Free Culture Foundation a lease until 2006, but the mayor, Anatoly Sobchak, got fed up of the situation because the artists didn't have the money to maintain the buildings. In 1994 he signed a declaration entrusting Pushkinskaya 10 to the local Channel Five television company for its employees to live in, on condition that Channel Five would find investors for the necessary renovations.

Channel Five's deputy chairman, Anatoly Margunov, was not impressed by the Free Culture Foundation. 'The Soviet Writers' Union had 5000 members,' he said. 'Do you think there were really 5000 writers in the Soviet Union? I don't. There are more than 100 artists at Pushkinskaya 10. They cannot all be genuine artists.'

The Free Culture Foundation did let some of its rooms to commercial organisations: it would have gone bankrupt if it didn't. In return for their studios the genuine artists were supposed to pay 25,000 roubles (£3) per month, but many couldn't even afford that and were allowed to stay without making a contribution. Bella remembered how someone once came to her door collecting for the family of a Pushkinskaya 10 artist who had just died. She told him she couldn't give a single rouble because she didn't have enough to buy a loaf of bread for herself or milk for her baby. So the man went away and came back later with a jar of money. He'd taken up a collection for Bella.

One of the businesses supporting the Free Culture Foundation was the ADM travel agency. In stark contrast to the spartan artists' studios, it had all the conveniences of a modern office - telephones, fax, photocopier and its own heating system. Outside its door the windows were broken. Downstairs, gallery owners sat wrapped up in overcoats.

'Why should we repair the building if we're going to be thrown out?' asked ADM's director. 'If they told us we'd be here for the next five years we'd fix this whole wing.' Challenged to explain his company's qualifications for being a member of the Free Culture Foundation, the director turned a few logical somersaults. 'St Petersburg is a city of culture and we arrange tours of St

Petersburg. Everything connected with this city is connected with culture.'

Anatoly Margunov had no sympathy for this view. 'I can't understand how our employees are less needy than those people who are in the building at the moment', he said. About 150 journalists, directors and camera-people from Channel Five were waiting in the city's queue for accommodation because they had less than six square yards of living space for each member of their families.

The dispute between the Free Culture Foundation and Channel Five was taken to the St Petersburg court of arbitration and the legal processes were on indefinite hold. Members of the Free Culture Foundation had no intention of repairing the building while the court could take up the case again at any moment and rule that they should leave Pushkinskaya 10.

When the mayor's declaration in favour of Channel Five was first published, he was inundated with letters and telegrams from promoters of the arts in Russia and America asking him to support the Free Culture Foundation's existence. In addition to the artists, some of Russia's greatest 1990s rock bands broke their first guitar strings at Pushkinskaya 10. Russia's minister of culture also intervened for the Free Culture Foundation, saying it had state significance.

'The question of the cultural centre and the question of the building are completely separate,' the head of the Mayor's Office committee for culture told me. 'We have a positive attitude towards the cultural centre and we are trying to find alternative premises for it. But in all civilised countries such centres are located in old factories or barracks, not residential property.'

He said he had considered several properties in the city, including disused public baths, but none of them were suitable. The final twist in the saga was that the Free Culture Foundation and its artists were themselves prepared to move elsewhere. 'I looked at all the premises suggested by the mayor and they were in worse condition than our building,' said the president of the Free Culture Foundation, Sergei Kovalsky. 'If there is a place we like then we will move there, but the city can't offer us anything.'

Way out in the suburbs of St Petersburg, 90 minutes from Pushkinskaya 10, lived another artist who had come into conflict with the city's conservative establishment. What made Dantsik Baldayev unusual was that he once *was* the establishment - he was a 70-year-old retired policeman - but his art had the capacity to shock to an extent that made Pete Moss look as dangerous as Val Doonican.

For forty years Baldayev had a secret which he shared with no one except his father: his meticulously drawn caricatures of subhuman existence in the Soviet labour camp system, the Gulag. 'This work was like a noose round my neck with which they could have hanged me at any time,' Baldayev explained. 'I didn't tell my friends about it because that would have created a whole circle of 'enemies of the people' who could also be punished.'

Sections of Baldayev's *Everyday Life in the Gulag* series, which he began to draw in 1948, were accepted by the St Petersburg Museum of Political History for exhibition in 1995, but he was distressed that the museum wouldn't take his work in its entirety. Baldayev left nothing to the imagination, filling sheet after sheet with scenes of torture, mass rape and murder. The museum's administrators decided that his naturalistic style made it too difficult to look at some of the most gruesome pictures.

Visitors' sensibilities should not have been spared, Baldayev said - everyone must know about what happened in the Gulag. The sheets displayed in the museum could hardly be called restrained. Churches and monasteries exploded, a naked woman was interrogated by gleeful guards, the bodies of the newly executed lay unburied and prisoners listened to lectures on socialism under the slogan, 'Only through honest labour will you win the right to early release.' Baldayev himself was a tough cookie. His Mongol face made him a constant target of racial insults, 'but when someone makes a comment I just roll up my sleeves and challenge them to a fight,' he said. 'I can still sock 'em one like I could when I was 20.'

The first exhibition of Baldayev's caricatures was at the Peter-and-Paul Fortress in 1989. 'People took their hats off and walked through in silence as if they were at a funeral,' he said. 'After a week, the KGB closed it down.' Baldayev made four trips on the

Trans-Siberian Railway to Vladivostok between 1949 and 1960, stopping at camps on the way to make sketches and meet political prisoners, known as zeks. 'The camps were like beads dotted all over the country,' he recalled. He had privileged access to them because he was a policeman, and he made his preliminary drawings in a small notebook that would not be noticed. The zeks showed him their tattoos which depicted everything from reproductions of Biblical scenes by classical artists to Soviet leaders in obscene poses, and Baldayev redrew them for publication in a book. The camps were full of highly skilled artists and such was the demand that zeks would wait for two or three years for their turn to be tattooed.

As a policeman Baldayev arrested common criminals, not political dissidents. He socialised with drunken KGB officers in their holiday homes and turned their bragging reminiscences about camp brutalities against them in his art. Baldayev's father was a Buryat-Mongol ethnographer and playwright who came to Leningrad from Ulan-Ude, having spent ten years in a Stalinist prison. Until he died in 1979 he was Baldayev's chief source of encouragement, urging him to preserve as much material as possible on the camps so that they would not be forgotten. 'Russia will be a free country only in 50 years' time. The Russian people are very conservative, they have slavery in their blood,' Baldayev told me. 'Come and see me more often,' he added. 'I'll make you a cup of tea next time.'

Unlike the struggling artistic community, St Petersburg's theatres had the advantages of support from the city authorities. If anything, the problem was that they had too much support. There was no need to worry about whether a play would attract audiences or not, because the state, as in Soviet times, paid for it to run for weeks or months regardless. 'We are deeply concerned about *Woe From Wit*,' a spokesman for the Mayor's Office cultural committee told the press at the beginning of the 1996 season - but his department continued to fund the play. It had already cost the city half a billion roubles - £75,000.

Griboyedov's early 19th-century comedy *Woe From Wit* was one of hundreds of staid classics being plodded through by St Petersburg's repertory companies. Anything new and innovative, such as *Claustrophobia*, about life in 1990s Russia, went on tour to the West to earn real money. If *Woe From Wit* wasn't gruelling enough, you could try sitting through an adaptation of Dostoyevsky's novel *The Devils*, which took nine hours on a Saturday or Sunday to perform.

English literature was also a hit amongst St Petersburg directors, who put on six Shakespeare plays in 1996 as well as productions based on the stories of Oscar Wilde and Rudyard Kipling. The great thing about watching Shakespeare in Russian was that the colloquial translations were usually easier to understand than the original English. Problems of language occasionally resulted in surprises at the theatre, though. A friend of mine from England once bought us tickets to *The Constant Wife* by someone whose name in Cyrillic letters was pronounced 'S. Merm'. We sat down expecting to see a new work by Sergei Merm or Stanislav Merm, but as the duplicity of an aristocratic family in their English country manor house unfolded it suddenly came to our attention that we were watching a play by Somerset Maugham.

A rare contemporary gem in St Petersburg was a farce called *Kremlin Chimes, or, Well, Come Back In Ten Years Or So...* In it a foreign writer visited Russia sometime during the age of feudalism and his first encounter was with customs officers who ordered him to take off his hat, coat and trousers. They turned the clothes inside out, ripped them and gave them back to him. The writer reached the court of the tsar, where everyone was on their knees with a fixed grin on their faces. The writer found this rather suspicious and asked the tsar if the Russian people were really happy. The tsar brought on some merry peasant folk dancers in national costume. 'I'm still not convinced,' said the writer.

'We do have our revolts and famines,' the tsar conceded, 'but I've nearly finished sorting out the country. Come back in ten years or so and everything will be in order.'

The writer waited a while longer, returning in 1917 to be greeted by customs officers who ripped his clothes and gave them back to him. Lenin popped out of his haystack to say hello, and when the writer started to ask questions Lenin said he needed his advisers, so Lenin's wife, Gorky, Dzherzhinsky and the rest of the

Bolshevik mob trooped out of the haystack. 'We are on the eve of a dictatorship of the proletariat,' Lenin announced to the writer.

'That's fine,' said the writer, noting it down, 'but I have noticed that the proletariat hasn't got much electricity. Are you going to do something about that, too?'

'Electricity?' said Lenin. 'How do we make it?'

'You need to build some power stations,' the writer told him. Lenin consulted with his advisers and they assured him that if he built power stations the nation's lights would go on.

'We shall build power stations!' Lenin declared. He had to think up a slogan to advertise his latest stroke of genius. 'Soviet power plus the electrification of the whole country equals com-,' he paused, waiting for his advisers to join in. They were stumped, not knowing what he meant.

'Complete anarchy?' Gorky suggested.

The writer wasn't impressed and when he asked Lenin how long it would take to modernise Russia, he got a familiar reply. So he came back at the beginning of the 21st century. In New Russia, Inc., as the country called itself, the customs officers were the same as ever. 'I know the procedure,' the writer told them, ripping up his own clothes to save time. The president of New Russia, Inc. was a multimillionaire businessman who was just about to unveil the prototype for an improved human being. The writer arrived in time to witness New Russian hatching from a mechanical egg. Unfortunately he had a fault and went berserk, knocking down all the television cameras and insulting the assembled dignitaries. 'We haven't got things exactly right yet,' the president apologised, 'but come back in ten years or so...' The writer, confined to a wheelchair in his old age, declined the offer.

'I think I've seen enough,' he said.

There was more mayhem to be found in puppet theatre, a long tradition in Russia. I couldn't resist visiting the St Petersburg Theatrical Academy's puppet theatre department, to find out how the mastery of grotesque and ridiculous dangly creatures had been turned into a subject for serious academic study. The head of the department, Anya Ivanova, said that new students had a choice of four disciplines - actor, director, stage designer or puppet technologist. The latter became the Guiseppes to Russia's Pinocchios, experts in the mechanics of puppet-making.

Puppet theatre in Russia developed from street entertainment, similar to our Punch-and-Judy shows, and the first eyewitness to write about such a spectacle was a German traveller who was in Moscow in 1636. Bible stories and mythology were common themes. Puppets remained on the fringes of Russian culture until the 1920s, when the Soviet government in its wisdom recognised their crucial role in building a socialist nation (they distracted people from going to see subversive flesh-and-blood actors). A number of special puppet theatres opened up around the country.

The Soviet government had overlooked the fact (or perhaps no one was brave enough to tell them) that puppets are manipulated by real human beings. They were considered politically harmless and from the 1960s onwards many artists transferred from conventional theatre to puppet theatre because through this genre they could express ideas which could not be discussed openly on the stage. The St Petersburg puppet theatre department was the first of its kind in the country, opening its doors in 1959. Its graduates went on to found similar institutions in towns such as Yaroslavl, Ekaterinburg and Nizhny Novgorod, but to this day there is no such department in Moscow.

During my visit to the puppet department second-year students on the acting course were demonstrating their ability to control the flailing limbs of marionettes and give them voice in outlandish accents. In their first year the students had worked with glove puppets and their progression to marionettes posed a considerable challenge as each one had up to 20 strings attached to the various joints of its body.

One slip of the performer's wrist could have dire consequences, as acrobats entangled themselves in an unwanted embrace or a horse was spontaneously decapitated. But when things went right the interaction of humans and puppets was hilarious to behold, as for instance an enraged husband chased his wife's lover around the house and in the confusion the two male actors swapped marionettes.

The main problems Russian puppet theatre faced in the era of free speech were a lack of plays specifically written for puppets, and technical backwardness, according to Anya Ivanova. Her advice to potential puppet playwrights was that they should work closely with the puppet designers to understand how their characters could move and what could be left out of the script - only the most essential words should be spoken. As for the technology, she had been to England and saw that here, special effects such as flames or an underwater kingdom were relatively easy to realise. 'In Russia, even if we have the ideas in the first place, we don't have the equipment to put them into practice,' she said regretfully.

The only way of seeing high-budget special effects in St Petersburg was to go to a cinema and sit in a cold, popcornless auditorium watching a dubbed Western film. The dubbing was better than it had been in Voronezh or Minsk, where all the characters were read by a single voice, which tended to spoil the endings of thrillers when the same person said, 'You are the murderer. Who, me? No, not you, you! I didn't do it - he did.' In the St Petersburg cinemas there was usually at least one male and one female, so there was a great improvement on the dialogue in sex scenes, at least.

Russian cinemas made no concessions to bodily comforts. They were never full, but even so it was particularly bad when three of us went to see a new French release and weren't joined by anyone else. The projectionist obviously wasn't feeling optimistic and started the film the moment we walked in. A while later two more people sidled in but couldn't be counted in the audience figures for that night because they gave up half-way through.

After the film we discovered why this cinema was so unpopular. We emerged into the bright lights of virtual reality arcade games: St Petersburg's answer to the Trocadero in London. A segregated section of the hall was full of teenagers seated at PCs zapping CD-generated aliens, and the rest was a gimmick-seeker's paradise of video Dodge City shoot-outs, luminous table ice-hockey, Mortal Kombat II and the bash-the-leaping-frogs-over-the-head-with-a-rubber-mallet game (my personal favourite). I achieved a startling degree of success in it after I gave myself the psychological edge by naming each frog after a colleague at work, or a friend who hadn't written for a year, or representatives of the Student Loans Company, who wrote every week.

When our tokens for the arcade games ran out, we progressed to the Wild West saloon bar, a Disneylandish plastic recreation of a St Petersburg drinking-hole during the little-known 1880s gold rush. Its authenticity was confirmed by a cactus, a saddle and a noose swinging idly in the corner. No one had got round to finding a game to play with these items yet (Russians have missed out on the improvisational comedy show *Whose Line is it Anyway?*), so the saloon's customers had to be content with using a prime working model of a US pool table, circa 1996, one of only a handful in the city. With such a range of attractions on offer, I could quite understand why people had come to this cinema to do anything but watch a film.

St Petersburg was a hot location for making a film, though. Filling the void left by Russian production companies, most of whom were taking an enforced holiday because they had no money, Western crews descended on the city to take advantage of its stunning architectural backdrops and relatively low costs. James Bond led the charge with a tank chase along the city streets in *Goldeneye*. Then came the first Western film to be shot entirely in Russia since the collapse of the Soviet Union: *Anna Karenina*.

By now I expect the results of this reinterpretation of Tolstoy's novel by Mel Gibson's production team are known to the public. When Gibson's partner, Bruce Davey, and his costumed cavalcade arrived in town, I was dubious. Wouldn't the plot have to be tweaked a little to provide US audiences with the happy ending they are accustomed to? Tolstoy wrote so many words, a few more could hardly be out of keeping. Why not scribble in a miners' strike in the Urals that causes the train to run out of coal and screech to a halt seconds before Anna flings herself under it?

The company's plot synopsis for journalists reassured me on that score. The changes weren't so drastic. Melodrama and violent death were there in spades:

'Russia - 1880. Handsome young cavalry officer, Count Alexei Kirillovich Vronsky (SEAN BEAN) succeeds in the conquest of Anna (SOPHIE MARCEAU), whose passionate nature matches that of her spirited suitor.' Tragically, Anna is a married woman.

Her husband is a big-eared bore of a civil servant and he's determined to win custody of their son by proving Anna's moral depravity.

'...Anna and Vronsky begin to feel the pressure of their situation. Society forbids them to be seen out together until the divorce is final and Anna cannot go out alone. As she becomes more dependent on liquid morphine, the tension increases. They begin to row.' Now that things have got tough, Vronsky skedaddles to the country. Anna decides to follow him.

'...As the steam from the locomotive swirls around her face, Anna's mind drifts back to when she was a child steeling herself to plunge into a cold Russian lake. She falls forward... onto the track. Realising where she is, she tries to get up. But it is too late. She is hit from behind and crushed under the wheels. Her life, like the flame of a candle, is snuffed out for ever.'

In the black-and-white Russian film, that's the end. But the Americans still had a trick or two up their sleeves. Some more weeping and then a chance to forget all about Anna the adulterous drug addict and admire the domestic harmony of a family Newt Gingrich would be proud of:

'Autumn 1883... Unable to come to terms with Anna's death and welcoming the prospect of laying down his life for a cause, Vronsky has volunteered for the Serbian war. He feels he has lost too much. All he asks is to be able to remember Anna as she once was, when he first met her. He tries to bring back those moments... but he cannot. He cannot see her face. He can only see her in the railway shed where they took her, laid out on a table, mangled.

'Levin (ALFRED MOLINA), who is against the war, believing it wrong to kill innocent men and women, cannot save Vronsky from his fate. He returns home to Kitty (MIA KIRSHNER) and his son, to a house full of hope and a life full of love.'

The shooting of *Anna Karenina* began in the week when my parents were visiting. I'd planned a packed itinerary of palaces, museums and concerts for them, but they'd seen the reels of film arriving at the airport and what they really wanted to do in St Petersburg was to spot a famous British film star. Luckily we didn't have to look very far. On their first evening I took them to hear the Russian National Symphony Orchestra at the

Philharmonia. Three seats down from us, a pair of boots attached to long legs in scruffy jeans stuck out conspicuously. 'These tourists have no respect for great Russian institutions,' I said.

In the interval the boots and jeans got up and we caught a glimpse of their instantly recognisable owner. 'You know what,' Mum said excitedly, 'That's that actor I really fancy. It is! Can you believe it?' Ever since I could remember, Mum had had a crush on one of the Fox brothers, James or Edward. Ever since I could remember, she hadn't been able to decide which one he was. As this Fox sexily sipped a glass of champagne, Mum tried to identify him. 'Well, there's a tall one and a short one, and the tall one's definitely Edward.'

'Is this the tall one, then?' I asked her.

'Er...,' she said. I offered to stand next to him at the bar and shout 'James!' to see if he jumped, but Mum wasn't keen on drawing attention to herself so early in their relationship.

'You're right, it won't work,' I said. 'He's probably so used to it that he answers to both names.' We concluded that James did war films and Edward did Chekhov and Tolstoy, so this must have been Edward. Mum was still uncertain about whether he was her heartthrob.

The next day I phoned the publicity officer for *Anna Karenina*, enquiring about the cast's availability for interview and hoping to solve our dilemma at the same time. 'You know who the stars are, of course,' he said. 'Anna's being played by Sophie Marceau.'

'Oh yes,' I said knowledgeably. Pretending to be informed is a cardinal sin in journalism - it can get you into hellish trouble - but the temptation to boast about my new showbiz awareness was too great. 'I bumped into Edward Fox the other night.'

'You mean Jimmy, don't you?' the publicity officer corrected me.

'Exactly, yes, Jimmy. So is he doing interviews?'

He wasn't - it was too early on in the production. But we hadn't seen the last of Jimmy. Dad was writing a business travel article and for research purposes the manager of the five-star Nevskij Palace Hotel had given my parents a room. They were James Fox's neighbours. When they ate their breakfast, he was on the table next to them. When they wanted to make a phone call, he was there booking a taxi. As he paced up and down in the lobby one evening we joked that he was worried about being late to the same opera we were going to see. His cab screeched up to the doors of the Mariinsky Theatre 30 seconds behind ours. James Fox was around so much that Mum's interest in him waned and she was pleasantly surprised when she had the chance to witness Alfred Molina cashing some travellers' cheques.

While Western stars lived it up in the Nevskij Palace, the Russian film industry was in a sorry state. This was unwittingly illustrated during a Russian film festival in August 1995, *Long Live Russian Cinema*. On the opening day of the festival, a montage of jolly clips from the glory years of Soviet cinema called *Great and Unrepeatable* was due to be projected to the masses on an outdoor screen in Palace Square at 8 pm. *Invisible and Unshowable* would have been a more appropriate title. Between the Hermitage and the column which honours Alexander I, a couple of hundred people had assembled in broad daylight to see if some new form of technology had been developed to defy the laws of nature.

It hadn't. The film started 20 minutes late but the sun showed no sign of going into eclipse or modestly retreating to another hemisphere. Instead of leaving, most of the audience were mesmerised by the blank screen and stayed around to laugh at this extraordinary event and listen to the rousing Soviet music. When the sun went behind the clouds, faint shadows of strapping farm workers strumming banjos and passengers chatting to each other on a train flashed in front of us momentarily. The festival had an audience of satisfied customers, who'd been more entertained than they would have been in an ordinary, old-fashioned, dark cinema.

Cinema was doing badly in Russia, but was the country's supply of literary genius drying up, too? I talked to Andrei Balabukha, president of the Belyayev Fund, which awarded prizes for new works of science-fiction, fantasy and popular science. The reward was financial, unlike other Russian science-fiction prizes. 'Russian writers need money,' said Balabukha. 'We won't say exactly how much the prizes are worth, but it is nothing by Western standards. They are in the region of £175 each, which gives the winners an opportunity not to think about where their bread is coming from for a month or so.'

The Russian market had been flooded with pirate publications and cheap Western detective novels, so 'good literature' had been swamped. There was a copyright law and a presidential decree allowing literary organisations to pay lower taxes, but enforcing those laws was another matter. Balabukha and his friend Alexander Bransky, vice-president of the Belyayev Fund, could cite numerous examples of their acquaintances being deceived by Russian publishing companies. 'There are two reasons for this, incompetence and deliberate avoidance of payment,' said Bransky. 'A translation by one of my friends was published in a collection without his name even on it, and on another occasion a writer wasn't paid because the publishing company didn't know where to find him.' Sometimes publishing companies would produce pirate editions of books and then simply liquidate themselves and disappear so that no legal action could be taken against them.

Balabukha started working on a novel in 1993 about the psychological condition of people in a chemical catastrophe, but he had been unable to finish it because he spent most of his time writing criticism for magazines and translating. This earned him a maximum of between £75 and £100 a month. 'Poets are in the worst situation,' said Balabukha, 'because poetry is not profitable.'

Despite the cash crisis, the recipients of 1995 Belyayev prizes weren't short on inspiration. I asked some of them how they imagined Russia would look in the year 2010. Sergei Ryazantsev, author of *The Philosophy of Death*, was confident of living to see a reunited empire with its medieval state names printed on the map again. 'Russia will be a rich, strong, great state,' he said. 'She will have its traditional Baltic, Caucasian and Central Asian guberniyas [provinces] which will be known by their original names such as Lifland, Kurland and Estland.'

This harmonious situation would not come about through war, Ryazantsev assured me. The various nationalities would agree to live together democratically and form an economic union. Indeed, six months after this prediction, the presidents of Russia and Belarus signed a treaty of unity. 'People will speak whichever language is most comfortable for them,' continued Ryazantsev. 'This small Russia which exists at the moment is only temporary.

We need the territory of Central Asia for its grain, gold and important installations - the Baikonur space centre in Kazakhstan, for instance.'

Ryazantsev was convinced that Russia would catch up with Western European standards of living and that e-mail and the Internet would be in widespread use. As for his special subject, death, he didn't foresee an immediate cure. 'The question of immortality will not be solved within the next thousand years,' he said. 'However, religion will have more influence in the Russia of 2010, especially Orthodox Christianity and Islam.'

Science-fiction writer and sinologist Vyacheslav Rybakov wouldn't commit himself to any definite predictions but said he had already conceived several alternative scenarios. 'There is the way I would like Russia to be in 2010 and there is the very frightening picture, but I can't choose between them and say which will come true. There is also the middle way, but that's very boring.'

Rybakov's dream was for Russia to become more stable, 'leaving extremes behind and at the same time not making Russia a completely European country. Our politicians have to learn to find a compromise between the historical traditions of Russia and the real world in which she has to live.' He shared Ryazantsev's opinion that Russia was bound to re-establish close ties with her neighbours. 'An empire like the USSR doesn't just collapse. The Baltic states had to go but the Orthodox Slavic civilisations can unite again, at least economically. When different nationalities mix there are very bad repercussions, such as in Yugoslavia, Ireland and Quebec.'

Fantasy writer Svyatoslav Loginov thought that Russia in 2010 would be the same as Russia in the nineties, 'except maybe she will make a bit more noise.' Loginov, a chemist by training, said that scientific 'progress' wasn't worth discussing because it made no difference to the quality of life. 'Our famous comic writers of the 1920s Ilf and Petrov said that with radio there would be happiness, but there was radio and it did not bring happiness. Happiness has no relationship to science. Sandwiches make people happy.'

Society

Russians say, 'Without papers, you aren't a person'. Few truer statements have been made about the country. Russian citizens have an internal passport which they carry around with them at all times, and if they want to go abroad they have to apply for a separate foreign passport. The internal passport is stamped when they get married and stamped with their home address whenever they move. A lost internal passport is like gold dust to criminals - they can use it to start a company in someone else's name and that person takes the rap if the company goes bankrupt or does anything illegal.

In the 'democratic' 1990s, Russians who lived in a town other than the one on their official residence stamp couldn't go to the doctor, get a job or send their children to school. They could also be detained by the police for up to three days in case their unannounced presence was part of a Chechen terrorist conspiracy. A blow was struck for human rights in 1996 when a journalist who had moved from the provinces to work for a newspaper in Moscow won her court battle against the city council, which had told her a Moscow residence permit would cost several thousand dollars, but in general the Russian population continued to cringe in the face of authority.

Respect for papers worked both ways. A St Petersburg newspaper ran the headline, 'As metro prices rise, so does the number of students'. It referred to the extraordinarily high proportion of people who were passing themselves off as students to get cheaper tickets. The number of survivors of the Siege of Leningrad (who travelled free on public transport) was also increasing mysteriously. For many working people a month of full-price journeys on the metro cost the whole of their salary. But the metro needed money, too. The man in charge of it told the press he could no longer guarantee the safety of passengers as there was nothing to fund routine repairs. All his available resources had been diverted to a collapsed tunnel in the north-eastern suburbs, which had severed the last two stops on the line from the rest of the underground system.

The metro was once known for its cleanliness and architectural beauty. The grand neo-classical columns, the statues and the mosaics were still there; the ideal of a metro without litter bins had been preserved by an unwritten social contract which compelled people to carry empty cans and paper bags with them until they reached ground level - and then drop them next to a bin - but the floors were grimy with dust and the trampled black remnants of chewing-gum.

Capitalism enlivened the metro with newspaper stands, kiosks, old men selling wooden tortoises whose heads nod until Doomsday ('You can have it for free if you get it to stop') and old women selling real tortoises. I bought one for 40,000 roubles (£5) and was given a free milk carton to take it home in. 'They're very intelligent,' said my baby's ex-owner. 'In a few weeks she'll recognise her name and come when she's called.' The other piece of advice I was given was to feed it raw meat twice a week. The reliability of my information was cast into doubt when little Ninja completely ignored me and ate only lettuce. 'Tortoises are deaf, aren't they?' someone suggested helpfully. I should have bought a wooden one with a nodding head - it would have been more fun.

If you had spare change on the metro and didn't need a newspaper or a pet, there was a beggar or a busker to give it away to every few paces. The beggars had scrawled signs in front of them to denote their level of piteousness. A mother and baby: 'Please give money for cancer operation.' A young man with no hands: 'I served the Motherland. Please help.' A Gypsy family: 'We are hungry.' A babushka in a shawl lingered next to one ticket counter, meekly approaching each passenger as if to ask them the time, 'Excuse me -,' and then, tearfully, 'Please, just enough for a loaf of bread, God bless you.'

Some of the buskers were, quite literally, virtuosos. An accordionist playing Gershwin and two keyboard players doing a Bach fugue as a duet had me rooted to the spot. You could be treated to anything from a penny whistle to a jazz band. So if you were hard-up yourself, how did you decide who to help? I asked Rozanna her opinion, as she was studying sociology and had done a project on beggars. 'Beggars are all professionals,' she said, like a true Thatcherite. 'I only give money to buskers. No Russian would really beg, it's beneath them, they'd go home and knit something to sell. These people you see on the metro live in big houses and drive expensive cars.' Especially the ones with no hands, I thought.

Most Russians were cynical about beggars because there didn't seem to be any before 1991. Therefore they were either proof that capitalism had made people poorer or they were frauds. Not everyone remembered, or chose to remember, that the lumpenproletariat of the Soviet Union were simply picked off the streets by the police and escorted to a place where no one would see them being poor and miserable. In a television debate about how to cope with the proliferation of beggars, someone said that the reason why there were remarkably few cripples after World War II was because they were shot by their own government when they returned from the front.

The man who organised St Petersburg's first night shelter for homeless adults accused President Yeltsin of killing people through his failure to reform the laws which linked access to basic necessities with the residence stamp. 'It is difficult to describe the policy of the Russian government in relation to homeless people other than as concealed genocide,' Valery Sokolov said in the report he sent to the UN Committee on Human Rights. In 1995 a total of 1066 homeless people in St Petersburg died in streets, yards, basements, stations and attics. Only 76 died in a hospital. The government's warning when temperatures in Moscow and St Petersburg plunged below -20° was: 'Be careful when you go outside at night. Don't fall asleep on a park bench or you may never wake up. Every walk could be your last.'

Homeless people were always outside at night. The St Petersburg city budget provided money for children's shelters but didn't fund a single adult shelter. At Pushkinskaya 10, where Sokolov's organisation was based, clothes and soup were handed out and a lawyer gave free advice. The charity, Nochlyezhka (Nightshelter), also had a doctor and a few beds for elderly people. 'This isn't a real night shelter,' said Sokolov. 'We have appealed to the Mayor's Office so many times for funds but they have never given us anything. The money goes to high-profile events such as the Goodwill Games or the 50th anniversary victory celebrations.'

Nochlyezhka relied entirely on private donations. Sokolov hoped to raise enough cash to build dormitories for 60 people.

Sokolov was homeless himself from the age of 19 while he was avoiding military service. When I met him he was 28 and had been registered as a St Petersburg resident since 1993. In 1995 he stood as an independent candidate in the parliamentary elections. 'At least in prison homeless people had a roof over their heads, work and food. In that sense things were better during the Soviet era,' he said. 'But in terms of human rights, of course, the situation was even worse than it is now.'

Unresolved family disputes were a major cause of homelessness in St Petersburg. People didn't like turning to outsiders for help. After 70 years of state interference in their personal lives, they preferred to be left alone. Paroled prisoners were another group of people who commonly got left out in the cold: the government had the right to reclaim their flats if they spent a long time behind bars. Sokolov pointed out that this breached the guarantee in the UN Declaration of Human Rights that no one may be punished twice for the same crime. Russia is a signatory to the UN Declaration.

Sokolov pointed to piles of letters stacked up on a table. 'We get a bundle of these every day from prisoners,' he said. 'They all say the same thing - you are our only hope.' In response Nochlyezhka gave out parcels of clothing to released prisoners. In every parcel there was a leaflet detailing their rights.

Nochlyezhka doctor Vladimir Podkolzin depended on whatever out-of-date medicines were given to the charity. 'It's horrible,' he said. 'Sometimes we get good antibiotics, but we have no bandages. People come here infested with parasites and I can do nothing about it.' One thing homeless people could do to help themselves was to sell Nochlyezhka's magazine *The Depths*, as the homeless in Britain sell *The Big Issue*. Representatives of *The Big Issue* went to Nochlyezhka and were so disturbed by what they saw that they donated a proportion of their sales revenue to their Russian counterpart.

Chabo the Caucasian brown bear was luckier than many of St Petersburg's human inhabitants. When Asya Makhomateva went to visit relatives in Grozny during a lull in the war in Chechnya, a hunter gave her Chabo. He was a 16-inch baby, orphaned by the fighting. Makhomateva brought him back to St Petersburg with her on a plane.

Five months later, Chabo was three foot three and his adult teeth were beginning to grow. Makhomateva took him out on the street every day for fresh air, and that's where I met them. Chabo chewed on her hand unrelentingly, thinking he was being affectionate but frequently scratching her. He was becoming a problem child. Makhomateva was desperately looking for a zoo or a circus to buy her overgrown pet before he gnawed through her front door.

'We must take you for a bath today,' Makhomateva told Chabo sternly. She said he hadn't washed for three weeks because whenever he heard water running he would roll onto his back and refuse to be moved. Makhomateva's latest ploy was to drive the bear and some shampoo to the Gulf of Finland and toss him in there, where the bath was already full.

Chabo lived in Makhomateva's flat, happily playing with her three children. He ate fruit, vegetables and dairy products but wouldn't touch meat or honey. Makhomateva had succeeded in pacifying the neighbours, who called the police when they first found out why such loud chomping noises were coming from their building. The police approved - 'No problem, some people like to have dogs as pets - you have a bear.'

My own neighbour threatened to call the police when I sabotaged her redecorating and nearly caused her ceiling to collapse. As her ceiling was my floor, I was as anxious as she was to keep it from turning into a mushy pulp, but this was easier said than done. A pipe in my kitchen had sprung a leak which no bucket was big enough to contain while I was asleep at night. I couldn't call the plumbers straight away because my landlady was afraid that if anyone found out she had a foreigner renting her flat she'd have to pay extra taxes, so I had to wait for her to do it.

Russian plumbers never said what time they were coming, they said whether they were coming in the morning or the afternoon. The landlady offered to sit in my flat waiting for the plumbers to arrive while I was at work. She didn't promise to stay until they'd finished the job, though. When I came home in the evening it seemed she'd opened the door to the plumbers and then left. The original leak was worse than ever and there was now water flowing from several more pipes which had been intact until the plumbers got at them. The unopened bottle of vodka which had been in my fridge was standing on top of it, three-quarters full. My downstairs neighbour came to visit me again, this time demanding money.

Some of the pipes that were leaking were so low down that no bucket or even jar would fit under them. I dragged my spare mattress into the kitchen, hoping that during the night it would soak up some of the water and save my neighbour from being crushed to death by my cooker, although after she screeched at me the second time, that prospect didn't seem entirely unattractive. But I needed the cooker.

The next day I called the plumbers myself and waited at home for them to burst in with the tax police. Instead, I got one little old man who looked as crumpled as my mattress. He slapped a coating of cement over one of the leaks and splattered it all over the floor. 'Is that your usual method? Shouldn't you put in a new pipe?' I asked him.

'Narr, that'll see you for a good few years yet. Getting a new pipe's expensive. No need to do that.' He got up to leave.

'Hang on,' I said, 'what about all the other leaks? I can see water dripping.'

'That's not dripping, that's condensation, that is.'

'No, it's definitely dripping.'

'Well, in that case I'll put my glasses on.'

After eleven months in St Petersburg the stresses were beginning to take their toll on me. Each day a different joint would ache and from time to time my hands shook. When I'd convinced myself it was the onset of a terminal disease, I felt ready to make my first visit to a Russian polyclinic. Like plumbers, doctors didn't make appointments. In sophisticated polyclinics you took a scrap of paper with a number on it and that was how you knew when your turn was. In my polyclinic each new arrival looked around the waiting room and said, 'Who's last for door 32?' and the last person in the queue for door 32 identified himself so that this new person knew who was going in before him. But to get to the waiting room you had to get past Reception.

Before Reception there was the cloakroom. You couldn't enter a public building in Russia wearing a coat. I took mine off and handed it to the babushka on duty, who was supposed to give me a token. Instead she shook the coat at me, fuming. 'I can't take this! Look at it! Where's the hook?' It was broken and I hadn't got round to sewing it up. 'You knew you were coming here, you should have done something about it!' How foolish of me to worry about my illness when I should have been taking care of my coat. I tried to look as if I was going to burst into tears, which wasn't difficult, and the babushka shoved a token over the counter with a glare.

Reception consisted of a desk where three women sat engrossed in conversation. I loitered nervously in their vicinity, hoping someone would pay attention to me so that I wouldn't get shouted at again for interrupting them. They ignored me. When my shaking and hyperventilating became too distracting, one of them turned round. 'What did you want?' she snapped.

'I would like to see a doctor, please,' I said in my heavy English accent.

'Oh my God, a foreigner. What sort of doctor? What's wrong with you?'

'I have pains. I'd rather explain it to the doctor. Could I see one, please, I feel very bad.' The Receptionist sighed with frustration and disgust.

'A surgeon, a neuropathologist, an endocrinologist, a cardiologist, what? Have you got an injury?'

'No, just pains.'

'I don't know what you're talking about. Go to room 26 on the second floor.'

The doctor took my blood pressure and found it was low, so she prescribed something in a bottle that sounded like Electrocock and was supposed to perk me up in the mornings. To investigate the rest of me she ordered me to have a blood test, a urine test and a lung X-ray for good measure. I wasn't allowed to see the X-ray but I was given a piece of paper which said 'Everything fine' on it. Getting the results of the other tests was an eye-opener. I was already dubious when the nurse who was sticking a needle into my finger shouted at the nurse in front of her, 'No, no, you're doing it wrong, you don't put that needle into that liquid, it's not sterile!' The results, of course, had to be collected from Reception.

I asked the Receptionist where my results were. 'They could be anywhere,' she said. 'Anywhere around here. Look for them. You don't expect me to do it, do you?' Someone on crutches was rifling through a drawer full of test results.

'They should be in here,' he said. 'If they're not, they'll be with the doctor.' I had to look through the test results of all the people with surnames in my section of the alphabet. I could see their name, address, and whether they were HIV positive or had hepatitis. If I'd wanted to, I could have picked one out and taken it with me to use as future proof of my excellent state of health, or blackmailed people about their not-so-excellent condition.

My results were with the doctor. This time when I went to see her the queue was longer. Each person who joined it said, 'I'll just nip in ahead of you. I'm not here for treatment, I'm picking something up', or, 'I've got a quick question to ask her, it's hardly worth me waiting', or, 'I survived the Siege of Leningrad, I'm allowed to go in first.'

I waited an hour for my turn. I was exhausted with worry and slumped on the torn canvas chair next to the doctor while she argued with the group of people who had charged in with me. One couldn't find his doctor and wanted mine to pay immediate attention to his bleeding hand. Another was too old to wait any longer. The doctor's curt replies were enough to disperse most of the crowd but she had to physically escort one person to the door. She left me alone with the woman who was too old. I had my head in my hands. 'What's the matter? You've probably got a temperature, dearie,' the other patient advised me sympathetically.

There was nothing wrong with my blood or my urine. I said I'd been drinking the Electrocock but it hadn't done much for me. Apparently I had to get through several bottles of the stuff. 'I feel terrible and I've started twitching,' I said.

'You've got a syndrome!' the doctor announced triumphantly, and marched me downstairs to see a neuropathologist. The neuropathologist tapped me a few times with a hammer and asked me if there was any unpleasantness in my life.

'Seeing the doctor has been a little traumatic,' I said. He sent me out to the corridor while he considered my syndrome. A few minutes later he emerged with a prescription, which he read out to me and everyone else in the corridor.

'Your nerves are out of order,' he said. 'You have to take tablets. Half of Amytripylin twice a day and one of Agapurin three times a day. Off you go.'

For a short time after this I was thrilled - at last someone other than an elderly patient had recognised that something was wrong with me. As soon as I had the tablets in my hand my pains and twitching went away. I took them for a few days and I was fine. Then doubts crept in. Why were my nerves out of order? How long would they be out of order for? What were these tablets? Would I die if I drank alcohol while I was taking them? Why hadn't the neuropathologist asked me to come back and see him so that he could check my nerves were in order again?

My symptoms returned, more forcefully than ever. At the same time I was cut off from the world because my telephone had gone dead. On this occasion the landlady really was the only person who could do anything about it. She lived in a flat in the same building as me and had installed a telephone in my flat on the same line as hers, running the wire over the roof. The wire had broken, cutting off my phone but not Lena's. I dragged myself off my sickbed every day to knock on Lena's door, but she either wasn't in or she was in a foul mood. She couldn't deal with my telephone because she had her own troubles raising £2000 to bail out a friend who had been arrested for buying a gram of cannabis.

Alone in my silent flat one night, twitching, I panicked. Someone in the medical profession had to take some notice of me. Machines should be monitoring me. I needed a cardiologist and an endocrinologist. I should have taken them when they were first offered to me. I ran out into the street in the pouring rain and called an ambulance. I dialled 03, the emergency number, and was interrogated about the seriousness of my complaint. I couldn't think how to encapsulate the variety of my symptoms in Russian, so I said I'd been poisoned. 'What by, food, alcohol, drugs?' a voice barked at me.

'I don't know. I have pains everywhere.' The voice asked me where I was and then gave me the phone number of my local hospital, which I had to memorise as I'd forgotten to bring a pen. Two empty ambulances drove past me.

'I need a doctor urgently,' I told the hospital. I had a bleak suspicion I was talking to a Receptionist.

'I can't understand you. Find someone who speaks Russian normally. You need a doctor? They don't see patients at this hour. How old are you? Are you calling from the street? Then you'll have to dial 03. That's the emergency number.' I went home to bed. There was nothing I could do to get into a Russian hospital: not even collapsing in the middle of Nevsky Prospekt in broad daylight would have helped. There were so many people lying comatose on pavements that no one took any notice of them. Either they were drunk, in which case they would wake up with a headache and stagger off, or they were dead already, which meant it was too late to do anything for them. Thinking I was on the verge of a heart attack, I considered sticking a card onto the front of my coat: 'I am not in the habit of falling down drunk in the road. If I become immobilised in a public place, it's because one of my vital organs has ceased to function, so please call a doctor.'

I came back to England and saw my GP. He didn't even bother tapping me with a hammer. I told him I was having palpitations and my big toe had swivelled around on its own while I was trying to do relaxation exercises. Surely this alone justified a bed in intensive care? 'It's stress,' said the doctor. 'Your nerves are fine and you didn't need to take those pills - they were very strong anti-depressants. Go away and take things easy.' One thing that had been successful was the Electrocock: my blood pressure was back to normal. I can recommend it.

Much as I relished the challenges of living in Russia, the freedom to go home for a dose of boring old British common sense gave me the status of the only tightrope-walker in the circus with a safety-net to break my falls. I had to count myself lucky that I wasn't born in Russia. The Russian struggle begins in the maternity hospital, as I saw when I visited the oldest one in Europe, St Petersburg's Snegirev hospital.

The hospital was founded in 1776 but its methods in the late 20th century were just emerging from the dark ages. Women brought their children into the world in a room where up to nine others were in various stages of agony. With no space for relatives, it was the cleaning ladies and other hospital staff who yelled at new mothers to push harder. Anaesthetics weren't used and only one birth position was traditionally acceptable. The women were told to lie on their backs, which put pressure on the main vein in their spine, thereby decreasing the oxygen supply to the baby. It also meant they were pushing against the force of gravity.

The head doctor was anxious to change conditions in the hospital and sent an obstetrician, Ludmilla Bazhenova, to Sweden for a course on reproductive healthcare. 'We are doing everything that can be done without extra material support,' Dr Bazhenova told me. 'For instance, we try to get acquainted with women during their pregnancy, we are introducing a choice of positions for birth and we start them on an immediate programme of breast-feeding.' Another much-needed step forward was the establishment of a visitors' lounge. In the past, relatives were completely barred from the hospital and used to pass presents up on a rope to mothers standing at the window.

The hospital also hoped to replace the dreadful communal birthing rooms with individual ones. Seeing and hearing the labours of others just a few feet away scared some women and stalled their contractions, especially as the Snegirev hospital accepted a high proportion of women with birthing complications. Denise Gaines, an American midwifery student doing work experience at the hospital, was so impressed by the staff's attitude that she wouldn't say a word against the place. She didn't even mind the cat which roamed freely around the hospital. Her most critical comment was that she would want 'a more participatory role' if she was giving birth there.

'It's important that the same physician who looks after you during the pre-natal period is present at the birth,' said Gaines. 'Russian women don't know the doctor who supervises their labour. And choices about whether or not to use drugs to induce contractions are usually discussed with the mother in America, but not here.' Dr Bazhenova agreed: 'In this country in all spheres of life decisions do not depend on you. I don't think that the woman can make choices, though, if she hasn't got enough education and information.' To further the education of pregnant Russians the hospital was going to open an ante-natal centre which would prepare women and their families for the big day through talks and films.

I did manage to find one satisfied mother, a 40-year-old accountant, who said the horror stories she'd heard about the Snegirev hospital had turned out to be untrue. Her husband had successfully sneaked in to see their baby daughter. 'I was afraid to come here at first, but the staff treated me wonderfully,' she said. Her only concern was that no one had yet shown her how to use the Italian breast-pump she had brought with her.

The breast-pump was an item of modern equipment which the hospital couldn't have provided. But the Snegirev did have intensive care units and lung ventilators for women in comas which no other hospital in St Petersburg had. Healthy babies lay constantly in cots beside their mothers - not so long ago they were loaded onto wagons so that they could be brought to their mothers for nursing during the day.

Another Russian doctor who said medical practices were gradually improving was AIDS specialist Asa Rakhmanova of St Petersburg's Botkin Infectious Diseases Hospital. She was the editor of a magazine called *AIDS, Sex, Health*, and her dream was to distribute it with free condoms. Dr Rakhmanova was keen to show me a rack of disposable syringes which she used to conduct HIV tests. 'It's perfectly safe,' she said. 'But it's hard to persuade Russians to come for tests because they think AIDS isn't their problem. Everyone wants to die of ignorance. If we continue to do nothing about AIDS then Russia will soon occupy the first place in the world for HIV cases.'

Russia still had a relatively low number of HIV cases - about 1000 in 1995 - because the country was cut off from the world for so long, not because the use of condoms was popular. Syphilis was far more common than HIV. When the Iron Curtain was raised and foreign travel was permitted, Russians immediately accused African students of introducing AIDS to the country, conveniently forgetting that traffic goes in more than one direction and it was just as likely that the disease could come in via a Russian who had been to America.

Instead of spending money on education to help people protect themselves from HIV, the Russian government thought up a law which was supposed to prevent HIV-positive visitors from entering the country or to deport them if they slipped through the net. On August 1, 1995, this illogical, unenforceable clanger of a law was due to come into effect. It demanded that anyone visiting Russia for more than three months, or wishing to extend their visa, produced a certificate proving their HIV-negative status.

There were so many reasons why this law was crazy that it's hard to enumerate them all. I'll have a go:

- People with HIV could enter Russia for less than three months and return as many times as they liked.

- Anonymous testing meant that you could use a friend's certificate as proof rather than one of your own.

- To be certain that you are HIV negative you must have a second test three months after the first one. The law didn't mention this, so there was no guarantee that people who had been tested in order to get a Russian visa weren't actually carrying the virus.

- There was nothing to stop foreigners from bringing in whatever other contagious deadly diseases they happened to have (or Russians taking syphilis with them on holiday, or the Russian government from selling automatic weapons to noxious regimes all around the world).

- If there had already been one case of HIV in Russia, then the virus was already in the country. If the government really wanted to forcibly keep control of people who were HIV-positive, it ought to have tested all 150 million Russians and isolated the infected ones, following the Cuban example.

- It is vital for Russia to attract foreign trade and tourism. Thousands of people who were considering going to Russia might have chosen another country when they found out they had to have an HIV test.

Rationality doesn't win many arguments in Russia, but the confusion surrounding this law rendered it virtually harmless.

'What are you talking about? We haven't received any instructions on this,' an official at the St Petersburg department of visas and registration told me when I telephoned to enquire about procedures. Embassies were also in the dark: 'I have seen the law but at the moment we cannot fulfil it and we have no instructions to do so,' said Russia's consul-general in Brussels.

Dr Rakhmanova said the saddest aspect of the law was that it included a number of more enlightened articles which the government couldn't afford to implement. The law theoretically obliged the government to regularly inform people about AIDS through the media and to provide insurance and psychological help for patients. AIDS patients were guaranteed free medicine, confidentiality and the right to be protected from discrimination.

The deputies of St Petersburg's city assembly were aroused by a different ethical issue: what to do about the bright pink signs which had sprung up around the old haunts of Dostoyevsky and Tchaikovsky, garishly pointing the way to sex shops. Churchgoers could stroll across the road after a service to pick up inflatable dolls and bubblegum-flavoured condoms for a Sunday afternoon's relaxation. That had upset the local politicians - it wasn't right for employees of sex shops to be intimidated by having God for a neighbour. Or perhaps I've got that the wrong way round.

Anyway, not to be outdone by the government's crackpot AIDS law, the city assembly debated a law which would have prohibited sex shops from operating within a mile of churches and other bastions of moral authority such as educational institutions, kindergartens, clinics and historical monuments. You didn't need an intimate knowledge of St Petersburg to realise that there were enough of these virtuous hotspots to push sex shops right out into the Baltic Sea, which is exactly what the city assembly wanted to do.

Marina Tsigankova, a middle-aged whale with a moustache, was the director of a sex shop around the corner from the Cathedral of St Vladimir, not far from a statue of Pushkin. Tsigankova said she used to be a pharmacist. Her shop was in a cellar and had no window display. Children were not admitted. 'This law is not rational,' said Tsigankova. 'Perhaps there are pensioners who are shocked by us, but there are also many single people in this city. I can't understand why there is so much prudishness. If there really was no sex in the Soviet Union for 70 years, where did our population come from?'

Fortunately for Tsigankova, if not for St Vladimir, the deputies of the city assembly developed an obsession with a law on local self-government and stopped thinking about sex. The citizens of St Petersburg must have wondered what all the fuss was about. They were engaged in far more wholesome pursuits, such as searching for buried treasure. For - twisted, smashed, rusted, rotting - the ghostly hulks of doomed warships lay buried in sand and silt under the murky waters of the Gulf of Finland. Even the most modern underwater equipment could discern only shadows, which to one observer appeared to be the outline of a submarine, and to another just a trick of the light.

This was the vast and unforgiving world whose secrets were the spoils in a contemporary battle between a naval history society and a scientific research company, INTAARI. The history society, Memory of the Baltic, had been investigating the inhospitable region for six years, ever since some fishermen accidentally came across a British minesweeper. Then INTAARI got involved, when a mysterious client paid the company to make a series of high-technology surveying expeditions.

The minesweeper, HMS *Myrtle*, exploded in 1919 near the island of Saaremaa (now Estonian territory) whilst on a mission to help the anti-Bolshevik forces in the Russian civil war. Skin-divers from Memory of the Baltic reached the wreck at a depth of 120 feet and recovered a magnetic compass and mechanical log. The bow of the ship was ripped off and the crew from Memory of the Baltic couldn't find it.

The compass from the minesweeper, with its manufacturer's stamp, 'Dobbie McInnes Ltd, Glasgow', still clearly legible, was given to the Kaliningrad Museum of World Oceans. Konstantin Shopotov, the former naval captain who founded Memory of the Baltic, was excited at such an early success, but the Greenwich National Maritime Museum in London showed no interest. He was only able to get background information about the *Myrtle* when he made contact with someone from England at a St

Petersburg international fishing expo. 'The British have a devil-may-care attitude to their own sailors,' said Shopotov. 'There is no way we can find out who died on the *Myrtle* as all the literature is in England.'

For Memory of the Baltic, which Shopotov called a 'military-patriotic organisation', the Russian civil war was of secondary importance in comparison with the triumphant victory over the forces of Sweden's King Gustav III in 1790. The Swedes, who had never forgiven Peter I for stealing land at the mouth of the river Neva a century before, were attempting to seize St Petersburg but were repelled by Catherine II's Baltic Fleet under the command of Admiral Chichagov.

When news of the raid first arrived at Catherine II's court, she was asked by a French envoy if she intended to move to Moscow, where she would be out of reach of the Swedes. The empress swiftly rebuffed him with the words, 'I shall not leave, you can be sure.' Thus all the diplomats were obliged to remain in St Petersburg out of politeness.

Russia suffered no losses in a battle described by one British historian as a 'Baltic Trafalgar'. Somewhere at the bottom of the Gulf of Finland there were seven Swedish battleships, three frigates and more than 50 galleys. Memory of the Baltic found a number of these vessels. One of their trophies was the 74-cannon battleship *Louisa Ulrika*. Amongst the artefacts retrieved by Memory of the Baltic were a bottle containing a statue of a royal personage on a horse, ceramics from the facing of a hearth, pieces of mast and a massive section of a keel.

The exploratory activities of Memory of the Baltic were limited because it was a voluntary society. It didn't have the enormous funds which would be required to raise whole ships to the surface. 'It would cost millions and in the first place you have to decide why you want to bring these ships up,' said Shopotov.

But someone was willing to spend big money on old relics. INTAARI wouldn't name their client and couldn't let me go on board the ship which was making the reconnaissance trips because it belonged to the navy and was being leased illegally. But I did see sketches of the new equipment INTAARI designed to do the research. Hydrolocators and custom-made underwater photography devices were the scientific answer to Memory of the Baltic's divers and 200-year-old maps. The scientists found a German ship which sank in World War II, an unexploded torpedo and the Swedish ship *Charlotta*, buried in mud at a depth of 85 feet. INTAARI initially involved Memory of the Baltic in their investigations. When valuables began to turn up they excluded the historians, infuriating Shopotov. INTAARI's photographs could be examined in minute detail on their computers, but their client wouldn't allow the pictures to be published. The only conclusion that could be drawn from all the secrecy was that there was still something very valuable in the Gulf of Finland.

As I wasn't able to have an adventure on the water, I bought a map of the region around St Petersburg and set off with Kostya for a spontaneous journey into the countryside. The largest lake in Europe, Lake Ladoga, was about 25 miles east of St Petersburg and I'd never set eyes on it. The railway line from the city bent around it to the north, splitting like pincers to circumvent the lake on the east and west sides. We took the west side, because it was nearer and because Kostya had once met someone who owned a hotel in a town in that direction.

My other Russian sleeping and drinking partner, Dima, once said that whenever he couldn't think of a subject for a news report, he took his tape recorder and microphone to a train station because the whole of life was there. On Saturdays, Sundays and public holidays, hordes of urban Russians who spent their weekdays in a stuffy office or a sweaty factory pulled on their wellington boots, picked up a spade, a hoe and a sack, packed a pound of sausages and shuffled off to dachaland.

Families may have been building their dacha for ten or twenty years, bestowing upon it the architectural purity of Worzel Gummidge's hat, but it was the centre of their lives: it doubled as a tranquil retreat and a source of cheap food which insulated them from the alternating Russian plagues of empty shelves and rampant inflation. The dacha meant work. Digging potatoes to fill those sacks. Wandering in the woods through swarms of mosquitoes to gather mushrooms. Cultivating tomatoes, onions, cabbages, radishes; breeding rabbits and chickens, and in one case I heard of, water rats for shashlick.

83

When strawberries, raspberries and redcurrants were ripe, people boiled them in a pan full of sugar and poured them into foot-high jars so that they would provide a winter's supply of the stickiest, fruitiest jam imaginable, varenye. Also for the winter, cucumbers were pickled and fish were salted. There was no need for an industrial refrigerator - most flats had a balcony which kept the dacha haul cool. Spare produce could be sold on the street corner, sticking another stack of roubles under the mattress.

At the railway station on dacha days business was brisk. Here were old people who were merging into their sacks of potatoes to become a single amorphous entity. I saw two babushkas who looked like a pair of rumpled handkerchiefs, walking side by side along the platform, red babushka and blue babushka. The same chubby fingers, the same swollen legs in woolly socks over torn tights. They must have been sisters, or perhaps mother and daughter, as one face was merely wrinkled and the other could have been a map of the rock formations in the foothills of the Himalayas.

'If you don't bring it with you, then you ain't got it', was the phrase to bear in mind on trips to the Russian countryside. That was why entrepreneurs at the station sold socks, bras, personal stereos, books on meditation and books on dog training, dogs (to go with the books) - new-born puppies cradled in the arms of their owners - greasy mincemeat in pastry, spit-roast chicken, mushroom pies, alarm clocks, Kodak film, Coca Cola, nail scissors, busts of Lenin and you-name-it whatever else. If you looked hard enough it was even possible to find a ticket.

Kostya and I had chosen to go on May Day. Logical, because the weather was fine and I had three days off. So logical that the rest of St Petersburg had decided to go too, as they also had three days off. When we got onto the train it was standing room only, but there was enough space between the carriages to stretch our legs, lift a beer bottle and breathe. Ten minutes and twenty people with baskets later, breathing was an optional extra. Sprinting through quicksand would have been easier than getting out before the doors closed. We survived as far as the last station on the outskirts of the city and made a break for it when the force of other exiting passengers pushed us towards fresh air.

The next train was miraculously empty, but it wasn't going to our town, Losevo. It took us a fair distance in that direction and then we got onto a bus. Bumping up hill and down pothole, we eventually reached our destination. No Lake Ladoga yet, but golden fields of hay, a spreading sunset and rapids unleashed by the onset of spring more than made up for it. The hotel we were looking for, a two-storey concrete building, was the town's central business district. It may once have been thronged with tourists clamouring to see the Film of the Day, advertised on a board in the lobby ('The Film of the Day is ----------'), but we were alone apart from the bleary-eyed manager and a picture of an elk, which probably had something to do with Losevo as an elk is a los in Russian.

There could hardly have been two people more likely to get ripped off in Russia than a foreigner and an Ossetian who looked exactly like a Chechen. Kostya's friend, Albert, had sold the hotel, so we were at the mercy of the manager. In small towns such as Losevo, £30 a month was a decent salary. I expected to pay about £5 for a hotel room. The manager wanted £20, and added that there was no hot water and no heating. We asked her if she knew where Albert was and she directed us to his flat.

Albert wasn't overjoyed to see us. He was celebrating May Day with his mother and aunt, and hardly knew Kostya but remembered he was a friend of racketeer Ruslan, and Albert had apparently sold the hotel because visits from Ruslan's men were causing his financial troubles. However, Albert was Ossetian and this meant he had to offer us a cup of tea and help us find a bed for the night. Albert said he'd drive us north to the larger town of Priozersk, where there might be a hotel with heating.

Once we were locked inside his car, Albert's mood improved enormously. He liked showing off. Thick fog had suddenly descended, reducing visibility to the front of the bonnet. Albert put his foot down and zoomed into oblivion at 80 miles an hour. Then he picked up a mobile phone beside him and asked me to give him a number in England, or Australia if I liked. 'Come on, who do you want to call? I've got a satellite phone. It was very expensive, but worth it, because there's no way of tracing the numbers I've dialled so I never get a bill.'

I rang my brother in England. We parked in a layby so that Kostya and Albert could get out for a smoke, and as I was chatting away mindlessly I noticed I was sitting next to a tank. 'I'm calling from a satellite phone in a complete stranger's car on the road to Finland in a layby in the fog next to a tank,' I said. 'What's new with you?' My brother was revising for his French A-level and Albert had worked in Morocco for several years, so they greeted each other enthusiastically in French.

Albert said the tank had been abandoned during the 1991 coup. A panicked army officer drove it out, intending to use it in support of the coup leaders, but when he discovered he was on the losing side, he left it by the riverbank and ran away. Its doors had been welded shut and it was in peaceful retirement; the army officer was probably still hiding in a haystack.

The cost of a hotel room in Priozersk was £25 a night and it had no heating or hot water. We paid up. The room had three single beds in it with two blankets between them, and a view of a rubbish tip. The hotel was in the town's main square and we were woken up by loudspeakers blasting out the Internationale. The local Communist Party had organised a May Day rally; a few hundred people were gathered around a lorry adorned with red flags. 'Let's tell those democrats we don't need their Snickers bars!' an angry speaker shouted at the crowd. True, we don't need Snickers bars, I thought, but amongst the multitude of dire threats to human existence, I would place them fairly low down on the list.

I think the Communists were just jealous, because there weren't any Snickers bars in the shops in Priozersk. I know - I went into both of them. One shop sold beer, bread, cheese and fatty salami. The other sold bread, cheese, fatty salami, coffee and horseradish sauce. The Communist Party was against the reforms, and yet it was strongest in the provinces, where there hadn't been any reforms. The real change which had upset people was that the price of the same sparse range of products they had always had was several hundred thousand times higher than it was before 1991. The advantages of the free market could be seen in the cities, but for the inhabitants of Priozersk, St Petersburg might as well have been the Gobi desert.

We bought ourselves a picnic and ate it on a rock in the woods, considering where to go next. I'd heard that Karelia was a beautiful, swampy district on the shores of Lake Ladoga. If we'd been on the east side of the lake we could easily have gone there. On the west side we had a problem, because this part of Karelia was in no-man's land, a customs zone in the part of Russia which used to belong to Finland until World War II. Priozersk was also a Finnish town, known as Käkisalmi. Russians consider that the war began for them in 1941, when Hitler invaded. Finns know only too well that the Soviet Union was fighting in 1940, on the same side as the Nazis. Stalin's troops seized 16,173 square miles of territory and killed nearly 20,000 Finns.

Karelia was difficult to reach, but aside from any romantic notions I was harbouring about it, the last railway station on the line was there. It marked the apex of a triangle, so if we got that far we could stop at Vyborg on the way back to St Petersburg, down the other length of the triangle. If we couldn't get through, we had to go back the way we'd come, via Losevo.

The woman at the ticket office in Priozersk slammed the door of the hatch in my face. She was bored of listening to me arguing that Karelia was within the Russian Federation and I should be allowed to go there. 'You need a pass, I don't know where you can get a pass from, and there's nothing I can do for you.' I asked a taxi driver outside the station if he would mind helping us smuggle ourselves across the 'border' and bringing us back if we failed. He said we didn't have a hope, but he'd do it for the familiar sum of £20. It was worth £20 to avoid seeing Losevo again.

'Have you got St Petersburg residence papers?' the driver asked me. I shook my head.

'My friend has,' I said. Kostya was waiting at the hotel - the driver hadn't seen him yet.

'Well, that's something, but you really need a pass and you can only get that if you have an invitation from somebody who lives in the customs zone. If there are only one or two guards at the crossing we might have a chance. You'll have to think of a good story.' As Kostya got into the car, the driver laughed cynically. 'Let's see your passport,' he said. 'You say you came from the

Caucasus quite a while ago? If I were you I'd save your money and take the train back to St Petersburg.'

I insisted; perhaps a bribe would get us through. The less possible the trip sounded, the more I wanted to do it. My foreign passport was a definite hindrance, so Kostya decided I'd be his 16-year-old daughter asleep in the back and he'd be a prospective house buyer who wanted to look at a property. Again, we'd chosen the wrong day to travel. At the barrier there were several soldiers and their commanding officer. 'Oh, you hardly ever see an officer!' the driver exclaimed. 'Must be because it's May Day. You've had it.'

Kostya spun his line - no dice. A group of Finnish backpackers also came to a halt. They sat on the grass and passed a water bottle around while they were being scrutinised. I whispered to Kostya that he should take the officer to one side and ask him if we could grease his palm, but he was incurably incorruptible. My small ambition to go to Karelia and see Lake Ladoga wasn't destined to be fulfilled: I didn't have the right papers.

Law and Disorder

This is what the UK Foreign Office advises travellers to Russia: 'Incidents of mugging, sometimes violent, theft and pickpocketing in all cities, especially St Petersburg and Moscow, occur. Be vigilant and dress down. Be particularly wary in Moscow of groups of young children/vagrants. Keep expensive jewellery, watches and cameras out of sight. Use officially marked taxis which you should not share with strangers. When travelling by train store valuables in the compartment under the bed/seat. Do not leave the compartment unattended. Ensure the door is quite secure from the inside by tying it closed with wire or strong cord. Do not accept food from strangers as it may be drugged.'

I wonder what the Russian Foreign Ministry has to say about Britain. Probably something like, 'The Gloucestershire constabulary have confirmed that they do not expect to find any more human remains under patios. Massacres in Dunblane and Hungerford hardly ever happen. The IRA bomb which exploded in the centre of Manchester was noisy and blew some glass around but didn't kill anyone.'

There is crime in Russia as there is everywhere else in the world, but there's no need for paranoia. It has become accepted practice to stick out your thumb and hail a private car, whose owner will charge half or a quarter of what a professional taxi driver would ask. Most would rather earn a few thousand roubles honestly than have the burden of a dead body in the boot. As for trains, it's fine to tie the door of your compartment shut if you're the only person in it, but what happens if you're with other passengers who wake up in the night and want to go to the toilet? And if you have to spend 18 or 24 hours on a bunk bed with a stranger, it can be pleasant to share their food, especially if the restaurant car is closed 'for technical reasons'.

As for mugging in Moscow and St Petersburg, shall I compare thee to New York, Washington, Rome, London...? Of course, the biggest Russian bogeyman is the mafia. The Western media has had various pet Russian topics - Gorbachev and glasnost, Yeltsin's drinking habits, Zhirinovsky's rantings, the war in Chechnya - but none of these have been milked more than the mafia. Bandits, as they are known in Russia, certainly grab the headlines. The entire nation mourned in March 1995 when popular television journalist Vlad Listyev was gunned down outside his Moscow flat by a hired killer. Leading bankers bite the dust nearly every day. It's not uncommon to see police in flak jackets, carrying automatic weapons, on patrol on city streets.

Media moguls and millionaires know they are the targets of bandits and surround themselves with security guards. Lesser mortals aren't in too much danger unless they get caught in the crossfire. To date, only one Westerner has been killed by the mafia deliberately, an American who was a major shareholder in the Radisson-Slavjanskaya hotel, Moscow. As the Foreign Office reports, 'Russian criminal gangs operate in major cities and this can occasionally result in violence between rival gangs. This violence is not directed against foreigners, but in February 1996 a shooting incident resulted in the death of a British businessman.' John Hyden had stopped into St Petersburg's Nevskij Palace hotel for a coffee. Unfortunately, so had the alleged boss of the city's notorious Tambovskaya mafia and his two bodyguards.

Two men with coats over their arms entered the hotel and flung the coats onto the floor, revealing loaded Kalashnikov assault rifles. They opened fire on the Café Vienna, killing the bodyguards (off-duty policemen) and John Hyden, who was on the next table. Their target recovered from his wounds in hospital. The assassins left the Kalashnikovs at the scene - their trademark - and made their getaway before the police arrived, three minutes later.

Poor John Hyden must have thought he was in the safest place in St Petersburg. I'm sure he never went anywhere near seedy dives such as the Baku restaurant or the 1001 Nights restaurant, or the dingy bar on Marat Street which has a collection box in the doorway for the 'Prison Brotherhood', or the Money Honey saloon, where 'clients have a habit of coming out with their faces rearranged', according to an English-language guide to crime in the city. I've been to those places and nothing ever happened to me, even when I was looking for trouble.

Money Honey wasn't a mafia haunt, it was just rowdy. A student from England who was doing work experience at *The St Petersburg*

Press came to me excitedly one day with the story that three other students she knew had been kicked out of Money Honey because one of them was black. They alleged that the manager invited a female student into a back room, where, in the company of another man who was punching the palm of his hand with his fist, he informed her that a customer had complained about her black friend and that they should all leave.

To test Money Honey's tolerance I spent an evening there with Tanzanian journalist Ali Nassor and a dictaphone discreetly positioned under my sweater. Nassor was eager to collect some recorded evidence of racial harassment. He had been beaten up on numerous occasions in unprovoked attacks and had told me, 'When I see a policeman I walk on the other side of the street. They always want to see my papers.'

No one blinked an eye as we walked into Money Honey. We took seats in the middle of the room, right in front of the bar, ordered two pints of beer and sat waiting to be hassled. Nothing happened. We drank another couple of pints and still nothing happened. We got up and danced to a rock 'n' roll band playing *Blue Suede Shoes* whose lead singer mumbled soulful gibberish until he came to the only line he could pronounce, 'Don't step on my blue suede shoes!', which he belted out every time. Nassor and I sat down and ordered more beer. By the end of the evening we were wasted, and so were the batteries on my dictaphone. Nassor was more disappointed than I was that we hadn't had a confrontation, and we promised each other to come back again for another intensive investigation session.

In the 1001 Nights Uzbek restaurant I was sure that blood was about to be spilt in my soup. The murky presence of imminent death certainly added spice to an otherwise bland and poorly-cooked meal, although the chef could have provided that sensation in a more conventional manner with a sprinkling of paprika. My Australian friend Karina and I were seated between three young toughs on one side and a solitary woman on the other. Solitary, that is, except for her two police bodyguards in bulletproof vests.

To judge by her drab denim jacket and scruffy tennis shoes, it seemed unlikely that this woman was a high-ranking government official. Perhaps she was a witness to a mafia killing and required constant protection. Karina's suggestion was that the woman's life had been threatened by the three other diners and that a shoot-out would soon ensue. Our sense of apprehension and the likelihood of Karina's prediction coming true increased as employees of the restaurant peered nervously at us from the door of the kitchen.

The waiter tried to hurry us along by telling us that most of the dishes were off the menu. Three kinds of soup and Uzbek speciality bread were 'off', so I settled for a dismal bouillon for starters. The main courses were also limited. 'I advise you not to order the roast chicken,' the waiter said, 'because you can get chicken anywhere but plov is an Uzbek dish, so I suggest you both have that.' Considering our close proximity to lethal weapons, we were in no mood to argue. As Karina was a vegetarian she asked for plov without meat. She could have it, the waiter said, but the price would be the same. Karina had a saucer of cold, greasy rice with carrots and I had the same delicacy with lumps of gristle in it.

For some reason no one in the restaurant felt like dancing to the taped Russian pop music which was substituting for the advertised Central Asian folk group with bellydancers. Karina and I swallowed our few spoonfuls of rice and got out of the restaurant unscathed, still wondering in whose illustrious company we had been eating. The lone woman also left quietly after her meal, with her policeman but without paying the bill. A sensible choice.

A Jordanian student once told me about the brush with death he had when he was living in a hostel in St Petersburg. His stereo had been stolen and the culprit was arrested after the student reported the theft to the police. A few days later he had a knock on his door: it was a bunch of Chechen bandits who were a little put out that one of their number was behind bars. 'My name is Kazbek and I have come to kill you,' said their leader. 'Before I do, I must know your name.'

'Mohammed,' said the student. Kazbek asked him what religion he was and Mohammed replied that he was a Muslim. Instead of killing him, Kazbek gave him a hug and sent his henchmen away. Soon Mohammed and Kazbek were bosom buddies over a vodka bottle; Kazbek said he'd happily bump off anyone in the hostel who Mohammed didn't like, but Mohammed said he liked everybody.

When I met the mafia it was strictly by invitation, in the company of Kostya. Although Kostya was adamant that his criminal days were over now that he'd found God, most of his friends were still practising their old profession. One of their dens was the café where I first met Kostya, which was owned by a diminutive Georgian called Gamlet (the Russian pronunciation of Hamlet: Shakespearean names are extremely popular in the Caucasus), who was known to his friends by his patronymic, Gyorg'ich. The café had one or two plastic tables outside it on sunny days and the only item on the menu was black coffee. The tables inside were reserved for pale young Georgian men with pistols.

There aren't too many sunny days in St Petersburg, so most of the time there was nowhere for the public to sit and the door was kept locked. To get in I had to knock on the door and say 'Nasha' - 'Ours'. I whiled away a few afternoons with these men, hoping at least to hear some tales of their bloody underworld activities. To my disappointment it was all pathetically banal. The gang I'd infiltrated were nothing more than armed estate agents. They sat in the café drinking vodka, playing cards or chess and discussing the 'job' they were hoping to do. It wasn't working out; Gyorg'ich would have made more money if he'd opened the café and served drinks to the families who were out for a stroll in the park.

Gyorg'ich did let a stranger in once, because he was begging for a vodka. He was a white-haired former KGB colonel who appeared to be stricken with guilt and self-pity. He held his wet fish of a hand out to each of us in turn: ironically, I was the only one who hadn't personally felt the cold finger of the KGB on my collar and the only one who balked at the idea of touching this man. I'd read my Solzhenitsyn and was resisting on principle. The hoods were glad to see someone who was a bigger loser than they were and shook his hand while Gyorg'ich poured him a drink. He downed it hastily and stumbled off.

Having taught me their card game, Idiot, Kostya's friends explained what they were up to when they left the café every three hours or so. They had found someone nearby who was trying to sell her flat for £20,000, and they wanted to get involved in the deal by persuading her to let them find a buyer who would pay £22,000, in return for a commission of £800. Their qualification for finding a buyer was their ability to hang around on street corners listening to gossip about the property market. I don't know what foiled their plan, whether the owner of the flat was unconvinced or they hadn't met anyone with a spare £22,000 on them , but nothing came of it.

Tengiz took us all out for dinner anyway. Tengiz was the Godfather of this group, a burly man with greying hair and a pumice-stone face. He had Marlon Brando's gravelly voice to a tee. We were in the dark, smoky Baku restaurant eating mushrooms in sour cream sauce out of aluminium dishes. Tengiz and the others told sad stories about the devastation caused by the Georgian war with Abkhazian separatists, which was what had driven them to the more lucrative business environment of St Petersburg. Then Tengiz invited me to go on holiday with him to Georgia. 'You must come to my city, to Batumi,' he said. 'There is no war in that area and it has a great beach.'

In spite of the tender temptations of Tengiz, Voronezh was the furthest south I ever went in the former Soviet Union. That was where I stayed with a policeman, Alexei, who had some candid words to say about his own operational methods over a cup of tea in the kitchen when he should have been on duty. In 1992 the Soviet quota system was still in force. Alexei's quota was five arrests each month; there was no point exceeding it because that would make it harder to fulfil the quota next month.

There wasn't much violent crime in the sleepy city of Voronezh, but what there was Alexei stayed well clear of. He was deeply concerned, however, about the quantity of illegal home-distilled vodka, samogon, in the possession of persons other than himself. He had embarked on a ruthless campaign to round up rogue bottles, ably assisted by local alcoholics. Alexei would approach a drunk on the street and ask him if he had been drinking samogon. The drunk would confess willingly, because he was drunk and because Alexei offered to pay him the magnificent sum of 25 roubles (15p) if the drunk showed him where the samogon was and bought some more to catch the crooks red-handed. After Alexei had made his arrests he confiscated the samogon and gave three litres of it to his informer to encourage him to keep up the good work.

Knowing that story, it wasn't altogether surprising that the Voronezh police were slow to respond when I thought I was about to be murdered. Alexei and his mother had gone to their dacha for the night and I was alone with two other female English students in the ground-floor flat. The doorbell rang. Rather foolishly (I was 19 years old and for 18 of those years I had lived in a village in Oxfordshire, so my crime awareness wasn't high), I opened the door to see who was there. It was a tall man in his twenties with a dirty face. I was taken aback and couldn't understand what he was saying until he rubbed his hands together and I realised he wanted to come in to wash them.

Suddenly my crime awareness shot up to a record level and I slammed the door shut. Instead of going away, the man started ringing the bell continuously, hammering on the door and shouting something that sounded like 'I love you'. The other girls ran to the kitchen and armed themselves with knives and an umbrella while I tried to keep watch on the man through the spyhole, but he went around to the side window to bang on that. This made one of the girls hysterical, frightening the other two of us even more, and I called the police. I could hardly remember a word of Russian apart from 'Crazy man, we are English, come now.'

Twenty minutes later the man was still banging and we thought he was about to break through into the living room. The hysterical girl started breathing at a normal rate for long enough to phone the elderly Russian couple she was staying with and ask them to come to our rescue. They hobbled over straight away but by that time crazy man had given up and gone to look for a sink elsewhere. 'You've been drinking red wine, have you?' the old woman asked us. 'Don't worry, dears, you can stay with us for the night.'

As we were leaving the flat two policemen approached us at a casual stroll. They said the equivalent of 'What 'ave we 'ere, then?' and our Russian acquaintances apologetically explained that these silly foreigners had imagined an intruder and called them out in a fit of panic. The next morning we saw Alexei and told him what had happened. 'Oh, yes, that's the neighbour from upstairs, he does that a lot,' Alexei said with a shrug.

For people who had lost faith in the Russian police, there were plenty of places to buy a gun. Before I went to Russia the only place I'd ever seen a handgun was on television and on the hip of a New York cop. In St Petersburg I found it hard to contain my curiosity as I walked to work every day past a shop which sold 'Weapons'. So I stopped in once and in the cause of journalism enquired about non-lethal gas pistols. I would never really have bought one, because they looked exactly like real guns and if you were to threaten an attacker with gas he might have retaliated with a bullet. And if a policeman saw you drawing a gas gun against someone who was unarmed, it would appear that you were the bandit and the policeman could shoot you.

The price of a gas pistol was £130 but the shop assistant said I had to have a licence before he could sell it to me. I arranged a meeting with the city's gun licensing boss, Yuri Krolikov. As was usual whenever I tried to track down a Russian official, I had to navigate my way through a maze of bureaucracy by telephone to get hold of Krolikov's number. But Krolikov cheerfully dismissed my suggestion that most foreigners would have trouble finding out how to get a licence. 'You just go to your consulate, or embassy in Moscow if you don't have a consulate here, and they give you a piece of paper which says you are not insane or a criminal. Then you come here and buy the licence for 55,000 roubles [£8].'

The British writer John Nicholson noted astutely in his book *The Other St Petersburg* that there were two entrances to every building in the city, the front entrance and the 'black' entrance, which led to the more intriguing back stairways and corridors. Likewise there were two ways to do everything in St Petersburg, one of which had absolutely no connection with the laws of the Russian Federation. To buy a gas pistol or even a real gun (which only the police and armed forces were authorised to carry), there was no need to deal with formalities such as paperwork. Why should you, when there were so many vendors waiting at Apraksin Yard to cater to a cautious traveller's every need?

Apraksin Yard was a sad remnant of the proud trading centre it used to be. Outclassed and overtaken by the flashy displays of Western-style department stores, this market had been left with racks of imitation leather jackets and tins of out-of-date spam shipped in as humanitarian aid. Apraksin Yard's reputation as a hotbed of criminal activity had grown to exaggerated proportions. A US Consulate crime and safety report of March 14, 1994 stated, 'All types of assault weapons, small mines, hand grenades and other anti-personnel devices are readily available and sometimes on open display in Mafia-controlled markets, such as Apraksin Yard.'

There were no weapons of any description 'on open display' in the market when I went shopping for a gun 18 months later. One could be forgiven for thinking that the place was a heavily-guarded military base as a row of men dressed in camouflage gear stood blocking the entrance. Their uniform was purely for show, as they had no official status and all they demanded was 1000 roubles (15p) from each visitor.

Just behind the border guards there were usually one or two people holding small pictures of the gas pistols they had on sale. When Karina and I went in, craftily disguised as naïve foreign tourists, in t-shirts and dark glasses, the people with the pictures were on their lunch break, so we decided to select the most sinister man we could find and ask him where to buy a pistol. Choosing the most sinister man in the place was no easy task, as there was a huge range. Opting to avoid a group of shaven-headed thugs in tracksuits, we went for the vinyl jacket-clad, black-moustachioed model.

Sure enough, Fyodor had a friend called Seryozha who could supply us with gas pistols for £100 or real guns for £300 each. Seryozha was young, friendly and easy-going - more like a student with a part-time job than a professional gun trader. Both men tried to dissuade us from buying real guns, saying there was no need for them and that we would go to prison immediately if we were caught with them. On the other hand, they pointed out that there were only two left, that they had been specially imported from Germany, and that they were 'even better than the guns that the police have.'

Gas pistols were 'the best thing for women,' according to Seryozha and Fyodor. Seryozha particularly recommended the Compact 9 mm revolver which fired not only gas but also buckshot. However, there was no way we could see the guns unless we promised to hand over our cash on the spot. The guys were none too happy that we had asked so many questions and were still not prepared to buy, but I told them I had to consult first with a friend who knew something about guns.

'I can give you a 100% guarantee that your friend will advise you to buy the Compact, so there's no point talking to him,' said Seryozha. He reluctantly agreed to come back and meet us the next day, but was worried that he might sell his last Compact by that time. I pretended to be concerned that the police would see us. Seryozha said this wasn't a problem. 'They don't bother us. Sometimes we have to pay a 'fine' or give them a litre of vodka, then they go away.'

Tourists who were thinking of buying a gun in Russia for self-defence could safely change their minds and spend the money on sets of Yeltsin dolls and Red Army overcoats, but for some businessmen a gun was an essential item of office equipment. A coterie of bandits with guns was even more effective when negotiating a difficult deal. When the American and Russian partners in a St Petersburg fast food business fell out, both sides brought in the heavy mob and in the end it was the Yankees who went home.

The Minutka sandwich restaurant on Nevsky Prospekt was for a short time known as the Subway sandwich restaurant, one of a large international chain. Its walls were still decorated with US subway maps a year after Russian entrepreneur Vadim Bordug seized control from his partner, Stephen Brown. When Brown took a week's holiday, Bordug transferred $70,000 from Subway Petersburg's account to a bank in Ireland. Brown claimed that when he returned to work, the restaurant's security guards tried to assault him and he had to take refuge in a locked office. He said Bordug told him to go back to America if he valued his life.

Brown left the country, but not before he'd filed a complaint to the US consul-general in St Petersburg and a civil law suit in Ireland. The executive vice-president of Subway's parent company, East-West Invest, commented, 'The illegal activities of Mr Bordug and his associates threaten to sour the investment climate in St Petersburg.' He said Subway had completely renovated the restaurant when the company took over, describing the condition of the premises as 'deplorable'.

Bordug's version of the story was quite different. He told me the Americans had deceived him about the division of profits in the business and because of that he took independent action - he sent the $70,000 to Ireland. Brown won his civil suit and the money was returned to Subway's account, but Bordug kept control of the restaurant. He lived in daily expectation of a criminal case. 'I am ready to go to court and prove my innocence. I have nothing to hide,' said Bordug.

Mikhail, one of the security guards who was on duty on the day of the incident with Brown, said the American didn't come to work alone: 'Mr Brown came to the restaurant with two bandits and wanted to bring them in. It was obvious they were bandits from the way they were dressed, although they were not armed. Of course we would have let Stephen Brown in on his own, but not with bandits.' Mikhail added that no security guards touched or threatened Brown. 'I knew that if anything happened to a foreigner I would go to prison.'

Bordug said he agreed to meet one of the Subway partners alone at the Grand Hotel Europe the night before the confrontation to sort out the dispute on a personal basis, without lawyers. 'I went there on my own but Mr Brown brought ten bandits with him. He wouldn't listen when I said I wasn't happy with the financial agreement we had.' Bordug was confident that he had improved the restaurant since his takeover. He had cut the price of sandwiches by a half and was particularly proud of the new 'Spasibo' signs on the bins under the words 'Thank you'. He said he had tried to persuade the Americans to add the Russian translation, but they had refused.

It was impossible to verify the truth of Bordug's claims, especially as Subway representatives would make no comment except, 'We haven't got our ducks in a row yet.' But Mikhail had good grounds for his fear of being punished for injuring a foreigner. There had been a police department specifically for crime against foreigners in St Petersburg since 1965, and it was remarkable how quickly the perpetrators of such deeds were arrested. The conviction of 18-year-old student Misha Glebov for the murder of an American businessman was one of the department's coups, given a special glow when the officers in charge of the case received an award from the FBI. But Dmitri Glebov, Misha's father, made his own investigation and presented the city prosecutor's office with the name of the man he believed was the real murderer.

Larry Jones, 44, was found strangled in his flat in November 1993, on the day he was due to leave Russia. In his last phone call to his parents, he said that the mafia had threatened his life. Larry and Misha were lovers and Misha never denied that he had been in the American's flat on the evening before his death. Dmitri Glebov argued that his son had neither the motive nor the strength to kill Jones. Misha was squeamish by nature - he had transferred from the medical institute to the chemical-pharmaceutical institute because he didn't like dissection. The year before his arrest he won a trip to Norway in a competition sponsored by Radio Roks, thanks to his expert knowledge of Michael Jackson's career. He had one of the best collections of Michael Jackson records in Russia. A month before the murder, Misha got married. He had everything going for him.

'Misha wouldn't hurt a fly,' said Britt Saunders, another American who 'dated' the student. 'He was afraid of people in general and there is no way a skinny guy like him could have strangled Larry Jones, who was a bodybuilder.' But Misha was sentenced to nine years in prison. Deborah, an American friend of his wife, Olga, was called to testify in court and was quizzed about whether she and Olga were lesbians. The prosecution successfully exploited the jury's homophobia: one woman juror said that if Misha was gay he deserved to go to prison whether he was innocent or guilty.

Amnesty International and the St Petersburg homosexual rights group Wings appealed for Misha's release, but it was Dmitri

Glebov's strenuous efforts which persuaded the prosecutor's office to re-examine the case in July 1995. Dmitri said the Russian legal system was saturated with corruption from the police to the prosecutor's office and that the police bullied Misha into writing a confession. 'The prestige of finding the killer of a foreign businessman was more important than justice,' he told me. Dmitri devoted most of his time to his son's case, practically giving up his job at the electrotechnical university. The stacks of information he accumulated made him fear for his family's safety. 'I know my phone is bugged,' he said. 'I'm not schizophrenic, I heard someone asking if the tape was recording or not.'

Unsurprisingly, the prosecutor's office and the police were condescending towards Dmitri Glebov's allegations. Roman Zubko, the investigator appointed to examine them, said, 'All of Dmitri Glebov's claims will be checked, despite the fact that the case has already been investigated thoroughly.' He pointed to a drawer full of folders relating to Misha's conviction. 'Mr Glebov probably didn't mention that the Russian Supreme Court upheld the guilty verdict. Of course, I understand that no father can believe his son is a murderer.' More than two months later, Zubko had come up with no conclusions and the prosecutor's office replaced him with a new investigator.

'I can't understand why there's so much fuss about this case,' a police officer in the department for crime against foreigners told me. 'Glebov is the murderer and that's that.' On the wall there was a photograph of Lieutenant Colonel Vladimir Karpenkov and Captain Valery Vasiliev being presented with an award for the conviction of Glebov by FBI director Louis Freeh. I tried to find out why the FBI had been so impressed by these particular officers but came up against a brick wall. A spokeswoman for the FBI in Moscow said she knew nothing about the award because at the time of Freeh's visit to Russia they hadn't started keeping records. FBI headquarters in Washington were also unable to provide details of the award.

Dmitri Glebov's 17-page appeal against the conviction described how his son signed a confession after more than seven hours of questioning in the department for crime against foreigners. He requested a lawyer but was not allowed to see one. Three days later he was interviewed again in another police station by an investigator from the prosecutor's office. A lawyer who had been hired by the Glebov family tried to find out where Misha was being questioned, but the prosecutor told him he didn't know and in any case couldn't give permission for the lawyer to visit him.

Misha's first meeting with the lawyer, Mikhail Telegov, took place behind glass and in the presence of several policemen. It lasted for five minutes. 'He told me he was not guilty but was afraid to change his testimony,' said Telegov. The lawyer added that the police hadn't needed to use physical violence against Glebov to extract a confession because psychological pressure was enough. 'They didn't have to beat him up, they could have just told him how he would be raped in prison.'

Telegov said the prosecution attempted to prove that Misha's marriage was a cover for the couple's homosexual lifestyles. The motive cited in court for the murder of Larry Jones was a row with Misha over sexual preferences. Dmitri Glebov discussed the case with a sexologist, who said that a couple who had known each other as long as Misha and Larry would be too familiar with each other's sexual preferences to fight about the issue. Dmitri's theory was that the real murderer was another of Larry's acquaintances who visited him after Misha had gone home. Misha's neighbours heard his stereo playing at 1 am, the time Larry was killed.

'If it turned out that the Jones murder was connected to business, that would have discouraged foreigners from coming here,' Telegov said. Dmitri's appeal pointed out that the fuel export business which Larry Jones was involved in was a prime target for Russian mafia groups in late 1993. In addition, Jones was careless. He liked to show off his wealth. 'As a homosexual, Jones was extremely undiscriminating in his contacts. He brought home complete strangers from the street to satisfy his sexual demands,' the appeal stated. 'In his search for partners, Jones visited dubious establishments of St Petersburg which were full of criminal elements.'

Olga was allowed to visit her husband in prison once every four months. She was lucky that he was only two hours from the city centre - he could have been transported two days away. She took a sack of clothes, books and food with her, and the latest Michael

Jackson album. On one of her visits Olga took a list of questions with her from me, and Misha answered them in writing. I began by asking why Larry Jones's passport was in Misha's bag when he was arrested. It was one of the most crucial pieces of evidence against him.

'I have no idea how the passport of Larry Jones ended up in my bag; I saw it for the first time after they removed me from the office where I was questioned. The bag from which the passport was allegedly taken remained in the office. The only explanation of this fact is that the passport was slipped in amongst my things by employees of the police station themselves.'

- Why did you sign the confession?

'We arrived at the police station at 11 am and I signed the 'confession' at 8 pm. What happened in that interval is painful for me to remember. This was the first 'contact' with the police I'd had in my life and I don't know if I would be alive now if I hadn't signed what they wanted me to sign.'

- Where were you when Larry Jones was murdered?

'I don't know the exact time of the murder of Larry Jones, so I can't say precisely where I was at that time. Most likely I was at home.'

- Which aspects of your trial do you consider were unjust?

'Prejudice. From the very beginning of the trial it was obvious that the judge and jury were disposed towards finding me guilty. All the facts upholding my innocence were not taken into consideration, and all the arguable facts were interpreted against me. The judge did not want to notice all the violations which were committed at the time of the investigation.'

- Do you know the murderer? What do you think the motive for the killing of Larry Jones was?

'I don't know the murderer. As concerns the reasons for the murder, there could be many different ones. A person leading the sort of life in our country which Larry Jones led always attracts heightened interest from the criminal world - from mere pickpockets to organised crime.'

- What are the conditions like in prison?

'There is nothing good in prison. A person can never understand or even imagine life here if he hasn't collided with it himself.'

- How do the other prisoners treat you?

'In prison each person is a wolf to other people. Here no one does anything for anyone else, it's every man for himself.'

- What hopes have you for an early release?

'If I didn't hope, then probably I wouldn't be able to endure this.'

- What will you do when you get out of prison?

'At the moment it's difficult for me to think about the future. I don't know when I'll get out, nor what Russia will become in that time.'

In February 1996, Dmitri Glebov had a heart attack caused by stress. His wife described his condition as 'serious', but added that he would continue working for the release of his son as soon as he recovered.

Earning a Living

Sveta, an accountant in Minsk, was earning £20 a month in 1994. She was thinking of starting a lottery scratchcard business and approached representatives of the local 'racket' to offer them a 70% cut. Oleg, a student in Moscow, was already in business that year. He had progressed from running kiosks staffed by disabled people (because they cost less) to importing swimming trunks and umbrellas from the United Arab Emirates. He chose that country because he didn't need a visa to go there and he could get a cheap ticket and hotel room by working for a travel agency. He brought back as much stock as he could carry in bulging sacks and paid an agreed bribe to customs officers every trip.

The nation which spurned bourgeois materialism for 70 years has taken to it with a vengeance. There is no other choice: millions of professionals simply can't survive on their state salary, or can't get a job in their specialist field. The unemployed receive £10 a month if they're lucky. To oil the cogs of the massive military-industrial complex, the Soviet Union created an extraordinarily disproportionate number of engineers. Now, with factories at a standstill, they are either having to retire to their dachas or find a new occupation. Yegor never even had a chance to begin his career as a space scientist. In 1996 he had recently graduated from university in St Petersburg and was qualified to design rockets. To support his wife and child he was working as a gas repairman, advising people on their dodgy cookers.

Lena, my landlady, was a chemist for ten years. Then she started her own one-person property business and made enough money to sponsor art exhibitions. Property was profitable but hellish. Lena sold communal flats to New Russians, a job which also entailed looking for separate flats for the occupants of each room and persuading them to move out. She was on the telephone from 8 am until 2 am, bouncing between buyers and tenants. It was a worthy cause, finding people homes of their own for the first time in their lives, but if one tenant refused to budge then the deal was off for the rest of them. Some old people couldn't bear the strain of being uprooted; for them, independence was synonymous with loneliness. Lena had little time to spend her money.

The director of Russia & World, a St Petersburg publishing company, used to be a doctor. I asked three other employees in the editorial department what they did before the company was founded in the mid-1990s: they had all been university lecturers. The average salary at Russia & World was £100 a month, although advertising salespeople could earn much more on commission. I was paid £100 as 'international communications manager', in charge of making contacts and gathering information from English-speaking countries, but I had to tell the director, Andrei, that I could only work three days a week because my monthly rent was £100.

'None of us have a contract, we are all volunteers,' said journalist Lola tearfully. She was upset because Andrei had thought of another task for me, selling articles from Russia & World's magazines to Western publications, and I said I would only do it if I was paid a commission. 'I wish I could stand up for myself like you do,' Lola continued. 'I can't, though, I wasn't brought up like that. I'm from an intelligent family and we're used to taking what we are given. I'm supposed to be an editor here, but I have sold advertising space, I'm owed money from last year, but I don't have the courage to ask for it.'

Another employee, a 22-year-old graduate called Sasha, was fluent in French and Spanish but her ability in those languages was useless because she was afraid to pick up a telephone or send a fax. Although she finished university at the same time as me, she hadn't been absorbing the culture of business since she was able to see and hear. She had no self-confidence and felt that if she talked to complete strangers they would think she was being a nuisance. To me it was obvious that people would be only too glad to publicise themselves in our magazines and when I asked for free books, brochures and photographs I made them believe I was doing *them* a favour.

The door of Russia & World was guarded by a policeman with a gun. I think robbers would have been disappointed if they had managed to overpower him and get to the safe. There was an air of nervous uncertainty on payday, as employees sat late at their desks, waiting for the accountants to call their names. We received our money in cash - roubles or dollars depending on the

106

accountants' whim. Part of our salaries was officially recorded as a 'food and accommodation allowance', which made it liable to less tax. Sometimes the company didn't have enough money to send magazines in the post, so packages were kept in the distribution office for weeks. For almost a month the telephones and faxes were cut off.

In the face of adversity, Russia & World was actually very successful. Andrei could justifiably be proud that his was one of a very small number of Russian companies which was producing something rather than importing, exporting or investing. A new magazine or almanac seemed to come out every week, much to the surprise of nearly all the sixty employees. Some, such as *Your Home*, a glossy guide to furniture, were just advertising vehicles. Others - *Marine Club* and *Matchball*, for instance - appealed to the new generation of wealthy consumers who could afford to indulge in yachting or tennis *and* to read about their hobby. Here, Russia & World was on risky territory because such people were in a minority. The editors of *Marine Club* thought it was the only boating magazine in the country, but just after the second issue had gone to press, the old Soviet boating magazine was relaunched with a 1990s capitalist look. *Marine Club* was in danger of sinking.

Russia & World published almanacs for the beer and spirits industries called *World of Beer* and *World of Drinks*. The next in the series was to be an almanac for the advertising industry, but the marketing department didn't think *World of Advertising* was an inspirational title. As often happened when someone in the company was stuck for an idea, everyone from the cook to the international communications manager was consulted for their suggestions. The marketing reps were looking for a single word which summed up the art of advertising. I said that in Russia there had always been a very powerful advertising industry, except that it was monopolised by politicians. My suggested title was *Propagandist*.

Business terminology gave the editors at Russia & World a headache at times. A huge number of English words had been assimilated into the Russian language over the past few years and Russians were not always sure what they meant or how to spell them. Occasionally English words were used in place of perfectly good Russian words because people considered English more prestigious - for instance 'interneshnl' instead of 'mezhdunarodny'. More logically, English words were adopted for concepts which didn't exist in the Soviet Union. 'Sarah, how do you spell 'franchising' in Russian?' one of the editors asked me. 'Is it 'franchising' or 'frenchising'? And if there is a word 'franchising', does that mean there is such a word as 'franchise'?'

I was taken aback one day when my English grammar was corrected by the combined efforts of a Russian and a German. Andrei, the director, was soft-hearted and took on employees in a rather haphazard manner: he invented a job for me because I'd asked for one after my parents met him at an exhibition in London. About a month later he introduced another international communications manager, a young German called Nils. He had also met Andrei at an exhibition and needed a job in St Petersburg because he'd just moved there and married a Russian. 'When did you get married?' I asked Nils.

'Last veek,' he said.

'How's your Russian?'

'Well, I'm starting to learn it. I haff a teacher.'

'Have you been to Russia before?'

'Oh, yes! I vas also here three months ago. Zat's ven I met my vife.'

Before Nils could do any international communicating, he needed a complete breakdown of the company structure in diagram form. This was patiently drawn for him by a secretary who spoke fluent German. Nils questioned the secretary in German about each section of her diagram and she explained it. I was a little puzzled about how Nils would fit in if we already had a native Russian speaker who knew German. His spoken English was passable, but he asked me to check a list of phrases he had composed. They were along the lines of, 'We look very much forward to hearing from you in the soonest future', and, 'I would like to present to yourselves our new almanac, which is calling itself *World of Beer*'. I rewrote them and at Nils' request told him exactly why they didn't sound right. The next day he showed me the list again, with some new notes on it in red pen. 'I haff discussed zees vis Zari,' he said. Zari was a Russian editor who knew English about as well as Nils did. 'Ve sink zat it vud be better like so. You do not mind?' I restrained myself from saying that the company structure might work more efficiently if Zari wrote his own letters in English instead of passing them to me through Nils and back to Nils again.

The name of the company caused its own problems. The Russian employees were expected to pronounce 'Russian and World' convincingly in English, not to translate it into Russian and call it 'Rossiya i mir'. Russians who heard this name on the telephone for the first time couldn't understand it and must have thought they were dealing with a foreign company. The name was also expensive. Russia & World was liable for extra taxes twice over, once because it had the sacred word 'Russia' in its name and again because the name was in a foreign language.

Taxes ravaged Russian businesses. 'Our accountants are geniuses. They have to devise so many ways to avoid taxes - if we paid all our taxes honestly we would be bankrupt tomorrow,' a secretary told me in 1993. The situation hadn't improved when I came to Russia & World in 1996, except that tax dodges had reached new heights of sophistication. Russia & World eliminated money in as many transactions as possible by bartering services. Advertisements in Russia & World's magazines were the payment for everything from a kitchen redecoration to international parcel deliveries. I asked the chief accountant if sharing a building with the district tax inspectorate meant the company had to be especially clever at bookkeeping. 'No,' she said, 'the tax inspectors don't come to see us too often; they assume that if we are right under their noses, we must be behaving ourselves.'

Other St Petersburg companies weren't so lucky. The tax police were in the habit of bursting into an office unannounced wearing balaclavas and carrying automatic weapons. InterOccidental Real Estate, an American company which had 3000 employees in Russia, was raided in late 1995. The tax police seized documents but returned them within a few weeks. InterOccidental made a complaint to the US consulate in St Petersburg and representatives of the company reported the incident to congressmen back home.

'American firms are not used to the type of audits which take place in Russia, and they hope the American government can influence the Russian tax police to change their procedures,' a spokesman for the US consulate told me. The president of InterOccidental, Don Corcoran, was philosophical about the raid: 'It was one of those mysteries of Russian life,' he said. 'It raised a lot of questions. We obey the law and have contributed significantly to the development of the real estate market in Russia. I can't understand why the tax police came in in such an aggressive manner, but we like Russia and hope to continue doing business here.'

I asked a senior tax inspector to comment and he said, 'Experience has shown that there are almost always infringements of the tax law in the property business, mostly mistakes rather than criminal evasion of taxes. Companies which have been raided have the right to ask why they were raided, but the tax police have the right not to answer.'

Martin Hupka, deputy director of the Bronze Lion distribution company in St Petersburg, said taxes were 'our A number 1 problem'. About half of Bronze Lion's time was spent on taxes. Hupka claimed, 'We are very unique as a 100% tax-paying citizen in the Russian Federation, and not many companies even try to say that. There are so many pitfalls and traps in the Russian tax laws; our director, Anya, is a lawyer and she has dedicated her life to taxes. We have to be more informed than anyone else, including the tax inspectors. Anya reads every law there is and asks for explanations - we don't want to pay too much tax.

'Times have come when we've had to challenge the tax police and we're not afraid to. We've never rolled over and we've never not paid. The tax police have been here but they were gone within twenty minutes, the tax inspectors respect us. The problem is that they don't differentiate between an honest mistake and tax evasion. On the other hand, Westerners who treat this place like the Wild West get treated as if they're in the Wild West.

'We've seen the catacomb of Russian business. We've fought every battle there is to fight, from unstable tax laws to Byzantine accounting, to customs delays, to security issues, and we're still here. Everything we've done has been utterly legal and we've survived. Russia is a kind of unique funky place - it's going to be fine but there's a lot for the country to go through, a lot of ghosts in the machine. 70 years of a certain system created a certain mindset, but at the same time you look around, you see the market forming.'

Russia & World eased the strain by holding regular parties on each employee's birthday. On these occasions work stopped at five o'clock and we all gathered in the office of the birthday boy or girl, where desks had been pushed together and covered with a tablecloth on which there was a fine spread of open sandwiches, cakes, fruit, champagne and wine. The honoured employee was presented with a bouquet of flowers and a present, and the editor of *World of Beer* recited a poem he had composed. A series of toasts were proposed, glasses were drained and refilled, and when the food was finished the desks were moved to the side of the room to make space for a dancefloor. Those who preferred a serious drink instead of a dance adjourned to *Marine Club*'s sitting room, which, like the captain's quarters on a yacht, had a cupboard well-stocked with cognac. These parties continued until eleven or twelve at night and some people dragged themselves to work considerably later than eleven or twelve the next day.

One more aspect of Russia & World worth noting is that their office humour was as bad as ours. We have pithy sayings such as, 'You don't have to be mad to work here - but it helps'. At Russia & World there was a sign above the toilet seat which read, 'At this moment you are the only person in the editorial office who knows exactly what they are doing'.

A US army veteran was in business just around the corner from Russia & World. Mel Sobel had battled his way through German and Chinese bullets; in Russia he was intent on making a financial killing. His mission was to brighten up drab Russian homes with Western-style armchairs, beanbags and pool tables. The 69-year-old entrepreneur was owner and president of Leathertouch, a company which he ran simultaneously in Philadelphia and St Petersburg. I interviewed him about his invasion of the Russian furniture market.

Sobel said Leathertouch was a learning institution because it taught local manufacturers about the latest models and styles from all over the world. 'We are also trying to teach Russians the Western way of doing business, which is based on honesty and integrity.' Sobel himself received an MBA from the University of Pennsylvania in 1948. His education was interrupted by World War II. At the age of 17 he fought in Belgium in the Battles of the Bulge and the Bastagne. He was wounded at Bastagne, where the United States suffered some of its worst losses of the war.

After Sobel graduated, his uncle, who worked in upholstery, handed him a piece of plastic and said, 'This is a good business.' Unlike Dustin Hoffman, who was given the same advice in *The Graduate* and responded by running away to have an affair with an older woman, Mel Sobel was gripped by a fever for plastic. He began by dealing in plastics for furniture and later progressed to manufacturing artificial leather.

Leathertouch's St Petersburg branch had almost 40 employees. They were all Russian, but politely greeted customers in English and called the company 'Lasertouch' because 'Leathertouch' was too tricky for the Russian tongue. The company used Western designs to make soft furniture specially adapted for small Russian flats. The most popular items were suites comprising a sofa bed and two armchairs, priced at around 3.5 million roubles (£500).

'Our prices are aimed at the middle class, not just New Russians,' deputy general director Marina Bevza told me. She proudly showed off the company's latest range of children's beanbags, manufactured in Sydney, Australia, by Sobel's son, Alan. They sold for £15 each. Pool tables were an experimental line - the game is hardly known in Russia. Like Russia & World, Leathertouch established a barter system. It gave fabric to manufacturers and they gave Leathertouch furniture to exhibit and sell.

Sobel was confident of success, despite the challenges posed by Russia. He told the US ambassador to Russia, 'Doing business in Russia is like gambling at a casino where you don't know if you get to keep your winnings.' But Sobel had already experienced tough times in China: when US president Richard Nixon opened the door to trade with the People's Republic, Sobel became the first American textile dealer to explore the opportunities there in 1972. This was the first of his 42 visits to the country, which ended in June 1990, when tanks crushed the pro-democracy demonstrations in Beijing.

Sobel had an office in the Chinese capital and four Chinese employees. 'Like everybody else, I got shot at when the troops were sent in to Tiananmen Square,' he said. Luckily he had already arranged visas for his employees to visit America that summer. They left China and have not been back since. In China, Sobel had access to the synthetic yarn PVA (poly-vinyl alcohol), which he believed was manufactured only in that country and in Japan. When he had to give up his business in China, he went to Russia to see if he could obtain PVA there.

With the help of a professor at the St Petersburg textiles institute, Sobel discovered a source of PVA and decided to set up shop in the former Soviet Union. He returned to the United States to find his 91-year-old Lithuanian mother-in-law on her deathbed. As a child she had fled from pogroms in the pre-Bolshevik Russian Empire. When Sobel told her where he had been she suddenly sat up and said, 'Are you crazy? Only crazy people go to Russia!' But with a newly-built factory in Luga (about 120 miles south of St Petersburg) and the huge retail centre which I visited, Leathertouch did not appear to be the brainchild of a madman. 'Russia is the last frontier in my lifetime,' said Sobel. 'Whatever I've done in my life so far has been preparation for my job here. It's a wonderful challenge if you don't get killed.'

Although Mel Sobel's comments about teaching Russians Western honesty and integrity had the ring of Uncle Sam idealism about them, there is undeniably an innate politeness in our service industry which Russians ought to import in bulk. It's quite simple for us: the customer is always right. If a shop assistant is rude, the customer goes elsewhere, the shop loses money and the assistant gets fired. The American insistence that you 'have a nice day' is grating in its falseness, but contrived pleasantries are ultimately less of a pain than indifference and hostility.

Djinn Shop was my local grocery store in St Petersburg. It was open 24 hours a day and sold almost exclusively imported goods (bread and mass-produced dumplings were the exception) for prices which were either the same as those in a British shop or much higher. A kilogram of frozen broccoli, for instance, cost about £5. Djinn Shop was one of the new shops set up like a Western supermarket, allowing customers to handle the products and put them into baskets themselves. Previously, all Russian shops had resembled top-security military installations. Such shops, concrete blocks called univermag (short for universal shop) or universam (short for universal something else) still exist but are rapidly losing out to the competition.

The first task in dealing with a traditional Russian shop was to remember the opening hours. Before I found Djinn Shop this was the bane of my life. It didn't matter what time I got to the universam, I invariably caught the hour-long lunch break - on some days between 12 and 1 pm, on others between 1 and 2 pm or 2 and 3 pm - and if I craftily avoided lunch then it was bound to be the second Tuesday or third Thursday of the month, which meant the shop was closed for a 'sanitary day'.

During the last 20 minutes of the lunch break people would start milling around outside the shop, asking each other what time it was due to open and what the time was now. Two minutes before the end of the lunch break they pressed themselves to the glass, looking for the shop assistants and trying to secure a forward position in the surge through the doors. Thirty seconds after the lunch break, according to the fastest watch, muttered grumbles and tuts would emanate from a crotchety middle-aged woman who had been perpetually irritated by the general decline in punctuality which had been noticeable ever since the threat of forced relocation to Siberia had ceased to exert an influence on the average working day.

When the doors did open everyone who was outside could usually get inside. At the most popular and most regimented shops, though, the number of people inside was limited strictly, as if the universam was a ride at Disneyland, and after the maximum was reached a person was admitted only when another had left. This wasn't because a large number of people would have been a fire hazard - it was more likely due to a shortage of shopping baskets. Usually you waited just inside the doors behind a turnstile, which was always operated by someone who took peculiar pleasure in making ambiguous hand gestures which could mean 'come on' or 'stop', and then locking the turnstile as you walked into it, causing a sudden and nasty groin injury.

Immediately after the turnstile you had to give all your personal property to another demonic babushka in return for a token - perhaps this was supposed to lighten your load, but I think it was designed to provide employment for another person and to make shoplifting an impossibility unless you had a lot of room under your sweater. In fact, purchasing an item legally was difficult enough. Everything was behind glass in different sections: meat, dairy products, fruit and vegetables, cereals and so on. You decided what you wanted by looking at it from a distance, however high up on the shelf it might be or far back behind the counter. Then you had to attract the attention of the shop assistant in that section, by pushing through the heaving masses, half of whom were in your situation, waiting to be served for the first time, and the other half of whom were waving receipts which proved they'd paid for the goods and could collect them.

The only way to induce the surly (and usually burly) woman in charge to do something for you was to shout 'Girl!' at her. Anyone with a weakness on the assertiveness side of their personality presumably ate very sparsely. There were various receipt systems in each universam, and this 'girl' certainly didn't have the time to explain hers to you. The worst problems occurred at the dairy products and cold meats section, where food had to be weighed. I would ask for half a kilogram of salami and receive 497 grams, which worked out at, say, 22,398 roubles. Then I would ask for a kilogram of cheese and receive 1092 grams, which cost 59,936 roubles. A generous shop assistant would write these figures down for me to save me from trouble at the next stage. The more sadistic ones, or those who didn't have a pen, left me on my own to rush over to the queue for receipts, jiggling up and down on my toes as I attempted to keep the prices in my head for long enough to repeat them to the cashier.

So in comparison with the rigours of the universam, Djinn Shop was indeed paradise on earth. But the luxury of serving myself and paying for everything at once was not afforded lightly. The assistants in Djinn Shop were selected primarily for the severity of their glare. Their piercing eyes followed you as you roved from the teas to the chocolates to the wines and spirits. Touch something. Take something. I *dare* you. I half expected to be punished by an electric shock as I reached for a jar of Swedish herring in tomato sauce.

The cakes in Djinn Shop were inside a glass cabinet, displayed like Fabergé eggs in the Kremlin Armoury. This was enough to deter me - I was afraid of triggering a laser beam which would signal a squadron of elite Interior Ministry forces to parachute onto the roof, drive pickaxes through the ceiling and slide down into the shop on ropes in defence of a Mr Kipling almond slice. I always circumvented the cakes cabinet by at least a foot to keep myself out of danger. My landlady, however, was determined to break in somehow. 'Can you believe that cakes cabinet?' she said to me. 'I wanted to buy one for my parents. I tried opening the window from the front but it didn't budge and the shop assistant just stood there watching me. I asked her how to get a cake and she looked at me as if I was an idiot and told me to go around the back. You have to go behind the fridge and squeeze in between the biscuits and the baby milk. Marvellous!'

Obtaining something in Djinn Shop wasn't the end of the matter. You next had to get past the women at the tills without being reduced to a gibbering wreck. They amused themselves by randomly stopping work without warning, so it would get to your turn in the queue and the one who was about to serve you would say, 'Go to the other till. That's it, I've finished. Get away from here. Did you hear what I said? Customers should know what to do by now,' (and to her friend on the next till, *sotto voce*), 'Doesn't it amaze you how ignorant they can be, Vera?'

I was scolded for my incompetence at asking for a plastic bag, which cost a few roubles. On my first visit to the shop I asked for the bag before the assistant started taking my purchases from the basket. By the time she'd added up all the prices she had forgotten about the bag and when I reminded her she was annoyed because she'd already printed out my receipt. The next time, I decided to dive in and mention the bag in the instant after she'd tapped in the last price, before she'd printed out the receipt. It didn't work. 'Couldn't you have asked for a bag earlier?' she huffed.

The place to go for impeccable service in St Petersburg was a five-star hotel. By 1996 there were three - the Astoria, the Grand Hotel Europe and the Nevskij Palace. Here the lackeys had been whipped into shape by their multi-millionaire employers. They refused to speak Russian; the doormen even tried to guess what nationality you were and addressed you in the appropriate language. I was greeted by a 'Good afternoon' and a 'Bonsoir', and waved off with a cheerful 'Arrivederci!' The public relations officer at the Grand Hotel Europe was an American who couldn't speak Russian, so I had to interpret when an editor from Russia & World met her to discuss advertising.

My parents and I had lunch in the Nevskij Palace with the British manager. A waiter came over to take our order and the manager said in English, 'I'd like a beer, please.' The waiter nodded uncertainly, hovered, and then said, 'Yes. What sort, red or white?' A waitress who overheard this exchange had a word in his ear, which turned bright red, and he discreetly retreated, leaving her to restore the staff's credibility.

Probably by the time you read this a fourth five-star hotel has opened in the city. The North Crown Hotel almost had the dubious distinction of being a massive failed business venture not once, but twice. It used to be a hollow carbuncle, a crumbling monument to two fallen empires, the Soviet Union and Yugoslavia. These former countries were jointly building a hotel overlooking the Karpovka Canal but work came to a halt in 1991. It started again in 1994 when Russian investors signed an agreement with a Turkish construction company, ATA, to complete the project. The hotel's glass lifts would rise to a restaurant in which guests would dine 'right beside Peter the Great, Pushkin, Lenin, Stalin and other historic figures of Russia', according to the publicity brochure. A night in one of the two presidential suites would cost upwards of £700.

Three months after the scheduled grand opening date of December 1995, these presidential suites had no running water and the North Crown's staff, some of whom had left jobs at other hotels, were sitting at home with no income. The builders had downed tools because ATA was owed £17 million by Bank St

Petersburg, which had recently splashed out on a televised celebration of its fifth anniversary in the Mariinsky Theatre.

'We didn't have a penny to pay for this project,' said Cengiz Duyar, ATA's boss on the hotel site. 'We were asked to finish part of the building for the bank's anniversary, so we worked very hard, day and night - they said many people would see it. Every day they told us they were about to find the money, but then it became a long story. Of course we should have known from the beginning that Bank St Petersburg is not reliable, it's not even one of the top fifteen banks in Russia yet. By the way, only four Russian banks are accepted as reliable in Western countries. I heard it on CNN this morning.'

Duyar was conciliatory and his company eventually worked out an agreement with Bank St Petersburg. He said that in future ATA would undertake projects in Russia only in partnership with other companies. Going it alone was too risky. 'The North Crown was our first project in Russia,' Duyar added. 'Before that we worked at home in Turkey and in Middle Eastern countries such as Libya and Jordan. We are not ready to work in Western Europe because of logistics and the strict legislation there. To be honest, we are not very well organised like American and German companies.'

In contrast to ATA, the Russian lorry company Sovavto was more concerned about the weakness of its competitors than its own deficits. The director of Sovavto, Vyacheslav Lazarian, said he wanted to protect the reputation of Russian firms so that they would continue to get foreign business. Sovavto was offering training to other Russian transport companies. 'Small transport businesses have started up with just one or two vehicles which their owners don't know how to handle,' Lazarian explained. 'We have a classroom where we teach people about the technical aspect of heavy lorries. We even help them buy lorries as we have good connections with Volvo. If we didn't do this, all Russian lorry companies would get a bad name.'

Lazarian boasted that in Sovavto's 30 years of existence, not a single driver had failed to return from a trip abroad. 'They know what it's like,' he said. 'No matter what country you're in, you still have to work, and in the West you have to work harder.' I was curious about whether the drivers would confirm what their director said. To further investigate their psyche, I travelled from St Petersburg to Stockholm and back on Sovavto lorries.

The driver who took me to Sweden was 38-year-old Sasha Grigoriev. He told me that in Soviet times drivers' loyalty to the motherland was proven by their obligatory Communist Party membership. To work for Sovavto they also had to be married and have at least one child. 'I like seeing other countries, but Russia's my home, it's where I was born and where my family is. Look -,' Sasha pulled out a photograph of his wife and daughters from his wallet. 'Come to dinner with us one day, so that you can say you have friends in St Petersburg.'

'Do you ever get out and walk around the cities you visit?' I asked him.

'No, there isn't time, and I have to stay with the lorry in any case. But it's the driving I love. I couldn't do a job where I had to sit behind a desk all day.'

Sovavto was never short of contracts to bring goods into Russia, from washing machines to humanitarian aid packages; but more often than not, lorries went out of the country with empty trailers. 'What could we take to them? In the West they have everything in the shops,' said Volodya Kuzmin, 52, who brought me back from Stockholm with a trailer full of chemicals. Sasha wasn't carrying anything when he drove there, which made it more difficult to control the vehicle on the icy roads. 'It's romance, romance,' he repeated with an unfazed grin as we reversed down a hill in a raging blizzard somewhere outside Helsinki. 'You never know what's going to happen next.'

Snowdrifts higher than the lorry, road signs which gave no more information than 'Murmansk - 550 km' and the tendency of young Russians to demand money with menaces on the road were some of the hazards of driving in the former Soviet Union. Although Sovavto had to go further and faster than ever to defeat its rivals, at least the drivers had hard currency in their pockets and visas in their passports. This gave them a considerable advantage over all but the richest of their fellow citizens. Dima, the radio journalist, was supposed to come with me to Stockholm to make a programme about Russians in Sweden, but his Swedish visa wasn't enough. He also needed a Finnish transit visa, and the

119

Finnish consulate in St Petersburg took a minimum of two weeks to process it, which was too late for him.

Having the right visas and stepping on the gas didn't guarantee that drivers would get to their destination quickly, though. A necessary element of the lorry driver's character was the ability to sit in one place for hours, or even days, without falling asleep. Volodya and I arrived at the Finnish-Russian border at 7:20 pm. Seeing the rear lights of other lorries gleaming through the snow far into the distance, we knew it was time to settle in for a long night. The temperature was -19° Celsius and the lorry's heater had just given up the ghost, so we had to keep the engine running to stay warm.

'Want to watch the news?' Volodya offered. I thought he was joking, but he unpacked a portable black-and-white television. His lorry was equipped with all the essentials for modern living, except a toilet. It had bunk beds, a gas stove on which Volodya warmed up the mushroom soup his wife had made for him, and a CB radio which crackled with updates on the movement and length of the queue, as well as a broad selection of Russian obscenities. 'Watch your mouths, I've got a female journalist from England in here,' Volodya chided his colleagues.

It was Christmas Eve, but long-distance drivers never noticed public holidays unless they coincidentally ended up at home. Sasha said he was on the luxurious Silja Line ferry to Stockholm one New Year's Eve and drank vodka all night, courtesy of the ship's captain, who treated the drivers. The next morning, no one was in a fit state to drive their lorries onto shore and they had to pay Swedish crowns to get someone else to take the vehicles off the ferry. All the Western drivers paid, but the Russians preferred to take the money home to their families and drove out themselves, completely inebriated, under the lenient gaze of the Swedish police.

The enforced 11-hour rest on the ferry was a welcome interruption in the heavy driving schedule. Whereas in Western Europe drivers must have a night's sleep after eight hours on the road, there was no such limitation in Russia. On the way to Sweden I had my own cabin on the ferry but on the way back I had to share with Volodya. He drank a bottle of beer and then got into bed in his vest and underpants. He looked dreamily across at me and said, 'Do you want to make love?'

'Sorry, not tonight,' I replied as politely as I could.

'Why not? Are you frigid?' he asked me, then burped and rolled over, disappointed.

There was no sleep for Volodya in the queue at the border crossing. There never was: if a driver dozed off, the other lorries would simply move past him. The most notorious queue was at Brest, where Volodya said he once waited four days to leave Belarus and another three days to get into Poland. 'We attached wires from the back of one lorry to the windscreen of another so that when the front lorry moved, the driver behind woke up,' said Volodya. My wait with him wasn't quite as long. We left Finland at 12:50 am and were waved through Russian customs at 10:15 am. 'Not bad', said Volodya. 'You were lucky.'

Sport

In a nation of sporting heroes, it wasn't immediately obvious how the ordinary mortal could keep fit. The public swimming pool, for example, was a daunting installation to penetrate, defended by fiendish babushkas with their hefty books of regulations. Most swimming pools demanded a doctor's certificate to show that you'd had a chest X-ray and a groin inspection and were free of skin diseases. Then you had to acquire a swimming hat from somewhere, inevitably a kiosk which had imported a shipment of reject pink flowery ones from Poland.

These twin medical and fashion humiliations were enough to deter me, but my friend Jane did go swimming and told me about it afterwards. 'The babusha said I had to buy a season ticket, but I only wanted to go once or twice. She said she didn't have a price for one session of swimming. I offered her 3000 roubles (50p) and she took it very furtively and put it under the counter. A few weeks later I went again and the same babushka was there. She repeated what she'd said before, a season ticket or nothing. I said, how about 2500 roubles for one session? - and she hid the money under the counter again.'

'Perhaps you'll get in for free next time,' I said.

Jane and her boyfriend Volodya, a political journalist, invited me to go cross-country skiing with them. We took the train to a village half an hour from St Petersburg and got off in a completely white landscape of hills and fir trees. An old man sitting in a shed was in charge of hiring out skis for 4000 roubles an hour. 'You're late!' he barked at us as we approached him. 'I'm shutting the door now. It's one o'clock, that's when we close. Can't you read the sign?' We charmed him into letting us be the last customers of the day and he thrust some pairs of long, thin skis at us. They were made of plywood, or something not much sturdier.

The village was called Kavgolovo. It was the usual cluster of wooden houses in the middle of a field. With beautiful scenery and heavy snow guaranteed for at least six months of the year, it could have been a bustling ski resort bringing in millions of roubles for the region. There ought to have been garish billboards all over St Petersburg screaming, 'Forget Switzerland, come to

Kavgolovo for a smoother ski! Relax in the après-ski cocktail bars and video lounges of our centrally-heated chalets!' But Kavgolovo was advertised only by word of mouth and foreign tourists had as much chance of stumbling upon it as they did of finding an Eskimo in the drinks cabinet of their hotel room. The après-ski facilities manifested themselves in the guise of a crooked little hut which sold boiled frankfurters, tea, coffee and vodka in plastic cups.

I shuffled forwards on my skis, sticks flailing, as Jane and Volodya glided on ahead. Soon my face was red and I was out of breath, not from skiing but from picking myself up off the ground when my skis were crossed over and half-buried in snow. But I made it to the Gulf of Finland. 'We're on the sea! We're on the sea!' we shouted at each other in astonishment.

'Hold on, I can see water over here,' said Volodya. 'We'd better turn around.' I turned around, fell over and snapped one of my skis in half.

Skiing on a frozen expanse of water was considerably easier than skiing on it when it had melted. In the tradition of new Blue Peter presenters, one of my first assignments as a journalist at *The St Petersburg Press* was to try out a dangerous sport. To me it was hair-raising. Andrei Smirnoff, a serious competitive waterskier, said it was 'completely safe'. He was adamant that the water in Pervoye Suzdolskoye lake was clean and the sport was ecologically friendly. I was happy for the environment, but what about me? 'The only danger is if you can't swim or try to go too fast for your ability,' Andrei assured me as he prepared to drag me through the water at 30 mph.

Being clumsy and uncoordinated put me in no danger at all, as there was little chance of my staying attached to the skis or the boat for more than ten seconds. 'Just lean back and enjoy it' was the succinct pre-ski advice Andrei gave me, but leaning back was easier said than done when a 200 hp motorboat was pulling you forward at the end of a rope. Eddie 'The Eagle' Edwards, the accident-prone British ski jumper who broke every bone in his body, would have been proud of me. The tanned athletes of the St Petersburg waterskiing club were rather less impressed. I had already amused them by struggling to squeeze myself into a rubber wetsuit. Still, going head-over-heels a few times in a lake wasn't as painful as it would have been on a mountain.

It was 7 pm but the water was warm and we managed to avoid the rainstorm which began a little later. 'You have to be a fanatic to waterski in St Petersburg,' said candidate fanatic Yuri Guzeyev. 'I am not as bad as some of the others. They start in April, while there are still no leaves on the trees, and ski until the end of October.' The club had about 20 members, most of whom had been skiing since childhood. Russian women are especially renowned for their waterskiing abilities - one was world champion recently - and at Suzdolskoye they demonstrated the grace and finesse that can be achieved with practice. Slicing the smooth curves of the slalom on one ski at the maximum speed of 58 mph, they continued to ski effortlessly to the shore even after they let go of the handlebar. From balancing on one ski the best athletes progressed to barefoot skiing.

When it was really freezing the club members simply moved over to the Spartak swimming pool, where there was an electric waterski training machine. Russia is the only country in the world where you can waterski indoors, and competitions are even held in the swimming pool. During the Soviet era the government invested huge amounts of money in sport and St Petersburg had three professional waterskiing teams. But without that help, the club's only hope of survival was to become independent of the naval base it was affiliated to and fund itself through fees.

'Sport in this country is dying because all the money is being spent on the war in Chechnya,' said Yuri. 'That's why we want individuals or groups to come here and pay to waterski. If more people became keen on the sport then they would bring their children and new champions would grow up. You can start skiing from the age of seven.' There are three forms of waterskiing. Slalom was the most popular, Yuri explained, because jumping was more dangerous and tricks required much more experience.

Members of the St Petersburg club competed in the Russian championships and performed in shows, such as the opening of the Goodwill Games in summer 1994. Andrei had a moment of glory as a waterskiing stuntman in a Russian film called *How to Become a Star*. The club's financial problems were its greatest concern, although it was dealt an additional blow a year before the Goodwill Games while the channel into the lake was reconstructed, making it impossible to ski.

Yuri hoped that the club's fortunes would be revived by encouraging companies to organise weekend excursions for their employees. But the waterskiers admitted that theirs was an exclusive sport - taking it up was an expensive business. Skis, wetsuits and the petrol for the boat all had to be paid for. The club could provide all the equipment and an instructor for about £30 per hour. The days when Russian athletes were guaranteed an income by the state were long gone. When he wasn't skiing, Yuri worked as a sales engineer for a Finnish company. Andrei sold waterskiing equipment.

Having demonstrated my ineptitude at two kinds of skiing, I decided I might do better at a sport in which someone else did all the work. I'd heard that microlites took passengers on short flights over the Gulf of Finland and so I set off in search of them. The beach they took off from was bisected by a river, and the water was waist-deep. I was ferried over in a rubber dinghy by a young man who happened to be floating around at the time. Then I had to pass a collection of nude, brown bodies, some of which were completely hairless, without running away in fright. The naturist section of the beach was marked by chequered flags so that those of a modest disposition could steer well clear.

There were up to six microlites on the beach at any one time, some single-seaters and some double. They looked like flying go-carts: the construction was so simple that they hardly differed from Leonardo da Vinci's 15th-century flying machine prototypes. These motorised hang-gliders just had to zoom along the sand for 60 feet and then they miraculously ascended into the air, wheels still spinning. On this beach there was no set runway - sunbathers had to scatter if they found themselves in the takeoff area.

The microlite pilots were members of the St Petersburg hang-gliding club. Their vehicles' 54-foot wings were manufactured in the town of Pushkin, 14 miles south of the city, and the engines were imported from Austria via Moscow. If an engine suddenly cut out, a microlite could glide safely down to the ground. 'There are more accidents in motorsports and on St Petersburg's roads,' said pilot Yuri Mishakov confidently.

To qualify as a microlite pilot in Russia, you had to be at least fifteen years old and have taken theory lessons in addition to ten hours' flying with an instructor. The pilot steered using a crossbar attached to the wings, exactly like that of a hang-glider. On the microlite there was also a gearbox. Normal cruising speed was around 40 mph, although a maximum speed of 70 mph could be reached. The microlites usually took passengers to a height of 300 feet.

Flying with the top of my helmet brushing the clouds wasn't a warm experience. In the winter I would see microliters zipped up in bright orange suits and masks like nuclear holocaust survivors. I felt chilly on a hot summer's day. But after a while I forgot the cold and my initial apprehension (to put it mildly) and began to appreciate the spectacular view. In any case there was nothing else to do as the heavy helmet and the loud vibrations of the engine made it impossible to chat with the pilot.

The vastness of the sea had a calming effect and I was able to relax my grip on the frame of the microlite. There was enough movement to keep you aware that contact with terra firma had been lost, but there were no sudden swoops, so it was less stomach-churning than a fairground ride. Aesthetics rather than thrills provided most of the pleasure. Certainly, the naturists were far more pleasing to the eye from a distance. With all my senses focused on taking in the scenery and fresh air, the minutes seemed to pass slowly. The gradual descent over pygmy tennis and volleyball players was one of the highlights.

Like the takeoff, the landing was also dependent on people having the common sense to get out of the way. Dogs were slower to respond and we almost skimmed over their backs in the last seconds before touching down. I braced myself for a jolt but the landing was as smooth as the flight. This was definitely my kind of sport: a passenger sport.

I trekked back in the direction of the train station. The man in the rubber dinghy had gone, and I wasn't inclined to wade across the river - the weather had cooled down and I was struck by the memory that Trotsky had lost his power struggle with Stalin because he caught flu from stepping into a Russian bog. I thought a short wander through the coniferous forest of the White Nights sanatorium would get me to the station dry and uninfected by a debilitating virus. An hour later I regretted this choice. I was still in the forest, along with numerous other lost walkers looking for the way out. The sanatorium was surrounded by a tall wire fence. Why was there never a microlite around when I really needed one?

Once I'd been in a microlite, there was nowhere else to go but up. The following winter I braced myself for a spin in an aerobatics plane. Even after communism, a select few pilots got intensive aerobatics training, courtesy of the state, so that teams from Moscow and St Petersburg could triumph in international competition. During the Cold War pilots from the capitalist side of the Berlin Wall could only watch Soviet aerobatic technique in amazement and wonder about the closely-guarded secrets of the Soviet aviation industry from afar. Now those secrets are open to anyone who wants to visit a Russian aerodrome - and any non-Russian pilot with a lust for near-death experiences and a full wallet can take aerobatics lessons in Russian planes from Russian pilots.

At the St Petersburg flying club the first lesson takes place in a classroom with the slogan 'Military pilot - a heroic profession' on the wall next to the blackboard. Many of the club's instructors were formerly officers in the Soviet air force, including deputy chairman Vladimir Chekirda, who showed me around. Another unusual aspect of this classroom was the presence of a Yakovlev-52 two-seater aircraft in the back row. Its outer casing had been removed so that students could fully acquaint themselves with the mechanical anatomy of the plane at an altitude which didn't necessitate the use of parachutes. 'You have to know why a plane flies,' said Vladimir. 'It's no use desperately trying to find the fuel gauge when you're a thousand metres up.'

Whilst some of the club's protegés were pilots who were soaring into the world of aerobatics for the first time, others were 16-year-olds who'd never flown before but had been chosen to train for the St Petersburg aerobatics team. The club used to take 60 new recruits a year, when the state had no trouble financing their five-year course, but in today's Russia aerobatics teams are low on the priority list for funding. In 1996 the annual intake was between 12 and 15 young people. Some of the expenses of their training were covered by the profits from giving private lessons to Swedish, Finnish and French pilots at £70 an hour, although at that rate the profit margin was minimal.

The club's aerodrome was to the north of the city, in a village called Lisy Nos on the shores of the Gulf of Finland. Vladimir invited me to sit in a Yak-52 for ten minutes while he hurtled it in all directions so that I could personally divulge to readers the bizarre sensations which made pilots mad about aerobatics. But first I had to survive the toe-curling experience of waiting in the club's wooden hut while snow was removed from the planes at a temperature of -20° Celsius. The pilots try to fly throughout the winter but they hadn't been up for some weeks because of a fuel shortage.

After three hours in the hut the snow was still being removed and the prospect of ascending to a height where the temperature was another ten degrees lower would have sent a chill down my spine if it hadn't already been too numb to feel anything. On that day I left the heroic professionals to their duty and decided to visit the warmer offices of Air France, where there was a person who could tell me his reasons for choosing aerobatics as a hobby.

Why not read a book or go fishing, after all? 'That's what my wife says,' laughed Dominique Cottin, Air France's representative in St Petersburg. 'When I was flying normally I had the strong feeling that I was only using 20% of the facility offered by the aircraft,' he said. 'With aerobatics you use 100% of its capacity. It's the oldest dream of man, to fly like a bird - except that's not quite right, because you never see a bird spinning!' Dominique had a private pilot's licence and had recently taken his first four-week course in aerobatics in France. He was having lessons at the St Petersburg flying club from an instructor called Mikhail Narbut.

Dominique's few words of Russian were matched by Mikhail's deficit in English, but when flying was the subject they understood each other perfectly. Dominique also found an affinity for the Yak-52: 'What I feel is the power,' he said. 'It's something like flying in a small warbird. It's a very healthy aircraft, not vicious; some planes don't support you if you make a mistake, but the Yak-52 forgives you.' Dominique's only complaints were that he was too tall for it - the top of his head was only a few millimetres from the roof of the cockpit - and his seat was uncomfortable because its back was vertical, not inclined at an angle as in most aerobatics planes.

By mid-March the airfield was still covered in thick snow but the sun was out and the temperature had risen to a blazing 0° Celsius. I returned to Lisy Nos for my date with destiny. The planes were mummified in protective sheets, icicles hanging from their wings and noses. Here were not only Yak-52s but also single-seater Yak-55s for competition, big Antonov-2 biplanes for dropping parachutists, and gliders which were released into the sky by the club's Vilga-35, a bright yellow Polish plane which resembled an underfed wasp.

I flew in the Vilga-35 with a trainee pilot and his instructor so that I could see the frozen sea and the grey outlines of the ships embedded in it from a horizontal viewpoint. I was slightly disturbed that the only one of us who insisted on wearing a parachute was the trainee pilot, who was flying the plane. It didn't fill me with confidence to think that he could jump out and let us plummet to the ground. Fortunately, he stayed in his seat, sparing me for the thrills and spills of the Yak-52.

'You press this button if you want to say anything to the pilot,' Mikhail explained as he strapped and buckled me in to the Yak-52. 'Take me home to Mum, for instance.' Mikhail looked on with a mischievous gleam in his eye as Vladimir taxied the plane and me to the runway. In front of me a throttle moved from side to side as if it were in the grip of some ghostly hand. I had exactly the same instruments as Vladimir - in this plane the pilot really could jump out to let a student fly solo.

To my right there were miniature sketches of the main aerobatic figures - corkscrews, Nesterov rolls, loop-the-loops - to be used as a crib sheet in case you had the plane at an angle of 180° and had forgotten whether you were supposed to be heading up or down. We took off smoothly and I immediately felt more at ease than I had been in the rattly Vilga-35. But the first two minutes of level flying seemed to drag on agonisingly as I imagined myself losing consciousness as soon as Vladimir launched into a dive. Instead, we started to spin, blue-white-sky-snow-blue-white, and my legs and arms lurched out to the sides of the cockpit, instinctively trying to cling on to something.

My brain was slower to react but it eventually signalled to my limbs that they might as well relax because I wasn't going to fall out no matter what the plane did. If we went down, we'd all go down together. For psychological reassurance I found it was just as useful to hold tightly onto the hem of my jacket. All that was left to do was to look through the glass roof of the cockpit in awe. Then we did dive and my head was forced almost into my lap by the g-force. (In tight turns, your weight increases and blood drains from your head to your feet.) I couldn't lift my head high enough to look through the roof but directly in front of me was a vision which could have been a frame in a Biggles cartoon: the back of the pilot's leather headgear, the propeller, and a maze of trees and houses rushing towards us at breakneck speed.

Suddenly I was elated, glimpsing something which by rights should induce a state of terror, safe in the knowledge that these probably weren't the last few seconds of my life. I wanted to press the button and say something to the pilot, but there was nothing to say. He had flown us into another dimension, where words were superfluous. What completely mystified me was that anyone could concentrate on flying a plane when the experience of aerobatics was so intoxicating. I was craving more even before the undercarriage made contact with the runway.

Aerobatics pilots don't consider their occupation dangerous or superhumanly demanding - it's all physics and aerodynamics to them, and once you understand the principles, you can do anything. Or so they told me. The only disaster at the aerodrome that day happened on the ground: a Yak-52 taxied too close to a snowdrift and its propeller was shattered.

Like anything in the world, it's possible to get used to aerobatics and again seek greater excitement. So what do aerobatics pilots dream of doing? The answer to this was on the wall of the St Petersburg flying club, a signed photograph of Sergei Krikalyov and his American comrades. Sergei trained at the flying club from the age of 17 and in 1994 flew in the space shuttle Discovery and walked in space. He was also the unlucky man who was left stranded in orbit when the 1991 coup took place, finding on his return that the country which had launched him into space no longer existed.

Russians play chess in space. They also play it in polar research stations, in prison, on ships, and, famously, on park benches. In Russia chess is officially categorised as a sport, and more people play this sport than any other. From the 1920s the Soviet government systematically developed a mass chess organisation which would train millions of children in the classrooms of chess schools and clubs so that a handful of them would become champions of the world. In Britain, the land of the stiff-upper-lipped loser, the idea of primary school kids volunteering to sit at desks in their spare time making notes on opening theory and memorising grandmasters' greatest games, sounds absurd. I've witnessed this phenomenon myself and I've been a victim of its effectiveness.

I've always liked chess because it allows me to combine two of my most finely-honed abilities: sitting down for a long time and staring into space. I was on one of the teams at university (OK, the third team, but who's counting?) and when I went to study Russian in Minsk, I hoped to find some new opponents. In Minsk there were three major chess schools, the school of chess and draughts Olympic reserves, the palace of Pioneers and the trade union school. In the school of Olympic reserves alone, 800 children studied with 17 chess trainers. The largest groups were of between 12 and 15 beginners, and the groups got smaller as the standard got higher. The strongest players had lessons five times a week, for a total of 20 hours. For those children who were considering a future as professional chess players there were specialists to help them at the Ministry of Physical Culture.

Once I'd been in the city for a few days I could understand why chess was so popular there. The other leisure activities in Minsk were pedallo rides on the lake, getting hammered on a 75p bottle of wine in Little Cellar Bar, getting hammered on 10p bottles of beer on Day of Liberation From Fascism, going to a concert by Russian rock band DDT in the football stadium (not so pleasurable for the more raucous members of the audience who were beaten about the head by police truncheons), going to the Theatre of Opera and Ballet, and changing money. The attraction of doing this every two weeks was that inflation was on the verge of making me a Belarusian rouble millionaire. At the beginning of my stay £30 was worth about 450,000 roubles; five months later it was worth over a million. I had to carry the wads of notes home in a sports bag and could hardly stuff enough money into my purse to buy a bottle of wine in Little Cellar Bar. Some of the British students in my group disrespectfully wallpapered their room in the hostel with banknotes. Before leaving, they threw the money out of the window.

Chess made Minsk less monotonous. I didn't dare approach the old men in the parks who played blitz - five or ten minutes each for all their moves - slamming the button on the clock as if they were dealing the death blow to a Fascist, shoving the pieces across the board so violently that anything teetering on the edge was sent flying onto the grass. I dread to think how they would have replied if I'd said, 'Excuse me, can I play?' They would probably have pointed their crutches at me and said, 'Young lass, it'll be your turn when you've fought in the Great Patriotic War, had your left leg amputated without anaesthetic, watched your children die of tuberculosis, learnt to live on a pension of 200 roubles a month and read the Giant Soviet Dictionary of Chess Gambits from cover to cover.' Or, they might have said, 'Sure, would you like Black or White?', but I'll never know.

I sought out a game at the city chess club. Some of the players there were under eighty. Encouragingly, some of them appeared to be under eight. I didn't know what the etiquette was, who to challenge, so I sat at an empty board waiting for someone to befriend me. A woman in her early thirties smiled at me across the table and asked if I would like to play with her pupils, two little girls. She introduced herself as Sveta, an accountant who also taught chess at one of the local youth clubs. She was a candidate master, 'but in your country I would be a master'.

I set up the pieces and took on the first little girl, who was nine. I built up a solid defence which she proceeded to knock down and march all over. 'Checkmate!' she announced, twenty minutes later. 'Have a go with Masha,' Sveta suggested sympathetically.

'She's only seven.' After a bitter tussle I defeated Masha, to my enormous relief - my first Belarusian scalp. Afterwards I got chatting with Sveta and she offered to give me chess lessons in return for English lessons, which I readily agreed to. Forget the third team, I'll be a candidate master by the time I get back to England, I thought, somewhat optimistically.

The problem with our 'lessons' was the highly influential presence of beer in them. The first thing I learnt from Sveta was that chess players and beer are inseparable. Strangely, it seemed to equalise the standard of our English, but not our chess. She won every time no matter how much we both drank. Except once. It happened when my thinking was so blurred that I didn't know what opening I was playing. On her first move as White, Sveta pushed her king's pawn forward. I confused it with the queen's pawn; it didn't help that Russian pieces were of a different design to British pieces, and the king and queen were very similar. I brought my knight out, believing I was playing the King's Indian, which I knew moderately well. 'Alekhine's Defence!' Sveta exclaimed. 'Interesting.' It turned out to be extremely interesting - without having a clue what I was supposed to do, I won the game. That's the only time I've ever beaten a candidate master, and it was also the source of a lasting personal attachment to Alekhine's Defence.

We had another beer experience when Sveta came to my flat with a chess master, a middle-aged man called Mikhail. He put down his heavy bag and unpacked from it his board, his pieces, his chess clock, and fourteen cans of beer. He poured us each a drink. 'Now we play!' he commanded. 'You will have ten minutes to make all of your moves, and I will have one minute.' I couldn't touch the beer during the game, because I couldn't afford to waste valuable seconds raising the glass to my lips. Mikhail calmly sipped his and in a deliberate voice managed to tell anecdotes about great tournaments he'd been in, whilst crushing me and Sveta in turn. In most of the games I saved Mikhail the nuisance of checkmating me by running out of time.

Someone who I could beat fairly regularly was Henry, a student from Uganda whose intention was to become a TV sports journalist. He had been in Minsk for six years and spoke Russian fluently. 'The Ugandan government pays for some people to study abroad,' he said. 'But it chooses the country and the university for us. I could have been sent to Britain or America; instead, I flew with a group to Moscow. A few people stayed in Moscow, others went to St Petersburg, and I was told I would be living in Minsk. I didn't know a word of Russian.' I was especially pleased with my chess victories against Henry because he said that as a child he'd toured Africa playing chess for his country.

One day as Henry and I were leaving the chess club he asked me if I'd like to meet some of his friends. We met them inside the gates of the football stadium, where they were selling tracksuits at an outdoor market. They had been sailors in the Soviet navy but when Belarus became an independent country their career disappeared - Belarus is landlocked. We went back to their flat for soup and more chess. The flat was in a village which had to be reached by train, and I was rather wary of going there in the evening with three young men who I hardly knew, so I told Henry that my room-mate in the hostel would be worried about me and made him promise that we'd leave for Minsk by nine o'clock. We drank nothing stronger than tea and went home on time.

After that I went on a picnic in the countryside with Henry and some more of his Belarusian friends. We drank our way through several bottles of vodka, the effects of which were unmitigated by a few mouthfuls of barbecued shashlick. Henry, who was married and had a three-year-old child, started picking up (literally) girls, running round a field with them and kissing them. When it got too cold and windy for these outdoor escapades, we returned to Minsk on the bus. We were all squeezed up next to each other and Henry was attempting to take advantage of the accidental proximity of my lips to his. 'We're going to a flat to 'relax' now,' he said lasciviously.

'Er, no, I can't, my room-mate, you know...,' I stammered, and jumped off the bus at the next stop.

Henry didn't give up. At 11 o'clock one evening he knocked on the door of my room. 'Who's there?' I said.

'Henry.' I opened the door and he traipsed in, followed by an assortment of drunk friends who draped themselves over the chairs and the beds.

My room-mate said, 'I'm just going to bed.'

I said, 'That's odd, I'm having an early night, too. I'm afraid you'll all have to leave.' Henry pleaded with me to have some beer. The only way I could get rid of him and his motley crew was by promising to meet him at the chess club.

'OK, I'll be waiting for you at 12 tomorrow,' he said. I never went to the Minsk chess club again and I never saw Henry again.

I visited the St Petersburg chess club during the 1995 Chigorin international tournament. Dedicated to the father of Russian chess, 19th-century champion Mikhail Chigorin, this used to be one of the most prestigious tournaments in the Soviet Union, attracting top players from all over the world. At the first Chigorin Memorial Congress, in 1909, the atmosphere was so inspiring that one of the contestants wrote a twenty-line poem in its honour. But in 1995 the prize fund was meagre and the tournament could cling on to the label 'international' only because the republics of the former Soviet Union were independent countries. 77 of the 78 players were from those republics - the other country represented was Switzerland.

Grainy black-and-white photographs of male and female world champions smiled down from the walls. The leading players sat on a stage at the back of the hall and their moves were plotted on giant demonstration boards. 12-year-old Dmitri Yakovenko wasn't on the stage, but the standard of his play suggested that he would be in the not-too-distant future. He finished with four points out of nine in the tournament.

While grandmasters racked their brains over the tasks he set them, Dmitri entertained himself and some of the spectators by watching his wind-up plastic bear toddle up and down the table. So young - and already so adept at psychological warfare. A tactic no doubt instilled in him by his coach Alexander Nikitin, who used to train a certain Garik Kasparov, as the little boy from Azerbaijan was known. Nikitin was based in Moscow and Dmitri lived 2000 miles away in the Siberian town of Nizhnevartovsk. Dmitri had his lessons on the telephone. The schoolboy was men's champion of the town, which had 250,000 inhabitants. He said he hoped to become an international master 'in a year or two'. Dmitri assured me that he did fit in some time for schoolwork around his travel schedule which had so far taken him to Germany, Hungary, Slovakia and Malta.

Going abroad was nothing special for Dmitri Yakovenko, but for Mark Taimanov it was a freedom which had been denied to him for decades. He was a world championship contender but never won the title. In 1971 he was knocked out of the competition by the American Bobby Fischer, in a 6:0 rout. When Taimanov returned to the Soviet Union after the match, he was searched at customs and found to be carrying a book by Alexander Solzhenitsyn and some undeclared money. It was unusual for chess players to be searched at the border but the Soviet authorities had to punish Taimanov for his defeat. His title 'honoured master of sport' was taken away and the Leningrad party authorities forbade him from making public appearances, writing and travelling. 'I'm playing more chess now than I did in my best years, because before I played where I was told to play,' Taimanov said to me at the Chigorin tournament. His increased activity had twice been rewarded by the title of world champion amongst seniors.

Judgments on aesthetic excellence at the tournament were made by 85-year-old Andor Lilienthal (after Miguel Najdorf the world's second oldest grandmaster), who still had the energy to divide his time between Budapest and Moscow and make guest appearances in St Petersburg. 'Russia is the El Dorado of chess,' said the old man who trained world champions Vasily Smyslov and Tigran Petrosian. Lilienthal grew up in Hungary but in 1935 decided to stay in the Soviet Union after a Moscow international tournament 'because of the beautiful women'. He married three Russian women (not simultaneously), and boasted to me that his present wife was 30 years younger than him. Lilienthal also claimed to have been the first grandmaster to play on a Soviet collective farm - he got there on a horse in 1939 and gave a simultaneous display on 30 boards.

Russians call chess a sport, but, true to national character, they also find deeper significance in it. World champion Garry Kasparov is adamant that it is an art and a science, too. That's why Kasparov is so devastated whenever he loses to a computer: apart from the dent to his ego, he believes that human creativity should always outwit the cold logic of a machine. Veteran grandmaster David Bronstein, who has written some of the most popular books on chess and played some of the most amazing games, now rejects the idea of chess as art which he once promoted enthusiastically. 'The Soviet government tricked us into thinking it was an art,' he told me. 'It isn't, it's just a game.' In my opinion, an excellent game to play over a pint of beer.

The Media

It isn't easy to understand the strengths and weaknesses of Russian journalism without having some idea of its extraordinary diversity: extraordinary, because until the beginning of this decade the media was completely under the control of the state, the Communist Party, or both, and of course regulated by censorship at every imaginable level. Mikhail Gorbachev was widely praised in the West for starting the process of liberalisation, but he didn't go far.

No mention at all of the nuclear explosion at Chernobyl was made in the Soviet press for days after it happened, even though Gorbachev knew how serious it was. His chief of staff, Valery Boldin, later wrote, 'The first official reports about Chernobyl that reached Gorbachev made it clear that there had been a disaster of epic proportions... It was already obvious that the human toll was monstrous and that the economy would have to bear a huge additional burden.'

One of my Russian teachers in Minsk recalled how she was caught in a sudden shower whilst pushing her baby in a pram one day in April 1986. When high radiation levels were discovered by Swedish scientists, small reports began to appear in Soviet papers, buried in centre pages. 'Everyone in Minsk has radiation phobia,' said my teacher, speaking in 1994. 'Whenever we're ill, we blame Chernobyl. So many of those children and babies who were out in the rain like mine now have a disease of their lymph glands. Why didn't our government warn us? We would have stayed inside on that day.'

The kinds of articles which Russians could read in *Pravda* in 1990 deterred all but the most avid followers of politics with lead paragraphs such as, 'On the 6th of April 1990 the Council of Ministers of the USSR in accordance with the work plan of the Supreme Soviet of the USSR presented for its examination a draft law on the introduction of changes and additions to the law of the USSR 'On co-operation in the USSR'.' Whatever historic reforms and events were taking place in the country, the paper submerged them in boring legal jargon. *Pravda* would have been torn up as a substitute for drastically unavailable toilet roll in millions of households before people had finished the task of extricating the key items of news from it. Newer papers, especially *Moscow News*, printed shocking revelations from Soviet history every day. Such stories made a mockery of Gorbachev's attempts to cling on to communism.

Victor Leontev was still suffering from the consequences of Gorbachev's lack of tolerance in July 1993. That was when he was released from prison after serving 18 months for insulting the Soviet president's honour and dignity. He hadn't done anything as vicious as throwing a bunch of flowers at him or punching him behind the ear (both of these things happened to Gorbachev when he was a deeply unpopular presidential candidate in 1996). Leontev simply displayed a caricature of Gorbachev in public.

By the time Leontev came out of prison, nothing was sacred. There had been a media revolution in Russia. Every politician was caricatured regularly; every possible issue was discussed freely and heatedly, from crimes and deceptions by the Communist Party, to the economic failings of the present government, to transvestites, to UFO sightings. I have made some selections from Russian newspapers which appeared between 1993 and 1996 to illustrate the phenomenal changes since the Soviet era.

Moscow News, a weekly paper published simultaneously in Russian and English editions, was one of the most progressive newspapers in existence under Gorbachev and remained so in the nineties. By 1993 it was not only at the forefront of political debate but also had a 16-page business section. In a copy I looked at, 1627 people were asked which items they had done without to save money. 52% said adults' clothes, 38% goods for long-term use such as fridges and washing-machines, 27% food for adults, 16% alcohol and tobacco, and 8% children's clothes. Children's food was sacrificed by 5% and medicine by 4%. Only 6% said they hadn't needed to make any savings.

In the same year, expatriates were also experiencing the hardships of Russian life. Voice of America's Moscow bureau chief and his wife reviewed a Chinese restaurant in *The Moscow Times*, the capital's leading English-language paper. The tone of the article was set by the title, 'Not a Chopstick in Sight', and the authors went on to bemoan the absence of 'the essential small flask of soy sauce'. They were irritated that the menu was produced on a photocopier and condescending towards the restaurant's failure to observe Chinese custom: it served 'black and white bread, which, as far as we know, is eaten with Chinese food only in Moscow.' Two bottles of wine were out of stock - 'We finally obtained a 1990 Medoc for $25.'

If going out to a restaurant didn't appeal, an advertisement in *The Moscow Times* offered to deliver a sex symbol to your home: 'Spend a night in bed with Madonna. Whatever you want. Five minutes or several hours. Enjoy her alone, or share her with your friends. It's up to you. With Madonna, tonight you're the master. Make her whisper or shout. It's your decision. Or if not Madonna, why not Diana Ross or even Michael Jackson!' Sadly for American businessmen stranded thousands of miles away from their families, this wasn't a travelling celebrity brothel - it was Kosmos TV, a satellite television company. To its credit, *The Moscow Times* provided a strong selection of Russian and international news. It was also a lifeline for those Americans who couldn't let a day go past without reading the latest baseball, basketball and tennis results.

Americans who could read Russian may have appreciated *Pyatnitsa*, a weekly St Petersburg paper devoted to entertainment. A 1993 issue printed a Raymond Chandler story and broke the news that rock star Tina Turner had started a fund for orphaned children. The LP *Tomb of the Mutilated* was reviewed, apparently a new release by the band Gannibal Corpse. (Cannibal Corpse? Hannibal Corpse? Any fans out there?) The Sex Pistols were the object of *Pyatnitsa's* attention, too. Under the headline, 'Shakespeare, Tolstoy and Johnny Rotten', the paper asked, 'Who would have thought 15 years ago that Punk No.1 would become a writer? But a fact is a fact - a book dedicated to the memory of the Sex Pistols will soon appear in the shops. The American shops, of course.'

The front page of *Pyatnitsa* was dominated by horoscopes. For Taurus: 'Getting acquainted with the object of your passion (hobby) might not please your older relatives at the weekend. Pedagogical problems will continue all week. In the middle of the week your outgoings (on pleasures) will noticeably exceed your income (from work).' For Cancer: 'Don't look in the mirror on Saturday morning - 'yesterday's' impressions remain on your face. It's best to leave your professional ambitions out of the programme for the weekend. At the beginning of the week consultation with a specialist (psychologist) would be useful. In the second half of the week don't show curiosity about other people's secrets.' Scorpios were warned, 'Road-transport unpleasantness at the weekend might even give you a migraine.'

More about the inner lives of Russians was revealed by St Petersburg's *Lvinny Mostik*, a small ads paper. The city's lonely hearts were brutally frank about themselves and what they wanted: 'Looking for a boyfriend-lover 30-45 years, good figure, not small, not indifferent to sex. Presence of mind, decency and self-consciousness in everything - obligatory. I am: 30-158-47 kg, petite woman, a brunette of the Eastern type. Interests various (from aerobics to philosophy), character abominable: a cat and a snake in the same person... Whoever isn't afraid, write to me.'

To qualify for the post of Nadyezhda's mate, it was necessary to have been born in 1936, in March or between very specific dates in September and December. She herself was 'born in the Year of the Dragon under the sign of Leo, education higher pedagogic'. Age wasn't the only stipulation she made: 'Those who are keen on alcohol or sexually preoccupied please don't bother. I want to bring into my life a real friend and fellow-traveller without housing problems.'

Two teenagers were less discerning. 'Girlies! If you want to know (for serious relationships) excellent 16-year-old lads, then two friends: Vovik and Alex are waiting for your letters with photographs (which we'll return.' But the spirit of true romance was burning brightly in a certain Mikhail Vagin, who said, 'Young guy offers his heart to a young lady up to 21 years old. I love to love and be loved, I love to give flowers and write poems to her. But up until now I haven't met the one I am looking for: a tall, enchanting, shapely 'American' in appearance, preferably with very long, blonde hair, but not spoilt by that. I'll give everything to such a girl - all the colours of the heavens and all the flowers of the earth.'

Assistance in flower-purchasing was at hand for Mikhail, courtesy of a company which advertised its services on the same page as his cry from the heart. 'Flowers with significance help men who can't explain themselves in words', the ad promised. Flowers could say much more than a mere, 'I love you'. A long list of flowers and their meanings included aloe - an insult; astra - secret intention; cherry flower - good upbringing; daisy - hatred; onion flower - run away from me; and white gooseberry - belief in eternal love.

Another section of *Lvinny Mostik* was called 'Looking for friends'. Some people knew exactly which friends they were looking for: 'Nice, modest and charming mother of five children wants to get acquainted with the president of the United States.' *Lvinny Mostik* dropped a hint to this woman on how to catch her man - it published a variety of potato recipes under her ad. If she wanted escapism, she need have looked no further than *Sovershenno Sekretno*, a tabloid which billed itself as an 'international monthly'.

The revelations of *Sovershenno Sekretno* in 1993 were a tasteless mix of supernatural sightings, gruesome crime stories and investigations into disastrous government policies from Lenin to Yeltsin. A cartoon of a zip-up King Kong dangling a bra from its claws leapt out of the front cover and was reproduced on the inside pages next to the headline, 'The Moscow apparition - maniac, zombie, or the missing link?'

In the same issue there was an astrological crime prognosis and an article on Russia's violations of the UN Convention on Rights of the Child. In 1996 there was a higher proportion of such serious articles in *Sovershenno Sekretno*. One which I found absorbing was the transcribed stenograph of a 1970 meeting in which Communist Party Central Committee members grilled former Soviet premier Nikita Khrushchev but couldn't force him to confess that he had sent his memoirs to publishers in the United States.

The official government newspaper of the Soviet Union, *Izvestiya*, had transformed itself by 1996 into a staunch supporter of the free market, with a section printed on pink paper called *Finansoviye Izvestiya*, backed by Britain's *Financial Times*. Multinationals such as Canon and Hewlett Packard advertised in this section and its headlines declared, 'IBM hasn't lost interest in investment in

Russia', 'The reformers have forgotten about the middle class', 'In the heat of the power struggle economic problems have been pushed to one side', and, 'Russians now travel as much as the French... and their spending in pounds sterling has increased by more than 1000 percent.'

Along with the rest of the Russian media (except papers owned by political parties), *Izvestiya* nailed its colours to Yeltsin's re-election campaign mast. A week before Yeltsin's second round run-off against Communist leader Gennady Zyuganov, *Izvestiya*'s front-page lead was an interview with the owner of a restaurant on Moscow's prestigious Arbat Street in which the journalist tried to persuade him to vote. Sergei Vrublevsky, a youngish man with cropped hair and a tattooed arm, was pictured smoking a cigarette outside his restaurant, wearing an open-necked, stripy shirt and dark glasses. *Izvestiya* considered him the epitome of affluent apathy. The headline was, 'If you don't vote, you lose!' and the sub-heading, 'My vote won't decide anything - that's how a 'New Russian' from the Arbat explains his determination not to vote. But he is mistaken.'

Vrublevsky said he didn't like any of the ten candidates who stood in the first round and saw even less point choosing between the remaining two. 'But this isn't as much a vote on personality, as the future course of development of society. That could be chosen for you,' the journalist protested. Vrublevsky wasn't bothered, despite having built up a successful business from scratch after private enterprise was legalised by reformers.

To shame people like Vrublevsky further, the President's Telephone of Trust (a hotline for voters to leave messages for Yeltsin) had an advertisement in *Izvestiya* which featured an open letter to the elderly population of Russia. 'You have lived your whole lives in fear and poverty. So think about your children and grandchildren! Let it be up to them to choose the regime they have to live with, not up to you. You have privatised and bequeathed your flats to your children and grandchildren. The Communists will probably take your flats away. Because, having been in power for 70 years without opposition, they couldn't provide homes for people.'

Housing was an issue which *Moskovsky Komsomolyets* drew attention to in its own way in a February 1996 edition. This paper was the nearest Russian equivalent to Britain's *Daily Mirror*. A photograph of a man in a dressing gown drinking from a bottle of beer with his sexy lover pouting beside him accompanied the headline, 'Yes, it's not my wife I love! I like her flat.' The story was about a 26-year-old man from the provinces who had got himself a flat in Moscow by marrying a 62-year-old woman - for an appropriate fee. The man's mother had been 'understanding', saying he was old enough to decide his fate for himself. The wife was very jealous, but the husband was satisfied with the way things had worked out. 'Other people are worse off than I am,' he said. 'At least she doesn't ask me where I've been all night.'

A less plausible scam was suggested by a reader of *Argumenty i Fakty* in 1995. The weekly national specialised in finding experts to answer readers' queries, but this letter needed no reply. 'I don't want my son to be drafted into the army. My husband didn't serve when he was younger and I was wondering, can he now join up instead of my son?' Reasonable enough, but - 'The only snag is, my husband doesn't want to go, either.'

I ought to say something about Russian television, too. Not a lot, because I only began to understand what people were saying on television when I was in Minsk in 1994; the television set I had there was black-and-white and doubled every image so that there were 44 players on the pitch in football matches. In St Petersburg in 1996 my television was green-and-light-green. If I was lucky I caught a fleeting glimpse of blue or red. It took five minutes to warm up and from time to time I had to stamp on the floor to stop the picture from jumping up and down.

Three years previously in St Petersburg I got to know some television producers and journalists. I was teaching English to Alexander the polar explorer at the time. I asked Elena, the secretary of the company, if she could help me find some journalists to talk to. 'We will put you in the media and you will find your way around,' she said. Two minutes later Alexander was on the phone to a friend of his, a television journalist called Olga. 'Are you doing anything tonight, Sarah? She's invited you to a party,' he said.

The party was in Olga's living room. Almost all of the guests were female producers and journalists, who thrust their business cards at me as soon as I walked in. The only man there was Olga's husband, who did something in the timber industry, and whose function at the party was to keep quiet and pour the lemon vodka. 'It's a little strong, isn't it?' he quipped as I spluttered and gasped. 'Sniff some black bread, it opens up your passages.' The vodka was home-distilled samogon. The words on the business cards I had accumulated were melting into a haze.

Later another woman arrived with her son, who was wearing a military uniform and apparently was training to be a cosmonaut. The woman sat me down next to him on a sofa and encouraged me to ask him questions. I'm sure I missed an excellent opportunity to hear about the ups and downs of cosmonaut life, but just then my passages began to open up belatedly.

My internal turbulence must have registered on my pale and vacant face, as Olga suddenly jumped up and said, 'I think it's time for you to go to bed, Sarah.' The cosmonaut was spinning around the room. Surely he was only supposed to do that in zero-gravity conditions? Finding my way around the media was more difficult than I had anticipated. Olga guided me to a bedroom and as soon as she turned her back I headed straight for the window. To add to my disorientation, it was still as light as day although it was somewhere around 10 pm.

My digested black bread with pickled cucumber and beetroot salad with mayonnaise doused in lemon vodka shot out onto the window ledge. I took off my t-shirt and used it to clean up the mess, then stood wondering how to get to the bathroom without bumping into a cosmonaut or a television producer. Olga came back into the bedroom with a basin. I used it and gave it back to her, hoping she hadn't noticed the disgusting crumpled-up t-shirt on the window ledge. 'Why don't you lie down?' she said, and I did, thankfully losing consciousness straight away rather than rolling around moaning, 'Oh my God, I'm dying, I'm so sorry, I'll never do it again, why is the music so loud?' as I have been known to do after heavy vodka sessions.

The next morning Olga made me cups of tea, which I gratefully accepted, and porridge, which I couldn't even look at. She started telling me about her work at the local television station, and how she'd been sent to Moscow in 1991 to cover some conference or other, but instead had found herself filming tanks rolling through the streets and anti-Communist demonstrators on the barricades outside the White House. She had a pile of photographs of Moscow during the coup: a tank with a rose sticking out of its gun barrel, soldiers chatting to the demonstrators, the tricolour Russian flag being waved fearlessly in defiance of the hammer and sickle. 'I've got plenty of these,' said Olga. 'You take whichever ones you like.'

I thought that my reaction to the samogon would abruptly terminate my acquaintance with the St Petersburg media, but Olga didn't seem at all disturbed by my revolting behaviour and offered to show me the television station the next day. There, in the coffee lounge, she reintroduced me to the people who had given me their business cards at the party. I remarked that most of the station's employees seemed to be women. Ludmilla, a producer, chipped in, 'In this country, women do all the work. Men do one of two things - they're either in prison or in the police force.' Ludmilla's view of the benefits of capitalism was equally sweeping: 'Today everything has been imposed on us by the Communist Party, but tomorrow everything will be like America. Lots of products.'

Journalist Nadyezhda said that interviewing the people who helped to put out the fire at Chernobyl was a revelation for her. She had made a programme called *What was the Cost of Chernobyl?* 'No one had ever talked about these things before. It was all new and unexpected. But we still don't know everything about Chernobyl, and we never will.'

The journalists were also keen to get their teeth into current political issues. On the show *The Thirteenth Question* one politician was interrogated by the audience in a format similar to our *Question Time*, and whoever asked the most difficult question was presented with a bouquet of flowers. Another discussion programme sent a van around the city to ask people their opinions on a particular topic each week. However, hard-hitting news programmes faced stiff competition from the wildly popular Mexican and US soaps *My Second Mother*, *Simply Maria* and *Santa*

Barbara. This didn't unduly trouble the women I spoke to. 'So what?' asked Ludmilla. 'I watch *Santa Barbara* every day. It's a very good programme.'

Santa Barbara was still going strong in 1996 and *The Secret of Tropicana* was a new favourite. National television broadcast an omnibus edition of *The Secret of Tropicana* (the secret revealed!) on the morning of the second round of the presidential election to induce people to stay home and vote instead of going away to their dachas. The television news was unwatchable in the weeks before the election. The ungainly figure of an artificially pepped-up Boris Yeltsin filled the screen in every other report. One day he was securing a £6.6 billion loan from the International Monetary Fund, then he was promising to pay out state salaries and pensions, another day he was commenting on the death of the Chechen leader Dzhokhar Dudayev and soon after that he was signing a peace treaty with the few remaining Chechen commanders. For the crucial months when Yeltsin's political future hung in the balance, Russian television manufactured a mini cult of personality for him, drawing on decades of experience.

On the rare occasions when Gennady Zyuganov was shown, he was usually speaking to a crowd of rabid Stalinists or placing flowers on a monument to Lenin, and these pictures were juxtaposed with black-and-white film of Bolsheviks firing on the masses and starving peasants having their last grain supplies requisitioned by people's commissars. 'Remember, that's what communism was like, folks,' newsreaders would interject. One political commentator entreated his viewers, 'Come on, now, make up your minds. You can't have communism, then capitalism, then communism again in the space of a few years. Let's choose a system and stick with it.'

Journalists justified their blatant campaigning for Yeltsin with the argument that there would be no more free press if Zyuganov won the election. Actual temporary censorship was used as a weapon against theoretical permanent censorship. Russia's democracy was a small and weak child of five - it couldn't be allowed to run around on its own yet. British kings and queens were tyrants for centuries before their subjects were gradually permitted to govern themselves, so how could Russia be expected to emerge from totalitarianism in half a decade? Democracy must develop gradually. This was a point of view which I heard many times in Russia. But look at the Americans - they gave themselves a constitution and a bill of rights as soon as their new state was born. And what guarantee is there that democracy will develop if it isn't put into practice? The saddest aspect of the 1996 election was that the media portrayed it as a straight race between Yeltsin (good) and Zyuganov (evil), whilst other candidates who were fitter, more capable and more democratic were almost entirely ignored.

In contrast, television did a sterling job of covering the war in Chechnya, making it the first item on the news nearly every day. Journalists pointed to atrocities committed by both sides in the Chechen war; chauvinism crept in only in the newsreaders' frequent use of the government term 'bandit formations' in reference to Chechen fighters. But Chechen civilians were depicted as innocent victims. Television, radio and print journalists risked and too often lost their lives in Chechnya. A moving documentary called *Three Hours from the War* reminded residents of St Petersburg that they were just a short plane journey away from Chechnya. In it, a cameraman was shot dead by a sniper as he filmed Russian soldiers making a dash between blocks of flats. His last words as he and the camera crashed to the ground were, 'They've killed me.'

Television didn't flinch at showing close-ups of dead soldiers sprawled in the mud or victims of violent crimes such as journalist Vlad Listyev and businessman John Hyden lying on the floor in pools of their own blood. Television cameras recorded prisoners speaking their New Year thoughts for their loved ones as a train transported them to Siberia, and cameras were in courtrooms to film interviews with judges, lawyers and defendants at every stage of a trial. But somehow news of executions rarely made it to the small screen.

I was vaguely aware that the death penalty was still in existence in Russia, but I only ever read one article about it. *Sovershenno Sekretno* reported in 1996, twelve months after the death of Listyev (whose murderer had not been apprehended) that the shockwaves of this event had hardened the president. Yeltsin was granting fewer and fewer pardons and in the past year had allowed 86 people to be executed by a bullet in the back of the head.

However sick it may seem that American television companies use fly-on-the-wall documentaries and excited countdowns from death row to boost their ratings, at least they show the public what cruelty is being done in their name. In Russia the media didn't make an issue of executions, and if journalists don't pay attention to them then no one else is likely to. There was no debate about whether the death penalty should have been on the statute books at all, or whether a more humane method of killing should have been adopted.

It was easier for me to get details of executions by contacting the human rights organisation Amnesty International in Britain than it was by watching the news in Russia. In February 1996 Amnesty International reported, 'Russia has one of the highest execution rates in the world... at least 28 people were executed during 1995 and a further 34 faced imminent execution in November 1995, after their petitions for clemency were turned down by President Boris Yeltsin. According to unofficial sources in the Presidential Clemency Commission, the number of executions in 1995 was 90. The Ministry of Internal Affairs of the Russian Federation, however, has stated that only 16 executions were carried out in 1995.'

The difficulties of getting official information were a daily headache for me and the other journalists at *The St Petersburg Press*, where I worked for seven months in 1995 and 1996. My colleague Nassor once showed me a piece of paper he'd filled with a mass of telephone numbers, arrows and names, some scribbled out and some circled. 'What's that?' I said.

'It's my day's work,' he told me. 'I've been trying to get a number and each person I've called has passed me on to someone else.'

I had a few scoops I was proud of at *The St Petersburg Press*, but my biggest triumph was my collection of candidates' telephone numbers and party manifestos for the December 1995 Duma election. I had an advantage over other local journalists: my paper could afford a courier who scoured the city's eight constituencies for these magic morsels at my request. Phoning up the city electoral commission and asking for information was pointless. By law the commission was required to publish the bare facts about who was standing in the state-owned newspaper *Sankt-Peterburgskiye Vedomosti*, in tiny, smudged print over a period of several months, and if I couldn't find everything I wanted in there, then that was my hard cheese. 'I'd just like to know the date of -,' I attempted on the phone to the electoral commission.

'Find out through the media,' a woman snapped at me.

'I am the media!' I said. She hung up.

There were 42 parties contesting the election. Half of the seats in the Duma were allocated proportionally to those parties which received more than 5% of the vote, and the other half were to be fought over by individual candidates in their constituencies. There were 152 candidates for the St Petersburg constituencies. Most of the parties had been formed within the past few months and some didn't have their own premises in the city. The candidates' own flats or offices were their headquarters.

To interview these people I first had to track them down. I discovered that the parties were all supposed to be listed at a place called the Department for Registration of Social Movements. I gave the department a call and asked if our courier could stop in to pick up a copy of the list. 'We don't have a copy,' came the reply. 'We only have the original.'

'Well, can you make a copy?'

'We don't have a photocopier.'

'Can our courier borrow the list for ten minutes and make a copy?'

'No, absolutely not.' Finally I won a concession. The courier could have a typed list of party names, but she'd have to write out the addresses and phone numbers herself. She kindly did this for me and over the next few weeks visited ten of the addresses picking up party manifestos.

I had the task of reading through these turgid booklets and reducing each of them to 400 words for our election supplement, *Decisions '95*. It took an entire weekend - I was in the office until midnight on Saturday and Sunday - and to my horror I found late on Sunday that the last party on the alphabetical list, Yabloko, hadn't provided enough material. I had managed to extract from the waffle of the other manifestos policies on the economy, land and property, law and order, welfare, defence and foreign affairs; instead of a manifesto, Yabloko had Ten Theses on loose sheets of paper and all ten of them were related to the economy. That was why in my summary welfare sounded suspiciously like economic policy ('Social policy can be the engine of the economy') and so did foreign affairs ('Attract credit from World Bank, EBRD and others'). They didn't even have a slogan, so I had to take a phrase from an election poster I'd seen - 'We will lead the country out of crisis'. As it happened, Yabloko ended up as one of the four parties with seats in the Duma, so perhaps Bill Clinton's motto was right: 'It's the economy, stoopid.'

The election posed huge dilemmas for Russian journalists. The state sector of the media was obliged by law to give exactly the same amount of coverage to all parties and candidates. Whoever drafted this law cannot have envisaged how many that would be. There was also a problem with politicians who already held office and celebrity candidates, of which there were many: was it legal to write about what they were doing outside the election campaign, or would their professional activities have to go unreported for the sake of fairness? Journalists also had to resist candidates' attempts to manipulate them. A candidate whose company had ripped off thousands of people in a pyramid share scheme promised to give all the money back if elected. When I rang his headquarters to ask for an interview, I was told I could speak to him only if his picture went on the front page and the text of the article was agreed with him in advance. I lost the interview; he lost the election.

St Petersburg journalists debated the perils of election coverage at a seminar which took place at the time of the prime minister's visit to the city. This was obviously the main news story of the week, but the journalists were timid about covering it. In the course of the discussion they came to the conclusion that it was probably OK to use common sense and put Victor Chernomyrdin on the front page. The seminar was run by two British journalists, Joanna Mills of the BBC World Service and Will Stuart, former *Daily Express* Moscow correspondent. They were travelling around Russia giving advice on how to cover elections, but it had quickly become clear to them that their experience in Britain was far removed from the situation in Russia. 'We've had decades and probably centuries to sort out some of the issues which you're trying to resolve in months and years,' said Stuart.

Mills pointed out that British journalists, unlike their Russian colleagues, rarely received death threats from unsatisfied candidates. Nor were they offered bribes worth ten times their monthly salary to write favourable articles about candidates. Strong pressure was also exerted on journalists by editors and owners of newspapers. Most privately-owned newspapers had few advertisements and sold for next to nothing. They were dependent on investment from rich companies and organisations. St Petersburg paper *Smena* was partly owned by the chairman of Astrobank, who was a candidate for the Democratic Choice Russia party in the Duma election. Later, shares were bought in it by the city council. Another local paper, *Nevskoye Vremya*, was financed by the mayor's office. This severely limited its objectivity during the 1996 mayoral election.

Three political journalists on the staff of *Nevskoye Vremya*, including a friend of mine, 25-year-old Volodya Kovalyov, were sacked from the paper because they had complained of censorship. They gave an interview to *The St Petersburg Times* (formerly *The St Petersburg Press*) in which they said that the editor of *Nevskoye Vremya* had refused to publish articles critical of the incumbent mayor, Anatoly Sobchak. 'This is not the 1970s!' Volodya protested. 'We are supposed to be witnessing democracy now. I would like to remind the authorities that our constitution guarantees freedom of speech and a free press.'

Volodya told me that the editor of *Nevskoye Vremya* had decided to support Sobchak because he had encouraged the establishment of the newspaper in the early 1990s, intending it to be the first independent democratic publication in the city. 'We weren't against backing Sobchak in principle,' said Volodya, 'as every paper has the right to take the side of a candidate. But a democratic newspaper must report objectively on events, regardless of its sympathy or antipathy towards a particular public figure. But during the election, *Nevskoye Vremya* and the other city papers failed to do this, as did the local television station, which showed Sobchak twice or three times on every news broadcast. Other candidates were hardly mentioned.'

Sobchak rewarded *Nevskoye Vremya*'s editor for her services. Volodya told me that she obtained a flat in the historic centre of St Petersburg for $7000, when its true value was closer to $35,000 or $40,000. The decree which allocated the property to her was signed by none other than mayor Anatoly Sobchak. The scandal deepened in 1997 when *Izvestiya* reported that Sobchak was under police investigation for corruption - he had allegedly connived with a property company to arrange for the flat next to his to be vacated and attached to his.

The sacked *Nevskoye Vremya* journalists received some consolation from the election result: Sobchak was defeated by his own deputy mayor, Vladimir Yakovlev. But opportunities in St Petersburg for unemployed journalists were few. Volodya had already worked for *The St Petersburg Press*, but he wrote in Russian and the editors eventually decided they didn't have the resources to translate his articles. He moved to *Smena*, and burnt his bridges there when he and the other journalists from the politics section moved overnight to *Nevskoye Vremya* without giving notice. They thought they would have a freer rein at *Nevskoye Vremya*, which was true to some extent.

The paper supported Volodya's ideas, paying him to go to Poland for the presidential election, to Estonia and to the Duma in Moscow. These were considerable expenses for a paper which for three months couldn't pay any salaries. Unlike so many journalists who were content to go to a press conference and report on it verbatim, Volodya chased politicians wherever they were, recording his interviews with them on the answering machine in his flat. He got hold of the home telephone numbers of party leaders and rang them for fun. 'I tried Boris Yeltsin's number, but that wasn't interesting because he has six security guards sitting by the phone. Then I called Grigory Yavlinsky [Yabloko leader] and his wife answered. She said, 'He's in the Duma often enough, can't you talk to him there?''

Volodya phoned Yabloko foreign affairs spokesman Vladimir Lukin at the Council of Europe in Strasbourg and the president of the republic of Ingushetia when the fighting in Chechnya looked as if it was spilling over the border. The leader of the Belarusian nationalist party, Zenon Pozniak, phoned Volodya to inform him that he had temporarily moved his headquarters to Ukraine because of the repression in Belarus.

I couldn't always make it to the end of Volodya's articles because they were so long. They often took up half of the front page and continued inside. 'Does your editor tell you to write these long articles all the time?' I asked him. I was very surprised to hear that the editor never gave him any clue as to word length.

'If an article is too long, they just save it until there's space for it on another day,' Volodya said. 'The more I write, the more I get paid, so of course I write a lot.' But if he or any other journalist made a mistake in spelling or grammar, their pay was docked and news of the penalty was posted on a board in the office. An economics correspondent lost a large part of her fee for one article because she incorrectly added an extra '0' onto a figure.

Conditions at *The St Petersburg Press*, which came out weekly, weren't too bad. Journalists were paid quite a high salary for St Petersburg in 1995-96, £300 per month. The Western companies which advertised in the paper could afford to pay decent rates and the paper also received backing from an American partner. There was no need for us to accept money from companies to write publicity articles about them in the form of news stories, as some Russian journalists did to earn themselves enough to live on. My landlady, Lena, paid a television crew to report on the art exhibition she was organising. Dima's employers, Radio Russia, instigated a policy whereby journalists had to find sponsors for the programmes they wanted to make. Another radio journalist told me that she lived with her husband and children in one room in a communal flat. Once she got so desperate that she stole a reel of tape from the radio station and sold it to buy food.

At *The St Petersburg Press* we could write whatever we liked, most of the time, without fear of retribution from an irate politician or mafia boss, because we were writing in English and the paper wasn't sold on the news-stands but could be picked up free in five-star hotels and expensive cafés frequented by expatriates. Nevertheless, the managing editor, a 31-year-old New Zealander called Lloyd Donaldson, was insistent that *The St*

155

Petersburg Press was a Russian paper and should be treated as such.

This view was logical because the paper was registered in the Russian Federation, distributed in the Russian Federation, and, according to a survey, 63% of its readers were Russian. 'If anyone has a problem with that, tell them it's just the same as a newspaper in the Tatar language. It's still Russian, no matter what language it's in,' I was advised by Yevgenia, another journalist on *The St Petersburg Press*. Someone did have a problem with that. His name was Victor Yugin and he was the press secretary for the city council. He turned down an application by me and Nassor for accreditation to the city council, but gave accreditation to Yevgenia.

Having made no progress with Yugin on the phone, I marched into his office one day, uninvited. Yugin was in his late fifties, with a balding head, a black moustache and a face twisted by years of being nasty to people and enjoying it. 'Hello,' I said, 'I was wondering if you could explain to me why you have accredited the Russian journalist on our paper but refused to accredit me and my Tanzanian colleague. You see, I am the chief political correspondent at *The St Petersburg Press* and Ali Nassor is in charge of health and education, so it's fairly important for both of us to attend sessions of the city council.'

'Foreigners can't understand politics,' Yugin retorted. 'I will not give accreditation to foreigners. Go and tell your editor to get a new political correspondent. Where do you live?'

'In the city centre,' I said.

'Right, but where do you *come* from? You don't have permanent residence rights, do you?'

'No, I have a visa. I come from England.'

'Ha!' he exclaimed. 'So you can't be a journalist in Russia. That's all there is to it.'

'What about Nassor?' I said. 'He has been here for six years, he's married to a Russian and has a son.'

'That's different, then.'

'So you'll accredit him?'

'I didn't say that.'

I put my press card on the table under his nose. On the back of it were quotations in Russian from the law on the media. One of them stated that journalists had the right to 'visit state institutions and organisations, enterprises and establishments, and public institutions or their press services.' 'What about that?' I said.

'What about this?' replied Yugin. He had his own copy of the law on the media and underlined a clause which said that journalists had to obey the rules of accreditation set by each organisation

'We obeyed the rules,' I said. 'We sent in our photographs and filled in your form.'

'I have another rule,' said Yugin. 'No foreigners.'

I was permanently accredited at the St Petersburg mayor's office and had been issued a pass at the Duma in Moscow, but the city council was out of bounds. Shortly after my head-to-head with Yugin, *The St Petersburg Press* received a fax wishing us well on the Day of the Press. It was from the chairman of the city council, Yuri Kravtsov - Yugin's boss. It read, 'I wish you all the best of luck and future success as representatives of our free, democratic press.' Soon after that, Kravtsov came under investigation for embezzlement of council funds.

Yugin wasn't the only person in the city who was determined to prevent the spread of foreign journalists. Before I got the job at *The St Petersburg Press*, I spent two weeks working for *Neva News*, a flimsy little paper in English for tourists. The editor, Alexander Kutcher, was bilious about *The St Petersburg Press*. 'That is a terrible paper,' he said. 'You must not write for it while you are working here. They print stories about crime and disease all the time - who needs that? We're trying to promote the city, so we write about its culture and architecture. Can you believe that *The St Petersburg Press* even has a Negro journalist?'

Kutcher knew Ali Nassor. *Neva News* was the first place Nassor went for a job when he graduated from St Petersburg University. As a test, he was given an easy translation to do from English to Russian. (I wasn't asked to do a test.) Kutcher told Nassor his translation wasn't good enough and he couldn't have a job. Nassor was puzzled. Some months afterwards, he got chatting with a journalist at *Neva News* who cleared up the mystery. 'Your translation was fine. But Kutcher said, 'No Negro is ever going to work here!', and that was that.'

Kutcher didn't inspire me with confidence in my ability to survive as a journalist in Russia. At my interview he said, 'We are not millionaires. We will pay you very little money. But look at my son - that's him in the picture behind my desk. He works for *Komsomolskaya Pravda* and other big newspapers in Moscow, and he has lost weight...'

I hoped to earn some extra money by selling articles to British papers. The *Daily Telegraph*'s Moscow correspondent, Alan Philps, was keen on stories from St Petersburg so I faxed a couple to him, on the Misha Glebov case and the dispute over the Subway sandwich restaurant. The next time I was in Moscow I stopped into Alan's office for a chat. I just had time to admire the shelves full of brand new hardbacks on Soviet and Russian politics and say hello to Alan's Russian secretary, Nelly, who made all the tedious phone calls to locate people which I spent half of my life doing, when Alan whisked me off to an American hamburger place for lunch.

Alan was a solidly fortified island of Englishness in the heart of Russia. He wore a tweed cap, carried an umbrella and drove a Volvo. 'Moscow has become inhuman in so many respects,' he said glumly as he opened the car door for me. In the restaurant we discussed my articles. 'I liked them, but they weren't quite right for the *Telegraph*,' he said. 'There was a certain something missing. How should I put it? Well, to be honest, there weren't any British people in them.'

I asked Alan about his job. 'British readers can only be introduced to one new Russian name a year, for instance Zhirinovsky and then Lebed. The elections here are a matter of complete indifference to our readers. I think Russia's time as a news hotspot has passed.' But as we said our goodbyes, Alan was encouraging. 'I'll get you into the *Telegraph*, Sarah,' he promised. 'Just remember, you're writing for the suburban fascist.' Alan kept his word - I contributed to his front-page story about the killing of British businessman John Hyden in the Nevskij Palace Hotel. Hyden had the misfortune to become the 'certain something' the *Telegraph* was looking for.

While the British have a limited interest in Russia, Russians couldn't get enough of the West. Russian editions of *Cosmopolitan*, *Playboy* and *Good Housekeeping* were doing a roaring trade for their Dutch-owned publishers, Independent Media. *Cosmopolitan* was Russia's bestselling magazine, with a circulation of 350,000. *Playboy* was selling well all over the country - but in St Petersburg the authorities considered its content too raunchy and would only allow it to be sold in certain shops.

When *Playboy* first arrived in St Petersburg, in 1995, vice police seized copies from street vendors, telling the distributors that an 'expert commission' had to ascertain whether it was pornographic. The vice police were enforcing a 1993 decree introduced by mayor Anatoly Sobchak in the absence of a federal pornography law. It stated that magazines with erotic content could be sold only in a restricted number of shops and kiosks. In Moscow and other cities no such decree existed, so pornographic literature was freely available.

Playboy failed to shock the mayor's experts, who concluded that it wasn't pornographic but had 'a certain erotic tendency'. Those fatal words were enough to place *Playboy* firmly under the decree and restricted licensed distribution followed. In fact, the Russian *Playboy* bore about as much relation to pornography as the French impressionists' nudes in the Hermitage. *Playboy* models were draped modestly in silk or lace, and much of the magazine featured celebrity interviews and stories by respected Russian writers.

Even the vice police chief, Captain Oleg Yuzhkov, thought the magazine was harmless and should have been on sale everywhere: 'Which other country allows everything to be shown on television but expects the police to censor magazines? My assistant and I have sole responsibility for censorship of pornographic and fascist materials. What do we know about that? I've spent the whole year trying to get out of this job.'

Martin Hupka, deputy director of *Playboy*'s American distributor, Bronze Lion, estimated that the decree was costing his company £80,000 a year in lost profit. 'We started packaging *Playboy* in plastic to protect kids,' he said. 'But the pictures are nothing like those in the American editions. Full-frontal nudity isn't acceptable in Russia. Russian *Playboy* is modelled on the *Playboy* of the sixties, which was a really good vehicle for literature and politics.'

'I have learnt not to put shocking words on the front cover of our magazine,' said Annemarie van Gaal, a partner in Independent Media. 'But Russians love to see them on the inside.'

Politics

'If anyone believes that our smiles involve
abandonment of the teaching of Marx, Engels and
Lenin he deceives himself. Those who wait for that
must wait until a shrimp learns to whistle.'
**First Secretary of the Communist Party Nikita Khrushchev, as
quoted by the *New York Times*, 18 September 1955.**

The shrimp was still practising in 1990, when I wrote a letter
with two other A-level students from my college to KGB chief
Vladimir Kryuchkov. We were about to leave for a week's trip to
Moscow and Leningrad. I received a very polite reply in English:

*On behalf of Mr V.A. Kryuchkov, KGB Chairman, we would like to
thank You and Your colleagues for having requested an interview*

*Your letter is a new proof of a great interest which the whole world is
taking in Soviet life, the process of enormous changes in all spheres of the
Soviet society. Understandably, we especially value the attention paid to
these events by the young people You belong to.*

*...Your interest in the issues related to the functioning of the Soviet State
Security bodies under perestroika is quite understandable. As future
journalists studying Russian and the history of our country, You
probably know that democracy and openness are again [!] becoming
guiding principles in the work of the KGB.*

*...As to Your request, Chairman Kryuchkov takes a positive attitude to it.
However, he can hardly give You a definite promise in view of the
impending full schedule.*

*In spite of that, if You and Your friends find an opportunity to visit our
country again the KGB Press Bureau will readily satisfy Your interest
(perhaps professional by that time) in our country and its security bodies.*

*We wish You and Your colleagues a successful graduation from the
college and realization of Your dream to become professional journalists.*

Yours sincerely,

A.V. Grinenko,

KGB Press Bureau

The subsequent fate of A.V. Grinenko is unknown to me, but I
certainly know where V.A. Kryuchkov was when I next visited
Russia, in 1992. He was unable to satisfy My interest in the

161

country and its security bodies because he was in prison along with the other leaders of the failed August 1991 coup. The collapse of communism has been called the second Russian revolution, but the speed of political change *since* 1991 has also been furious.

There was another attempted coup in October 1993, led by vice-president Alexander Rutskoi and the speaker of parliament, Ruslan Khasbulatov. President Yeltsin dissolved the Communist-dominated parliament by force, storming the Moscow White House with tanks, which resulted in the deaths of more than one hundred people. Rutskoi and Khasbulatov went to prison and the new Russian parliament which was elected in December assembled in a nondescript office block, not the symbolic White House. The lower house of parliament was known as the Duma, the name of the rubber-stamp parliament which was established as a sop to the masses at the end of the tsarist era.

The largest party in the Duma of 1993 was the Liberal Democratic Party of Russia (LDPR), led by 'Mad Vlad', ultranationalist Vladimir Zhirinovsky. When they voted for their Duma deputies, Russians also approved a new constitution by referendum. In the Duma election, President Yeltsin backed the reformist Russia's Choice party led by his former prime minister, Yegor Gaidar. It won 16% of the vote behind the LDPR's 23%.

The following February, the Duma pardoned the coup leaders of 1991 and 1993. V.A. Kryuchkov kept a low profile. Alexander Rutskoi, a former general, formed a nationalist political party, Derzhava, which contested the 1995 Duma election with the slogan, 'Alexander Rutskoi is your leader!!!' It won 0 seats. Ruslan Khasbulatov went to his native Chechnya to become a peace negotiator after the Russian invasion in December 1994. A year later, he unsuccessfully opposed the Russian government's candidate in an election for leader of the official administration in Chechnya.

In spring 1995, Chechen fighter Shamil Basayev, acting independently from his republic's military leadership, seized hostages in the Russian town of Budyennovsk. The crisis ended with many hostages dead and Basayev safely back in the mountains of Chechnya. In the December 1995 Duma election, Yeltsin gave his support to the party which represented stability, prime minister Victor Chernomyrdin's Our Home is Russia. The party advertised itself with pictures of sombre-faced Chernomyrdin making a roof sign with his hands, under the slogan, 'If your home is dear to you'.

During the election campaign the public gradually became aware that under the new electoral law a member of the government could not be a Duma deputy. This enabled Yeltsin to ditch his pro-Western foreign minister, Andrei Kozyrev, who was elected to the Duma, and replace him with former KGB chief Yevgeny Primakov. But it also became clear that Chernomyrdin had no intention of taking up his seat in the Duma, although he was number one on his party's list of candidates.

Number two on Our Home is Russia's list was the Oscar-winning film director Nikita Mikhalkov, who made and starred in the party's television advertisements in which he and a friend looked down at Russia from space and argued about which city had the most beautiful women. Immediately after the election, when Our Home is Russia had succeeded in becoming one of the four parties represented in the Duma, Mikhalkov announced that he would not be entering politics - he was only on the list to help Our Home is Russia get elected, and voters should have known that.

One other democratic party won seats in the 1995 Duma election, Grigory Yavlinsky's liberal party, Yabloko. But Yabloko and Our Home is Russia both received fewer votes than the Communist Party, led by a man who had denounced Gorbachev for betraying communist ideals, Gennady Zyuganov. In total, the Communists won 157 seats, Our Home is Russia 55, the LDPR 51 and Yabloko 45. Individual candidates representing the Agrarian Party (very close to the Communist Party) took 20 seats, independents won 77 and smaller parties 45. Out of 450 deputies, 44 were women. The Communists were surprise winners of the election and Zyuganov appeared to be a dangerous presidential challenger, especially as a Communist president had recently been elected in Poland. The Communist Party often had the support of Yabloko in the Duma, in opposition to an unholy alliance of Our Home is Russia and the LDPR.

Another Chechen hostage crisis coincided with the opening session of the new Duma. Salman Raduyev was the maverick with a death wish this time; but, like Basayev, he escaped alive. Basayev's raid on the village of Pervomaiskoye in Dagestan culminated in a bloodbath when Russian forces mowed down his men. The government claimed that no hostages had been killed, but this was impossible to verify and highly unlikely. Russian television didn't show pictures of the events in Pervomaiskoye until days after they had happened.

Vowing to finish the business he'd started in Chechnya, Yeltsin was re-elected in July 1996. A few weeks before the election, the Russian security service claimed it had located Chechen rebel leader Dzhokhar Dudayev by tracing the signal from his satellite telephone, and bombed the building he was in. It seemed that Dudayev had been killed and Yeltsin signed a peace treaty in the Kremlin with his successor, Zelimkhan Yanderbiyev. There were persistent, unlikely, rumours that Dudayev had actually escaped abroad. In 1997 his widow, Alla, commented on her husband's death to *Komsomolskaya Pravda*. 'On the eve of that missile attack satellites simply 'went wild' in the sky, there were about six of them,' she said. 'On those days Dzhokhar made regular trips to the field to make phone calls, and I had a constant feeling that clouds were gathering over him.' The missile which killed Dudayev was an American one, she claimed.

On the very day of Yeltsin's election victory, fighting resumed in Chechnya - Russian forces attacked the village of Gekhi. The Chechens retaliated by seizing their capital, Grozny. After 18 months of war, the Russian forces were no closer to victory. Yeltsin sent his new national security advisor, former general Alexander Lebed, to negotiate a peace deal with guerrilla leader Aslan Maskhadov. The question of Chechnya's independence was postponed for five years in return for a complete withdrawal of Russian troops. Russia had the worst of both worlds - it had lost control of Chechnya but also had to foot a staggering bill of something like 4 trillion roubles (£500 million) for reconstruction of the region. In January 1997, Maskhadov was elected president of Chechnya, defeating the extremist Shamil Basayev by a convincing 65% to 24%.

Lebed became so popular in Russia that Yeltsin, nervous about his increasing influence, sacked him. Immediately afterwards, Lebed received a standing ovation when he went to the theatre. The nationalist soldier, a controversial figure who preferred action to words and didn't touch alcohol, would be the clear favourite if a sudden election were called in the event of Yeltsin's death.

According to the constitution, if the president dies in office or is incapacitated, the prime minister takes over and a presidential election must be held within three months. If the president denies he is incapacitated, as Yeltsin has repeatedly done, there is nothing to force him to resign his post. But while Yeltsin was undergoing a triple heart bypass and then suffering from pneumonia, a new recruit to his administration was running the country - Anatoly Chubais, a radical reformer. Neither Chubais nor pen-pusher Chernomyrdin looked capable of defeating Lebed in an election. The only potential candidate with the resources and the popularity to mount a serious challenge to Lebed appeared to be Moscow mayor Yuri Luzhkov, a man of grandiose projects and similar ambitions.

Whatever happens next in Russian politics, it will probably happen peacefully. As has twice been shown, it is extremely difficult to stage a coup. On the other hand, parliamentary elections have twice been held successfully, and democracy has survived the victories of the LDPR and the Communist Party. Apart from media bias, the presidential election was also free and fair. Democracy has taken root in Russia, which is more than can be said of some of Russia's neighbours, including sad little Belarus.

In Belarus, democracy has fallen to its knees without so much as a whimper. Belarusian president Alexander Lukashenka believes that the Soviet Union can be revived. To this end, he signed a treaty with Yeltsin in 1996 creating a Union of Sovereign Republics - USR - which, as Yeltsin said, 'any other state can join, even Bulgaria if it wants to'. It was a response to pressure from the Russian Duma and large sections of the public to denounce the break-up of the USSR as illegal. The presidents of other former Soviet republics took the opportunity to reaffirm their independence, but Lukashenka was enthusiastic about a new

USSR. He has already unilaterally reintroduced some of the most repressive of Soviet policies.

In 1994 Belarus had a new red-and-white striped flag. Hardly anyone used the Belarusian language, but it was encouraged: the names of stops on the metro were announced in Belarusian, such as Ploshcha Nizhelezhnosti instead of the Russian Ploshchad Nezavisimosti, Independence Square. Lenin Prospekt had been renamed Frantskysk Skaryna Prospekt, after the man who translated the Bible into Belarusian in the 16th century. But as quickly as all this nationalism sprang up, it was knocked on the head by Lukashenka. He was elected when I was in Minsk - he defeated the Communist prime minister, Kebich. I had never heard of Kebich before I came to Belarus and whilst I could sympathise with the general animosity towards the prime minister, not being one of John Major's fans myself, I thought it odd that everyone said the same thing, 'Our prime minister is cabbage.'

Lukashenka was ridiculed for being an ugly, balding man with an oversized moustache who had difficulty stringing a sentence together and mixed up Russian and Belarusian. People voted for him because they found Kebich so unpalatable. All that Lukashenka had been in charge of previously was a collective farm; now he was in charge of the country. I have an ambition of visiting all the former Soviet republics and buying their flags. Lukashenka made that more difficult for me to achieve by changing the flag as soon as I had left the country: he reinstated the red Belarusian flag of the Soviet era. He clamped down on the vociferous nationalist party so hard that its leaders fled to Ukraine. Tax authorities targeted independent newspapers for alleged infringements, even the harmless English-language paper *Minsk Economic News*. A popular independent radio station was disconnected by the Ministry of Communications. Journalists who criticised Lukashenka were threatened with violence.

Belarusian citizens were told they must have permission to travel abroad and must register with the police in order to use the Internet. Lukashenka almost breathed new life into the Cold War in September 1995, when a Belarusian helicopter gunship shot down an American hot air balloon which was participating in a competition and had strayed over the border from Poland. The two balloonists were killed.

Naturally, the US government expressed outrage at these deaths, but after that unfortunate international incident Belarus sank into obscurity again, finishing one place behind Great Britain in the Atlanta Olympics medal table. It is small and insignificant to the West. Millions of people outside Belarus go through life in blissful ignorance of the country's existence. A journalist from Minsk recounted a story from his visit to Nottingham. A woman asked him where he was from and he replied, 'Belarus.' She looked at him sympathetically and said, 'Ah, yes, British people have very strong feelings about your country.'

'Why's that?' he asked.

'Because of the terrible struggle going on between blacks and whites there,' she explained.

It's harder for Western governments to ignore Russia, a nuclear superpower spanning two continents, physically the largest country in the world. But somehow Lukashenka's colleague Yeltsin has managed to get away with murder, too, in Chechnya. In the days when the Soviet Union was an evil empire, when dissidents were dissidents and oppressors were oppressors, politicians in Western Europe and the United States couldn't say enough about human rights violations in the USSR. Now they've shut up, because they can't work out who are the bad guys in Russia and who are the worse guys. When Zhirinovsky celebrated his party's election victory in 1993, I longed for the CIA or some Russian nutcase to assassinate him so that he wouldn't become president. But I realised the futility of this when I visited the Duma at its opening session in January 1996 and realised just how many extremists were queuing up behind Zhirinovsky to take his place as the politician with the most apocalyptic policies.

On the wall of the Duma there were photographs of some of the most colourful deputies from the previous session, including the leader of the Beer Lovers' Party and someone called Omar Omarovich, who was affiliated to the Party of Admirers of Stalin. A new deputy to grace the Duma's corridors, film director Stanislav Govorukhin, wasn't an admirer of anyone. Beady-eyed, with a permanent scowl on his face, he removed the pipe from his mouth only for long enough to make statements such as, 'We can't expect anything good from the intelligentsia. If they come to power there'll only be blood and tears. All foreigners are idiots, they can't understand the circumstances of this country. Young people these days don't strive for knowledge, or to defend their motherland. Schools and families have become weaker, great writers such as Jules Verne and Mark Twain are no longer studied, the new generation is indifferent to the fate of the motherland in which it is growing up.' Govorukhin's films, which included *The Great Criminal Revolution* and *The Hour of the Scoundrel*, showed how Russia had degenerated since the advent of democracy in 1991.

Communist leader Gennady Zyuganov assured me that his party's election success was good news for the West: 'We are for good-neighbourly relations with the West, maximum encouragement of business contacts and investment in Russia.'

'So there won't be a new Iron Curtain if you become president?' I asked him. He raised his eyebrows in horror and backed away from me.

'How could you suggest such a thing?' he exclaimed, as if I'd just called his grandmother a democrat.

The greatest foe of the democrats, Vladimir Zhirinovsky, had lost favour amongst Russian voters because of his increasingly outlandish behaviour. He physically assaulted a woman deputy in 1995 during a televised scuffle in the Duma. On a television chat show he threw a glass of orange juice in the face of a political rival. A worried pensioner once asked me, 'The clown won't be elected president, will he?' There wasn't much chance of that. But to the Russian and international media, Zhirinovsky was still a star.

All the Duma deputies stood around chatting in the lobby, among them big names such as Alexander Lebed, former Soviet prime minister Nikolai Ryzhkov and world-renowned eye surgeon Svyatoslav Fyodorov. From time to time they were surrounded by clusters of journalists. When Zhirinovsky opened his mouth, the media mobbed him. Journalists climbed onto tables to get him within range of their microphones and cameras. I felt the weight of someone's television camera on my shoulder and heard its owner say, 'Get down, you're in my way!' Zhirinovsky had been talking quietly to one or two LDPR deputies, but the media attracted more people to his group, and he raised his voice, deliberately bringing up contentious topics. An old opponent squeezed into the picture and a sparring match ensued, to the delight of the media.

Judging by his appearance, Zhirinovsky might have just been knocked out of a real boxing ring. His lower lip was swollen and bruised, the top button of his shirt was undone, causing his overlarge collar to jut out at acute angles, and his tie hung loosely around his thick neck. The voice of the ultranationalist was harsh and grating, as if his throat was lined with iron filings. Not content with the informal attention of the media, Zhirinovsky packed out a hall at a press conference. He was contemptuous of the journalists' concerns about the bloody hostage seizure in Pervomaiskoye. 'Millions of people die of hunger every day and you think that a few deaths in Pervomaiskoye is a tragedy,' he declaimed. 'There was no tragedy in Pervomaiskoye - it's the usual way of liquidating terrorist bands. The history of mankind is the history of wars. Conflicts will disappear only when the planet disappears. What would we do without them? Pace up and down our kitchens?'

I had ample opportunity to ask Zhirinovsky a question; he was constantly available, stopping for every journalist who buttonholed him, in contrast to the publicity-shy Lebed, who grunted at me, 'I've got to go, I promised somebody.' But I didn't have a question for Zhirinovsky. His opinions were already notorious, and I saw no reason to give him yet another chance to propagate them. It was only on the train back to St Petersburg that I thought perhaps I should have asked him a personal question, to test for myself whether he was genuinely angry *all* the time or just putting on a show. That evening he had stormed out of the Duma with the LDPR faction because he didn't like the procedure for electing the speaker. The question that came to me on the train was, 'Vladimir Wolfovich, is there anything in life that makes you happy?'

Zhirinovsky won a libel battle against a journalist who called him a fascist. To us he may seem to have all the attributes of a

fascist, but in Russia it is certainly possible to make the distinction
- real fascists are even crazier. They had a regular weekly meeting
in St Petersburg's Ostrovsky Square, just off Nevsky Prospekt and
in front of the Pushkin Theatre and a statue of Catherine the Great
surrounded by her lovers. There, with a captive audience on the
park benches - mothers gently rocking their babies' prams, young
couples whispering to each other, old men kicking their heels idly
in the dust - Russian Nazis stood to attention and recited their
litany of demands. Wearing black shirts or camouflage gear, they
were flanked by billowing, gold swastika banners. 'Return the
Baltic states and the Crimea to Russia. Eliminate Zionism. Join us,
we are the only people who can save Russia. We have some music
to play to you, please listen carefully, the meaning is very
important: this song is called *Light Anti-Semitism*.'

It was incredible to witness such a spectacle in a country which
lost 27 million people in World War II. Some of the people who
were relaxing in Ostrovsky Square fought Hitler's armies or lost
their parents in the Siege of Leningrad, but they listened to the
nineties Nazis with indifference. No one shook their fist at the
fascists, raised their voice against them or tried to tear down their
banners.

At their annual congress in St Petersburg, Russia's parties of the
far right announced they would support Yeltsin in the presidential
election. They were impressed by Yeltsin's patriotic position, in
particular his efforts to protect the unity of the Russian Federation
by conducting the war in Chechnya. Speakers at the congress
stood on a stage between two young men in quasi-military
uniform who held black, yellow and white nationalist flags in
their hands. A banner above the stage proclaimed, 'Nation,
Justice, Order' in large Gothic lettering.

Tapes of Nazi stormtrooper marches were on sale in the foyer
outside the congress hall. 'We're not racist,' insisted Eduard
Limonov, author of an infamous sexually explicit autobiography
and leader of the National Bolshevik Party. 'We are left
nationalists, not fascists.' The chair of the congress was St
Petersburg's own Yuri Belyayev, a bloated pig of a man who led
the National Republican Party of Russia. He was lucky to be at the
congress: a year previously he was hit by five bullets in an

assassination attempt and a day before the congress opened he was given a year's suspended sentence for inciting ethnic and religious hatred.

The conviction of Belyayev was the first of its kind in St Petersburg. Belyayev escaped imprisonment thanks to the 50th anniversary of the end of World War II - Yeltsin granted an amnesty to all minor criminals to commemorate the victory over Nazi Germany. In the Belyayev case this was remarkably convenient, as it allowed the judge to condemn his behaviour without making him into a martyr. He ordered Belyayev to pay one million roubles (£150) in legal costs.

Before the verdict, Belyayev and his supporters spent more than half an hour praying under the direction of an Orthodox priest standing on the court's main staircase. The inflammatory statements for which Belyayev was on trial included his claim that various Russian politicians were part of an international Zionist movement. The priest who blessed Belyayev told me he was opposed to religious strife and was not a member of the National Republican Party. 'I support anyone who comes to me for help, as Belyayev did,' he added.

In court, Belyayev argued, 'I don't agree with journalists who portray this ideology [Zionism] as a way of rescuing the Jewish people. I'm talking about the ideology and not the Jewish people. A Zionist can even be a Russian - I know some Russians who share this ideology and have looked me in the eye and said this. So I didn't accuse all Jews by accusing Zionism.' The judge was unmoved. He said that Belyayev had determined that the main task of his party was to fight evil, in which he included Jews. He had organised the printing and distribution of the newspaper *The Nationalist*, which insulted the honesty and integrity of Jews. He had expressed a negative attitude towards people of Caucasian nationality at a meeting in St Petersburg's Palace Square. The judge described Belyayev's activities as 'political hooliganism' which encouraged anti-social behaviour amongst young people and posed a hidden threat for Russia as a whole.

National minorities were not the only groups which were discriminated against by political parties. Homosexuality was legalised in Russia less than a decade ago, and society's attitude towards it remains overwhelmingly hostile. The most pro-Western, radical, democratic party of the 42 which contested the 1995 Duma election was Yegor Gaidar's Democratic Choice Russia (DCR). The party's slogan was, 'We've chosen an honest policy - now choose us!' In a bold and unprecedented act, the leader of St Petersburg homosexual rights group Gay Cities issued a press release to 50 newspapers and news agencies urging gays and lesbians to vote for DCR. But Alexander Bogdanov was told in no uncertain terms that DCR wanted nothing to do with him.

Before the press release was sent out, Bogdanov was asked by DCR not to publish it. Bogdanov went ahead with his campaign anyway, and afterwards visited DCR's headquarters in St Petersburg. Igor Soshnikov, deputy chairman of DCR's executive committee, verbally abused him and said he would be beaten up if he ever came back, Bogdanov told me. When DCR candidate and human rights activist Yuli Rybakov was asked about the incident at a public meeting, he replied curtly, 'That's a provocative question.'

Soshnikov needn't have worried, because the local media were reluctant to publicise Bogdanov's views. 'We didn't print this press release because we thought fewer people would vote for DCR as a result of it,' said Alexander Gorshkov, editor of the newspaper *Nevskoye Vremya*'s politics section. 'You have to understand the mentality of our society.' A spokesman for DCR repeated the same excuse. 'We can't ban anyone from supporting us, but I can't say we're delighted about this,' said the head of DCR's press service. 'In our society there's a definite prejudice and that has to be taken into account.'

But gays are voters, too, and DCR's refusal to acknowledge this may have cost the party dearly. It received less than 5% of the popular vote, too few to win seats in the Duma. Rather more than 5% of human beings are homosexual. The liberal party which did pass the 5% barrier was Grigory Yavlinsky's Yabloko. A Yabloko candidate in St Petersburg said he was relieved that Gay Cities hadn't chosen to support his party. Yabloko and DCR had much in common and many pro-reform voters who considered Our Home is Russia too reactionary were disappointed that the two leading liberal parties didn't make a pre-electoral pact. Apart from their differences in policy, the egos of their leaders were too inflated for one to make way for the other.

Yeltsin sacked Yegor Gaidar from the post of prime minister in 1992 because his attempt at a speedy transition to a market economy was causing widespread hardship. Grigory Yavlinsky was an adviser to Gorbachev who produced a wildly ambitious 500-day plan for reform of the economy. But Gaidar was adamant that their ideas were quite different, as he said in the magazine *Novoye Vremya*: 'Yes, we have economic disagreements. Their scope is global. By conviction I am a right-centrist, if we are using European terminology... Grigory Yavlinsky is a left-centrist - he is in favour of more state-led economics.'

Yavlinsky alienated many of his supporters by siding with the Communists in Duma debates, and he did badly in the 1996 presidential election, coming a poor fourth. He didn't help matters by cultivating the image of an intellectual who was selective about which journalists he talked to. His party held a congress in St Petersburg behind closed doors and afterwards Yavlinsky gave a press conference to about 10 specially invited journalists.

'He is tired, and besides that we don't have very much space,' was the excuse given by Yabloko's press spokeswoman for Yavlinsky's reticence. His eyelids were heavy and his face was pale. Nevertheless, the 43-year-old tousle-haired leader spoke engagingly about his politics and personal life. He said that he was not interested in becoming prime minister because 'with today's power structure the prime minister and the government don't have the power to lead reforms - only the president can do that.' Yavlinsky was scathing of Yeltsin, who had just announced his decision to stand for re-election. 'Boris Nikolayevich has always struggled for power, there was nothing new in his decision,' said Yavlinsky. 'It's interesting that he's now found money to pay for everything. If he knew where it was, why couldn't he have got it before?'

Yavlinsky was asked if seeming 'too intelligent' would be a problem for him in the election campaign. 'No, tell people not to worry, Yavlinsky can cope with the tasks set before him,' he said. 'Russia needs not only a strong arm but a strong head, too.' The person who had most influenced Yavlinsky's political views was the late Nobel Peace Prize-winner, nuclear physicist and Soviet dissident Andrei Sakharov. Sakharov was released from exile by Gorbachev and became a key political force in the final years of the Soviet Union. 'I can't forget that moment when he was speaking at the Congress of People's Deputies to a full hall. The delegates tried to drown him out by stamping their feet, but Sakharov continued to say what he thought was right.'

On the subject of his family, Yavlinsky said nothing about his wife but had 'two sons, my older son has graduated from Moscow State University and is looking for work, and my younger son is at school. I also have two dogs - there were lots of nice homeless dogs on the streets when the reforms started and I brought them home for my children. My flat is 41 square metres, it's on the 12th floor, I don't have a car and I don't have a dacha.'

'Do you have any security guards?' someone asked.

'No, if you want to tell everyone I don't have any security, please go ahead.'

Yavlinsky was set on becoming president and was unprepared to compromise his ambition by allying with other politicians. He remorselessly attacked the government, and this drew criticism from Gaidar, who backed Yeltsin in the presidential election. But Yavlinsky couldn't forgive Yeltsin for what he had done in Chechnya. Yavlinsky spoke out against the war again and again. At the opening of the Duma he answered questions from American journalists in English, in the wake of the hostage crisis in Pervomaiskoye:

'The tragedy that is a civil war in Russia shows that democracy in Russia is very far from the appropriate level. What's going on now is a development of the civil war in the Caucasus, it's an earthquake for the Russian political elite and personally for Yeltsin. I think that as a populist he is trying to be very close to the parties which win the elections. The war in Chechnya was a consequence of the victory of Zhirinovsky. What's going on just now is to some extent the consequence of the victory of the Communists.'

'Is it part of Yeltsin's pre-election campaign?'

'It looks like Yeltsin's pre-end campaign, but he thinks it's his pre-election campaign. There is no way to express to Yeltsin our attitude about the civil war which he started in the country and only a vote of no-confidence in the government can show Yeltsin how real that is. The situation for the government is very difficult because of the civil war in the Caucasus, which is in fact simply a crime.

'I sent a special plan to Yeltsin, I want to start negotiations about stopping the war in the Northern Caucasus in general, but in the present condition that might start with the releasing of the hostages, and for this Yeltsin can do a very simple step. Very simple. He simply can call Dudayev and say release the hostages and I'm going to take the troops away from Chechnya. This is the only way forward and Yeltsin does not want to do that. The hostages are just now in a terrible position. I was invited by the terrorists to be the man who would take part in negotiations and I was asking Yeltsin and Chernomyrdin to support me in this action, they didn't want to do that.'

'But their fear is that if they take the troops away from Chechnya the situation will get worse.'

'But every next day will bring them to the position that if the troops leave Chechnya later, the situation would be even worse than it is just now, so the only way is to do it as soon as possible. This is simply a crime, 40,000 people killed, no sense, no democracy, no future for such a policy.'

'And if the troops leave and Chechnya becomes an independent government?'

'This is an issue for the Chechen people, not for the people who are sitting in the Kremlin.'

When the Soviet Union was breaking up, Yeltsin said the fateful words, 'Take as much independence as you can swallow.' He was thinking of republics outside the Russian Federation, from Lithuania to Tajikistan, not autonomous republics within it such as Chechnya. He should have known from the experience of Gorbachev's blockade of Lithuania that extreme measures would only strengthen the determination of nationalists and increase their numbers. He should have known from the history of the Caucasus, Russia's battles to subdue the region and Stalin's mass deportation of Chechens, that they would fight to the death once provoked.

If Yeltsin recognised that the Soviet economic catastrophe stemmed from over-centralisation, then he should have realised that the same was true of the Russian Federation. He could have called Dzhokhar Dudayev's bluff and given Chechnya independence - one less troublesome region for Yeltsin to preside over. In all likelihood, Chechnya would have moved towards voluntary reintegration within a few years, as Belarus did. Even the proud Georgians asked for belated admission to the Commonwealth of Independent States. The small republics are quite capable of governing their own internal affairs, but collective security is essential for the former Soviet Union, where border disputes occur regularly and nuclear weapons are scattered over vast distances.

The conciliatory words of Chernomyrdin and members of Our Home is Russia belied the actions of his government. When Chernomyrdin visited St Petersburg in November 1995 he said, 'We are prepared to hold peaceful talks with those who really want peace, not those who turn around and shoot us in the back.' Alexander Prokhorenko, deputy chairman of Our Home is Russia in St Petersburg, didn't think that the government's conduct of the war contradicted the party's peaceful principles. 'What would happen if Texas wanted to secede from the United States?' he asked. 'It's a similar situation. Independence for Chechnya should only be possible if the Chechen people everywhere, including Moscow and other Russian cities, are given the opportunity to decide the question.'

Our Home is Russia's manifesto for the Duma election asserted, 'The most important state institution in need of strengthening is the Armed Forces... We will secure a heightening of the prestige of service and work in the Armed Forces and the country's defence complex.' To lighten the tone, the party resorted to conning Western pop stars into giving campaign concerts on its behalf. Britain's Glen Hughes, who used to play in the band Deep Purple, apologised profusely to his audience in Moscow when he found the stage adorned with giant posters of Chernomyrdin. Hughes hadn't even been told that the concert was linked with politics.

American rap singer MC Hammer was also enlisted unwittingly to the Chernomyrdin campaign. According to Prokhorenko, MC

Hammer's concert in St Petersburg simply aimed to encourage the city's apathetic young people to vote. Not necessarily for Our Home is Russia, of course, but the party's name was prominent on the publicity posters and Prokhorenko agreed that it was likely to penetrate the minds of MC Hammer fans along with his music. 'I don't believe that thinking people could go to a concert and then immediately vote for Our Home is Russia,' he said. 'But at least they will start to wonder who we are.'

Free concert tickets were distributed to St Petersburg schools, institutes of higher education, military academies and youth clubs. 'This should be an election for the generation aged between 20 and 40,' said Prokhorenko. 'They must determine their own fate or else the development of Russia on general world lines could slow down.' But the people who grilled their local candidates at public election meetings I attended were almost exclusively middle-aged or elderly. Yuliya, a public relations student at St Petersburg's electro-technical university, expressed a view shared by many young people: 'Politics isn't interesting. I haven't seen a politician on television I can trust when they say they will make a wonderful future. In their soul they are still communists, and Chernomyrdin is the oldest communist of them all.'

An elderly woman told me, 'Moscow politics is a dark forest to me.' But she was going to vote for a party called Communists-Labouring Russia-For the Soviet Union because, 'I want my former life back.' A middle-aged woman who worked at the till in a grocery shop said, 'We definitely need a dictator. One thing you can say for Stalin is that he built up the country in a short time after the war. Life was stable before.' Her knowledge of current political parties seemed sketchy: 'I might vote for the Communists but I also like Yavlinsky.' The woman's colleague was also in favour of a dictatorship. 'I don't want to give my vote to anyone, but I wouldn't mind trying Zhirinovsky,' she said. 'We don't have enough money - we don't live, we exist. This country needs discipline.'

Several candidates in St Petersburg were connected to military organisations, including the Union of Afghanistan Veterans, the Frunze Naval Academy and the Kalinin Artillery Academy.

Ensconced in the splendour of a mock Gothic castle which was once the home of an aristocrat, the city's deputy military commissar was bombarded with the complaints of impoverished officers and despondent conscripts. Lieutenant Colonel Stepan Zholovan stood in the Duma election to draw attention to conditions in the army. Zholovan, 39, was an independent candidate but previously he had been a member of the Communist Party. Born in Ukraine, he studied for six years at Leningrad State University, then worked on the railway in Kazakhstan before beginning his career in the army.

'The question of young people is most important to me,' he said. 'Their level of education is falling, their health is worsening and criminality is growing.' He believed that national service had its benefits, but he didn't think it too terrible that only a small percentage of St Petersburg's conscripts reported for duty. 'What *is* the purpose of conscription?' I asked him.

'Serving in the army cultivates patriotism. That means being prepared to stand up when you see your country's flag.'

The end of the Cold War should rightly have been followed by a reduction in Russia's armed forces, Zholovan said, but he added that other dangers still existed: 'We've got plenty of border conflicts. Our relationship with the West has changed, but there's been no change in our relationship with countries such as Turkey and China. There are no threats, but there are dangers.' Zholovan harboured few fond memories of the Soviet era. 'There were good and bad things then and there are good and bad things now,' he said. 'Life was no better under the tsars, either. I know several places in St Petersburg where people used to be sold on the streets. People!'

Zholovan wasn't elected to the Duma. Young people in St Petersburg must have been swayed by MC Hammer or perhaps a European Union-sponsored advertising campaign with the slogan, 'Wake up - there's no future if you don't vote!', because candidates from Yabloko and independent liberals swept the board in the city. Remarkably, one of the winners was 49-year-old Galina Starovoitova. Only four out of the 152 candidates in St Petersburg were women, and Starovoitova defeated 23 male opponents. Being nationally famous helped. The aggressive, padded-shouldered academic was once an adviser to President Yeltsin on international relations but was sacked in 1992 due to differences of opinion. 'Yeltsin has undergone a biological change and no longer represents liberals,' she said in 1995. 'He is not the man reformists supported and voted for.'

Starovoitova lectured at Harvard for a while, but turned down a job offer worth $100,000 from an American university because she wanted to stay in Russia. She founded the Democratic Russia and Free Trade Unions Party to contest the Duma election, but withdrew it at the last minute to help bigger liberal parties. So she won her seat as an independent, in St Petersburg's most heavily-contested constituency. She considered politics a creative business and obviously enjoyed it: 'What could be more wonderful than to build intelligent plans for people and see them come into existence?'

Strangers in a Strange Land

Hooray, there are no more closed cities in Russia; you can travel around without being glued to an Intourist guide spouting industrial production statistics, you can photograph railway stations without fear of imprisonment, you can drive a car without being followed around by a KGB grunt, you can make friends with Russians, get drunk with Russians, have sex with Russians, get married to Russians, work for Russians, employ Russians and write about Russians without having to change their names to save them from losing their jobs and being sent to Siberia. Hooray!

If there is a final frontier to boldly go to in this seen-it-done-it age, it's Russia. The Don and the Volga rivers, the Black Sea and the Arctic Ocean, the Urals and the Caucasus mountains, the steppe and the desert - if you have a train ticket, or a tent and a pair of boots, all this can be yours. But every country has its breathtaking scenery. For me, and for hundreds of thousands of other foreigners who have had their faces examined by the steely-jawed officers at passport control (some things never change), and emerged into a muddy autumn in Moscow, or a snowy spring in St Petersburg, the fascination of Russia is the onrushing tidal wave of opportunity for business and pleasure with Russians in their newly-awakened cities.

There are two main categories of foreigners who go to Russia: those who do things on their own, and those who have things organised for them. The latter group includes students, package tourists and people working for big charities, political entities such as the European Union, and multinational companies. I'll come to them in due course. First, though, let's see what becomes of the foolhardy souls who are inspired by the Sinatra Doctrine - 'I'll do it my way'. Do they all end up with imaginary diseases of the central nervous system, screaming, 'I've been poisoned!' to the ambulance services in the middle of the night?

I flew to St Petersburg in June 1995, on the day before the result of my final exams was published. (I wasn't fleeing from the result, I just misread the date before I booked my ticket, so my trip to Russia started as it meant to go on.) I had a flat in the northern

181

suburbs, near Pionerskaya metro station, but I was too late to be a pioneer myself. The flat had been found for me by Jane, who graduated from the same department of the same university as me a year earlier. She shared a flat with her boyfriend, Volodya; their neighbours were Becky, her husband, Volodya, and their daughter, Alice. Becky graduated with Jane from the Russian department of the University of Birmingham.

'I hope you don't think Volodya and I are too coupley,' Jane said to me once.

'No, Jane, you're very independent,' I replied. 'You go everywhere and do everything together, but other than that, you're completely separate people.' Volodya was paid erratically by his paper, *Nevskoye Vremya*, and later sacked for his protest over censorship, so Jane was lucky that her employer was more reliable. He was a British lawyer who had started a monthly property magazine for Eastern Europe called *Estates News*. Jane was the *Estates News* representative in St Petersburg, which meant distributing the magazine, selling advertising space and writing articles. 'I'm not a journalist,' said Jane. 'I'd really like to do something to help Russia, maybe work for a charity.' But working for a charity and earning enough to live on wasn't an easy ambition to fulfil.

Becky was once asked by a curious compatriot, 'Do you treat Volodya like a Russian?' Her husband did business deals with varying success, while she worked at an international kindergarten. Expatriates paid serious money to send their children there, but that didn't guarantee Becky's income. If you had a dispute at work in Russia, there was no one to appeal to. Becky's purse was stolen when she was looking after £100 of the kindergarten's money, and her boss docked it from her wages. Then the same woman abruptly announced that she was giving up the kindergarten and moving away. By this time, Becky had already decided that she and her family should go back to England. 'If you have a child, and you have the choice between living in Russia or England, then it's not fair to choose Russia,' she said.

Jane, Becky and I were in Russia because we liked it. Tina, a 28-year-old Australian, was in Russia because her mother liked it.

Tina's mother was Russian and thought it would be a good experience for Tina to study medicine in St Petersburg. In keeping with the style of her life so far, the course Tina enrolled on was cancelled a week or so after it started. Tina's previous misadventure was a failed marriage to a Czech ski instructor, by whom she had two sons, who were staying in the Czech Republic with their father while she was ostensibly studying. But when the course fell through, Tina moved into a freezing flat with a diabetic Ossetian called Morat. My Ossetian boyfriend, Kostya, introduced me to Morat and Tina. 'They'll be pleased to see us,' he said. 'All they do is watch videos and have sex.'

I'm not sure if Tina was capable of staying in one position for long enough to do either. While Morat sat engrossed in an episode of Rowan Atkinson's silent comedy show *Mr Bean*, Tina dashed from the kitchen to the living room and back, attempting to deal with all her domestic chores at once - boiling the cat, basting the teapot and feeding the roast chicken - or other permutations of these activities. 'This country!' she exclaimed breathlessly, tossing her straggly brown hair out of the way of her face. 'I can't stand this country! And *he's* useless,' she said, nodding at Morat. 'I call these Ossetians cave men, because that's what they're like, they expect women to do everything. He can't cook and he doesn't bother learning English, do you?'

'What?' said Morat, in English.

'He just sits there waiting for his friend Vadik the bandit to call.'

Morat gave as good as he got. When he was in a talkative mood he droned on endlessly about how Eastern philosophies justified spending all of one's life thinking - there was no point in doing anything for other people, it wouldn't make any difference to the world. Tina's Russian was feeble and she could understand very little of what he was saying, but neither of them seemed to care that all their conversations were one-sided. Since she met Morat and he asked her to marry him, Tina had devoted her life to searching St Petersburg for insulin and putting together the papers they needed to get married and go to Australia.

'I'd learn English if I knew I was definitely going, but I can't be sure,' said Morat. One evening, Tina phoned me in hysterics. I lived a ten-minute walk from their flat. 'Come over now, please, I can't cope with this any more, something terrible's happened, I'm packing my things and leaving him.' I rushed over there, but by the time I got to their door Tina had composed herself and changed her mind about leaving. 'He's gone out,' she said. 'I don't know where. He hit me because I told him to clean up the cat sick and he refused to do it. He gets like that when he hasn't had enough insulin, he has these hypos. And by the way, I'm pregnant.'

I'm hopeless at knowing what to say in other people's emotional crises, and Tina's stack of problems demanded the combined expertise of a domestic abuse centre, a missing persons bureau, a vet and a doctor, not to mention the Australian immigration services and Russian passport office, but fortunately I wasn't expected to advise, or even sympathise. Tina just wanted me to drink her tea while she embellished the details of all the mishaps she'd had in Russia. 'In the winter I fell over and cracked my head on the ice,' she said. 'I was taken to a mental hospital and I stayed there until I woke up one night with a naked woman leaning over me.' Another time, Tina was stopped on the street by a gypsy who wanted a lock of her hair to tell her fortune. Tina said no and the gypsy put a curse on her, which was probably a waste of a curse in Tina's case.

Tina's narratives sounded more like an omnibus edition of the Australian soap *Neighbours* than real life. Talking cheered her up and the row with Morat was forgotten. He came home late, sulking. A few days after this incident, the cat disappeared and Morat mumbled something like, 'I put it out on the street, but it knew where to go, it'll be fine.' Dispensing with celebrations, Tina and Morat signed a marriage contract and Tina went back to Australia, picking up her sons from the Czech Republic on the way. Morat couldn't go with her because he had to wait for his visa. He was worried that he would fail the medical examination and not be admitted into the country, but he got there in time to see his baby being born. He phoned Kostya to say he'd arrived safely in Sydney and Kostya told him to phone again in a year's time.

Jim, a cycling fanatic from England with a ring in his ear which he pulled and twisted whenever he was agitated, was another foreigner who had to improvise the arrangements for his stay in Russia. He was accepted as one of a small group of civilians to join a British army expedition to Lake Baikal in Siberia. He had passed a number of rigorous tests to get onto the team and then went with them to train in Germany. He had already been granted a year out of his university course when the army told him he couldn't go to Russia because of a medical condition he had.

To prove that he was fit enough to go, Jim surprised his former friends from the army by getting on a train and turning up at their camp. He told me Lake Baikal was wonderful, but the soldiers hated being there because they would only eat the revolting tinned rations they'd brought with them and wouldn't go outside their barracks to look at the lake or the countryside. They gave Jim a room for a week and after that time told him that if he didn't leave the next day, they'd throw his bags out of the window. So he went to St Petersburg, rented a room in a communal flat and got a job as copy editor at *Neva News*. That was where I met him. He was just starting to panic about the problem of his visa.

The Russian government didn't deport people very often, because it was expensive. Illegal immigrants from the Middle East and Africa who got caught by the police were put in prison until the money was raised to pay for their flight home. People from wealthy countries whose visas expired had a choice - they could pay a fine, or they could stay in Russia illegally - but they couldn't leave. This was a nice little earner for Russia, as the rules on visas were lengthy, complicated, and changed every few months. But the fundamentals were the same as they were in the Soviet Union, and that meant they did everything possible to discourage the independent traveller.

To get a Russian visa, you needed an invitation. If you didn't know anyone in Russia, you could pay a travel agency in your home country to provide an invitation from a Russian company. That was what Jim did. The Russian consulate in London issued his visa, and on it were the words, 'All visitors to Russia must register their presence with the police within three working days of arrival', so Jim obediently went to the police department of visas and registration (OVIR) in St Petersburg to register his presence. He wasn't allowed to register, though, because to do that he needed a representative of the company which had invited him to go to OVIR with a package of papers - this little difficulty wasn't mentioned on the visa. Jim's company was in Moscow and he'd never had any contact with it.

Rejected by OVIR, Jim didn't think about his unregistered presence until months later, when his visa was about to expire. He wanted to stay longer in Russia, so he decided to extend the visa. He went to OVIR again and was told, 'You can't extend your visa because you haven't registered it.' At this stage, Jim could probably have left the country without worries, as so few people succeeded in registering their visa that customs officials at the airport didn't take any notice. But he made the mistake of staying. Then he began to wonder how he would get out with an unregistered, expired visa, so he made another trip to OVIR to ask for advice on how to become legal again.

Flustered and upset, realising that his situation had become serious, he was sent from OVIR office to OVIR office in different districts of the city. At one point he blurted out in his undergraduate Russian, 'I simply want to go home.' The woman he was talking to shook her head and said, 'But for you this is not simple.' She couldn't help him. On the day before Jim's flight back to England, he phoned the office of the Ministry of Foreign Affairs at St Petersburg's Pulkovo airport, explained his problem and was given a hint. 'There's nothing we can do, of course, it's too late, but come to the airport with 250 dollars in cash anyway,' he was told.

Jim asked me to lend him the money and promised to return it by Western Union as soon as he got home. 'Are you sure you can afford it?' I said.

'I'll borrow it. I'll find it somehow, I'll just be so glad to be back. I miss my bike.' At the airport, Jim and I met the man from the Ministry of Foreign Affairs whom he'd talked to on the phone. He continued with his charade so that Jim would be in despair for the maximum possible time. 'I'm sorry, no, you have to go to OVIR to sort this out,' he said.

'I've *been* to OVIR,' said Jim.

'Ah. Well, prepare 250 dollars in cash, in that case,' the man said, and went away. I prepared the cash by taking it out of my purse.

When the man came back to collect it, he even gave us a receipt. As far as I knew, the law which forbade currencies other than the rouble to be used for payment on the territory of the Russian Federation applied to Pulkovo airport and employees of government ministries, but I thought it unwise to point that out.

The man from the Ministry stamped the visa and put an end to Jim's nightmare. Tears of relief came to his eyes as he hugged me goodbye. 'Take these,' he said emotionally, removing his disintegrating trainers. 'They're yours.' I asked him if he would ever come back to Russia. 'I don't know. I like it here, but that business with OVIR ruined my whole trip. It wasn't worth the hassle.'

After eleven months in St Petersburg, two visas and countless visits to OVIR, I knew what Jim was talking about. Like him, I was originally invited by a company in Moscow which I didn't know. I'd been in Russia before, though, so I brought the invitation with me just in case it would be needed again. An employee of *The St Petersburg Press* went to OVIR to register me, but she was turned away because I hadn't been invited by *The St Petersburg Press*, so the designers at the newspaper used the invitation to forge documents with the Moscow company's stamp on them, and the same person went back to OVIR with these documents, posing as an employee of the company which invited me. I was duly registered.

My visa was due to expire on December 19, and to extend it I would need more forged documents, so Lloyd at *The St Petersburg Press* advised me that it would be better to do things legally and start again with a new visa. To get a new visa, you had to leave the country. I went to Stockholm, arriving on December 20. At the Russian consulate I was told I could have a visa on the same day for $150, the next day for $100 or in three days for $50 - but the consulate was closing for Christmas in two days. I paid $100 and presented the pile of documents I needed for a six-month business visa: my Confirmation of Working Activity, the contract between *The St Petersburg Press* and the Ministry of Foreign Affairs allowing the newspaper to employ foreigners, a list of foreigners employed at *The St Petersburg Press*, the papers which proved *The St Petersburg Press* was a legitimate company registered in the

Russian Federation. All to no avail. 'You can't have six months,' said the consular official. 'You can have three months. New rule.' And to rub things in, he gave me an ordinary tourist visa.

Eight weeks later, my visa deadline loomed over me again, and I had moved from *The St Petersburg Press* to Russia & World. Russia & World had never employed a foreigner before and the boss asked me to find out from OVIR what papers I needed. I phoned OVIR and was told, 'We don't answer questions over the telephone.' I went there in the afternoon and found a sign on the door which stated that the opening hours were from 10 to 12 in the morning on Mondays, Wednesdays and Fridays. I went again at 10:05 on a Monday and joined a queue of about 20 people. Every so often, someone would charge in ahead of everyone else, saying, 'I've got a plane to catch in half an hour, I *must* get my visa now!' I waited for two hours until it was my turn.

In the office I was confronted by a woman in a grey uniform who was clearly still bitter about being made redundant from her job as a concentration camp guard. 'What are you doing here?' she said. 'We don't deal with foreigners. You should have a representative of your company -'

'I'm sorry, my company sent me here to find out what I need to do to get a new visa.'

'It's all in the waiting room on the noticeboard,' she said. 'Now get out of here.'

The noticeboard was covered with lists of rules, but it had nothing for people who had changed companies, which I knew already because I'd been reading it for the past two hours. I came back with a representative of my company on Wednesday at 9:45, to beat the rush. There was a new sign on the door: 'This OVIR now has a new address...' At the new address the sign on the door read, 'Visa enquiries for foreign citizens are dealt with on Tuesdays and Thursdays between 2 and 4 pm.'

When we did get to the right place at the right time, our enquiry established that I couldn't get a new visa until I had a letter from *The St Petersburg Press* which said the company had 'no material pretensions' towards me. When we came back with this letter, my visa had already expired and we hadn't progressed very far towards putting together all the papers from Russia & World. The concentration camp guard was most distressed that I accompanied the representative of my company to OVIR and participated in conversations about my visa. 'Why does she go all over the place with you?' she asked my boss. 'She has been asking questions and complaining. You've been to Russia before,' she said, turning to me. 'You should know how to behave here.'

My boss and I hung our heads in the hope that our remorse would shut her up. But the lecture was just getting into full swing. 'You were here on a tourist visa and you were working. Now your visa has expired and you are here illegally. You have violated the visa regime twice, and under the Soviet law, which is still in force, you could go to prison for a year. You are a criminal.' I couldn't help reacting to that. 'But the visa hadn't expired a month ago when I started coming to OVIR to find out what to do about it! You wouldn't tell me! It's not my fault. Do you want people to come to Russia?'

'Yes.'

'Do you know that there are people who say they'll never come back because of the way they've been treated at OVIR?' My tormentor was startled at my audacity. 'There's no need to get irritated,' she said.

I never did get a new visa because my nerves were out of order by that time and I went back to England. I couldn't afford to pay $250 at the airport, so I made two emergency plans. Plan A was to slip $30 into my visa as a bribe to the official who checked it. But she opened the visa, saw the banknotes and gave them straight back without a flicker of interest. Perhaps she was incorruptible, or perhaps she thought I'd left the money there by mistake, because she only noticed afterwards that the visa was out of date. 'Madame -' she began, and I cut in straight away with Plan B, which was to garble, 'I couldn't extend my visa because I've been ill for the past month and haven't been able to get out of bed,' and pull out a wad of doctors' notes which verified the existence of my mysterious 'syndrome'. It worked. I was through passport control before I could even twitch.

During the weeks when I was a fugitive from OVIR's merciless brand of justice, I arranged an interview with a senior official in OVIR, Margarita Tsibizova, to try and find out what exactly the new rules were. She said they were available to anyone - you just had to ask for them. So I asked for them and she handed me 25 pages of badly-photocopied fine print. I longed for the day when the Russian civil service produced the kind of leaflets we have in dentists' waiting rooms and driving test centres: 'PLAQUE! Ten painless procedures for cleaner teeth', and, 'YOU HAVE FAILED FIVE TIMES. Which way now?' But in five years of democracy it wasn't possible to wipe out centuries of secrecy, an entirely pointless secrecy which surrounded even the most mundane pieces of information.

'It isn't easy to get a Russian visa, is it?' I said.

'Russians have to wait several weeks for visas to most countries,' Tsibizova replied. 'When all borders are opened to us then things won't be so difficult here for foreign citizens.' It's certainly ironic that so many countries built invisible barriers in their consulates as soon as the Iron Curtain was raised. When Western Europeans and Americans travel abroad, they expect the world to assume they are going for a visit - they couldn't possibly want to sneak in permanently to a country full of foreigners. For all the Russian rules, at least visitors weren't subjected to questioning about their jobs and relationships when they applied for a visa. But Russians who wanted to visit the West were treated as potential immigrants until they could prove otherwise.

Kostya was desperate to go to the World Cup in the United States in 1994. The US consulate had just opened in St Petersburg, so everyone in the city had to apply for a visa there, not at the much larger consular department of the embassy in Moscow. The consulate in St Petersburg only had one telephone line; Kostya and I took turns dialling the number for an average of an hour a day until I got through after a week and was given a time for Kostya to go to an interview. Our efforts were wasted, as he was rejected and had to watch the football on television.

Kostya had also been turned down for a British visa twice - he wanted to visit me. 'It would be easier to swim there,' he said the first time, when he called me in Birmingham from St Petersburg. The second time, I went to the consulate with him. He walked in vowing to take a bunch of flowers to the Queen, and came out with a rejection slip in his hand: 'We are not convinced that you have a secure job.' I wasn't too surprised, because Kostya, a divorced, unemployed alcoholic from the Caucasus with a criminal record, must have been fairly close to Chikatilo the serial-killing cannibal on the priority list for a visa.

A British student in the queue with us at the consulate was devastated when his female friend was refused a visa. He banged on the glass which separated the powerful from the powerless and demanded to see the consul-general. 'I've stayed with this girl's family for three weeks and now I want her to stay with me for ten days,' he shouted. 'What's the harm in that? She doesn't know English, so why on earth would she try to live in England? She'd only be able to work as a prostitute!' Someone important from the consulate came out of an office and dismissed him with the indifferent politeness which the British excel at. 'I'm afraid there are no appeals against our decisions,' she said. 'Your friend may apply again if she wishes.'

My landlady, divorced and self-employed, was also refused a British visa. But even strong ties to Russia didn't guarantee a US visa for the wife of Vyacheslav Lazarian. He happened to be the director of Sovavto, the largest lorry company in Europe, and when I interviewed him he showed me the letter from the US consulate which denied his wife permission to visit America. In response to criticisms of their visa policies, the American and British authorities quoted statistics which demonstrated how many Russians did receive visas from them. The British embassy in Moscow issued 100,000 visas a year, more than any other British embassy in the world, and the consulate in St Petersburg issued 20,000. So who was getting them? 'Russians must prove that they don't intend to settle in the United Kingdom by showing they have the finances to return home,' said Sir Andrew Wood, the British ambassador to Moscow.

We'll see how Russians get on in Britain in the next chapter. For foreigners in Russia, the way to avoid OVIR was to be looked after by an organisation which dealt with visas on their behalf. Students, for instance, never even had to hear the word 'OVIR'. But then, some of them hardly heard any Russian words as they sat in their rooms all day listening to BBC World Service and writing letters home. One such person was Anya, a whinging blonde girl with nerdy glasses who was in Minsk with me. Her parents were from Poland and I think she was studying Russian only because it was similar to Polish; certainly not because she liked the country.

Anya's hatred for Minsk rivalled Hitler's. She would have happily razed it to the ground again if she'd had a Luftwaffe squadron at her disposal. She marked each day which passed with a red cross on a giant wall calendar, and the date at the end of our three-month course was decorated with a cartoon of herself grinning and waving. Anya worshipped Poland. Everything in Poland was superior to everything in Russia. 'Russian people are smelly!' she said, crumpling her face like Miss Piggy. 'The clothes they wear - ugh! No taste! The food is dis-gusting. You should see Polish cakes, oh my God, they're luscious, I just wish I had one now. The water here is brown. It's all horrible, horrible. Men keep coming up to me, but I wear this ring, you see, I shove it in their faces and say, 'U menya muzh!' - 'I have a husband!''

Anya had a Mexican boyfriend in England called Dan who was going to become a rich lawyer, marry her and take her away to a huge house in Mexico, where they'd have lots of maids, just like in a soap opera. But first he had to greet her at Heathrow airport when she arrived from Minsk, and he had to be carrying a bouquet of roses and a piece of Cheddar cheese. Everyone who knew Anya in Minsk was sick to death of Dan after hearing about his beauty, wit and talent for hours every day, but he managed to redeem himself by phoning Anya to dump her just before she flew back.

Anya's other obsession was cleanliness. Her mother sent her air freshener in the post and Anya was engaged in a constant crusade for greater hygiene in the toilet which she shared with her neighbour, a Syrian Kurd called Kawa. Unfortunately for Kawa, he was a man. He didn't always aim straight when he used the toilet and Anya reprimanded him about this by putting up a sign, 'Don't piss or shit on the seat!', decorated with a cartoon of herself grinning and waving.

I thought things would improve when my friend Amy came to visit me in Minsk. We always had adventures together in Russia. One very sunny day in St Petersburg, we set out for a picnic in the

Central Park of Culture and Rest, which we'd never been to before. It turned out to be half-an-hour's walk from the metro and by the time we got there, a violent thunderstorm had started. Soaking wet, we sheltered in the nearest building, which was deserted downstairs and had a billiard hall upstairs. We thought we might find a place to sit down, so we walked through the billiard hall and came to someone's private flat. 'Hello, my name is Boris,' said the someone. 'Would you like some tea?'

Tea was exactly what we needed; we accepted gratefully. Boris went to his ensuite kitchen and returned with a pot of tea in one hand and a bottle of cognac in the other. My only memory of our conversation is that Boris said he was 40 years old, came from Samarkand in Central Asia and was renting the rooms in St Petersburg for the summer. Between 2 pm and 11 pm everything went black and I moved from a sitting position on a chair to a prone position on a sofa. The blackness was interrupted occasionally by an appalling apparition of hideously magnified guitar strings being strummed inches from my face. 'Turn the music down! Please, somebody, turn the music down,' I begged.

At 11 o'clock Amy shook me awake. 'We've got to go now,' she said. 'I've been smoking hash with him, but I got fed up when he tried to touch my boobs.' As we didn't have the money for a taxi, Amy persuaded Boris to pay for one in return for our promise to come to his party a week later. Boris phoned us on the day of the party. 'I'll be seeing you later, then?'

'We're terribly sorry, we have to finish our essays on metaphor in the works of Tolstoy,' Amy told him.

'Deceit!' snarled Boris. 'Big, big deceit!'

Amy, who was studying in Birmingham with me, took every available opportunity to go to Russia, especially to her beloved Moscow. She had already lived there for a year between A-levels and university, so when the time came to spend a year in Russia as part of her university course, she preferred to organise the trip herself so that she didn't have to live in a hostel. She paid $1000 rent in advance for a flat, which surprised the landlord's mother, as it was her home. The landlord disappeared with the money and Amy had to find another place. Then Amy loaned the rest of her money to her friend Oleg, who imported swimming trunks from the United Arab Emirates, and he was supposed to pay it back over the year with interest, but he had to take it on the run with him from bandits wanting protection money.

Just before all these disasters, Amy came from Moscow with Oleg to stay with me in Minsk for three days. Also with her was a gay Asian man from London called Paul, who had passed his finals in medicine that month and was about to start practising. To recover from the sweaty overnight train journey to Minsk, Amy went swimming in a lake. Directly after that, she collapsed on my bed, delirious with pneumonia, and Paul had his first ever patient. He said that Amy needed antibiotics, but it was a Sunday and nearly all the chemists were closed. Oleg stayed in my room to watch Amy while Paul and I went to seek out a rota chemist with chess teacher Sveta: she knew where the chemist was, Paul knew what to buy, and I was their interpreter.

Sveta led us round the back of a block of flats, where a babushka in a white coat was standing in a stairwell behind an iron grille. She rummaged in a crate and pulled out two boxes of antibiotics. 'Which ones do you want?' Paul looked at them, chose one, and we hurried back to put Amy out of her misery.

'It was lucky that Amy brought a doctor with her,' I remarked to Paul.

'It certainly was,' he said. 'Those other antibiotics are quite dangerous. Some people have an allergic reaction to them and die instantly.'

I must give Oleg a special mention as the world's worst guest. He tried to teach me a hellishly complicated card game called Preference by process of elimination, making me play without knowing the rules in advance and scolding me when I broke one of them. He got in a bad mood because I couldn't get the hang of it and eventually gave me up as a lost cause. When he was buying the tickets back to Moscow he thought it was uncool to stand in a queue, so he made us wait until the last seconds before the train left by retreating into corners with shady characters and negotiating for tickets with them, finally getting some at twice the official price. As Oleg was standing at the train door he suddenly said to me, 'You owe me money! We all lived together, right? Communally. We all shared everything. But I spent more on beer and cigarettes than you, so you should give me something towards them.'

'Goodbye, Oleg,' I said. 'Thanks for letting me share my room with you.'

I stayed in Minsk for longer than the other British students because I found a job for the summer as a translator and administrator with a European Union agricultural project, or rather, several projects. 'Specialists', as they were known, from all over Europe, were based in the Belarusian Ministry of Agriculture to advise on meat, milk, flax and potatoes as part of the EU's TACIS programme - Technical Assistance to the Commonwealth of Independent States. All the specialists where I worked were men and most of them spent their lives travelling around the world, advising and writing reports, fattening their off-shore bank accounts and leaving their families at home in varying states of decay. A meat and milk specialist from France, Dominique Etiènne, made admirable progress in Russian, but the others couldn't get past the alphabet, so one of my tasks was to go downstairs to the shop and buy Coca Colas for them.

To spare them the indignity of having to use public transport, the specialists were driven from their flats to work and back, and anywhere else they wanted to go. Drivers and interpreters were paid local rates, earning in a month the equivalent of the specialists' *per diem* expenses. The EU paid phenomenal rent on the flats for specialists, around £300 per month, which was ten times the average monthly salary in Minsk. Our boss was Paul Wright, who can be instantly envisaged if you think of a bearded John Cleese impersonating a World War I colonel. 'Late again, how tiresome! We are here to show these people how to get to meetings on time and how to use fax machines,' he ranted, striding purposefully down the corridor.

The British were the most entertaining of the specialists, hidebound by anachronisms and a stubborn determination not to make any concessions to the fact that they were in another country. Mike Thornton, a food packaging specialist in his mid-sixties, said he was shocked by the short skirts of Belarusian girls. He obviously had a firm idea of the correct role in life for females: the person who would benefit from hermetically-sealed plastic bags of orange juice and clearly-printed lists of ingredients on boxes of porridge was, naturally, 'the lady who does the shopping'. I interpreted for him at a bottle-making factory and as we were approaching it he said, 'You'll probably be the first woman to set foot in this factory.' So he was rather surprised when we were greeted at the entrance by the chief technologist, a woman.

I hope she was better at her job than I was at mine. I was good at written translations, but interpreting was far more difficult, and my studies of 19th-century Russian poetry hadn't prepared me for the terminology of bottle-making. 'Now she's describing all the ingredients which go into bottles,' I told Mike.

'Well, what are they?' I couldn't understand any of them.

'Er - you know what goes into bottles,' I said.

'Could you ask her what source of energy the factory uses?' said Mike. The reply was 'mazut'.

'I don't suppose there's such a word as mazut in English?' I asked Mike, who shook his head.

'It's a kind of oil,' said the chief technologist.

'It's a kind of oil,' I told Mike.

Alan Taylor, a retail specialist whose mission was to set up a chain of Spar shops in Belarus, was overcome when he saw a plain blue van with the Russian word for BREAD on it. 'Can you *imagine* what that van would look like if it said SUNBLEST on it?' he marvelled. In general, Alan was the calmest and most rational of the British specialists. The most neurotic was Gordon Bailey, a lanky horticulturalist, whose hands shook as he lit his umpteenth cigarette of the day. Gordon wanted to make friends with me and Sveta. We met at his flat before going to a bar. He hadn't had dinner, so he shovelled down forkfuls of cold salmon from a tin and gave us a beer, a packet of raisins and a chewing gum each while we were waiting. 'Can you cook?' I asked him.

'I know two dishes: omelette, which I make by throwing eggs and other ingredients into a pan, and meat and vegetables, which I make by throwing meat and vegetables into a pan.'

Gordon was very worried about prostitutes. He was disgusted at how many of them there were in the former Soviet Union, or how many he perceived there were. I said there had been prostitutes in the Soviet era, too, and in any case they were hardly the region's most urgent problem. Prostitutes bothered him because they were visible evidence of male weakness. 'If I had to pay for it, I wouldn't consider myself a real man any more,' he confided in us unnecessarily. Then Gordon told us about a TACIS project he'd been on in St Petersburg, where most of the specialists slept with the project administrator, who turned out to be a KGB agent, and all of them except for Gordon (who didn't sleep with her) were sent home.

Gordon and some of the other specialists were uncomfortable about their privileged lifestyle in Minsk and were aware that not everyone reacted favourably to the presence of foreigners scrutinising their accounts and questioning them about their working methods. John Standingford of the European Bank for Reconstruction and Development, also based in the Ministry of Agriculture, said, 'If the West had lost the Cold War and a Belarusian specialist came to England to tell me how to do my job according to Marxist economic principles, I'd retire and go and pick strawberries in the forest. We are an occupying army.'

At least the EU was in the former Soviet Union to help, even if the effectiveness of its projects was difficult to quantify. The large expatriate business communities in Moscow and St Petersburg were there for one reason only: to make money. These people drank in Irish bars, shopped in Finnish supermarkets, watched Eurosport and CNN, had parcels of books and videos shipped to them regularly and flew home several times a year for a dose of 'civilisation'. In short, they did everything they could to avoid noticing that they were in Russia. It was remarkable how some of them got by for years without being able to string a decent Russian sentence together.

The social inequality created by the rapid transition to a market economy caused great resentment amongst the less well-off section of the population, and for this they blamed not only their own radical politicians, but also the West. If you imagine how you would feel if the majority of the brand names on London's advertising hoardings were in Japanese, if the only highly-paid jobs in London were for people who spoke Japanese fluently, then you have some idea of how Russians feel about the invasion of the

English language and Western multinationals. Foreigners are welcome to do business in Britain, but it is essential to speak English. Russians are welcome to do business in Russia, but it is essential to speak English. There seems to be a disparity here.

Westerners can blame themselves for giving the impression that all foreigners ooze money. That was why five-star hotels were constantly springing up in St Petersburg, while there was only one hostel for backpackers. And that was why it became accepted practice for museums and theatres to set a separate, higher admission price for foreign citizens. I have never heard of such a practice in any other country. Usually it was flexible - students with ID cards and people who spoke Russian could have a few friendly words with the ticket-seller and get in for the lower price. For tourists who were visiting the Hermitage for the first and probably the only time in their lives, it wasn't too much of a hardship to pay £8 instead of £1. But for a long-term visitor such as myself, living on a shoestring budget, if someone insisted that I pay the foreigners' price, then I simply couldn't buy the ticket. This happened to me at the Kremlin Armoury.

I was showing a girl from Minsk, Lyuda, around Moscow, as she'd just had her 18th birthday and had never been there before. Lyuda bought us two tickets to the Kremlin Armoury for the Russian price. But as I walked through the door, an angry babushka grabbed me by the arm and shoved me in the direction of the ticket booth. 'You go over there and pay extra,' she said. 'You're a foreigner.' She could tell because I was carrying an expensive camera. I'd been to the museum twice before and was only going there to keep Lyuda company, so I saved my money and sat on the grass outside while she looked around. In fact, if the babushka had somehow recognised that Lyuda was from Belarus (she'd have had to be draped in her national flag), then she, too, would have been charged the foreigners' price.

The rules for buying train tickets changed every time I wanted to buy one. Sometimes you needed to show your passport, sometimes you had to have your surname printed on the ticket, and sometimes you didn't need to do either. The most absurd rule (fortunately, it didn't last very long) was that foreigners couldn't buy the cheapest tickets for open sleeping carriages, known as platzkart tickets. Apart from the fact that they were cheap, I was keen to travel in the platzkart on the overnight train from St Petersburg to Moscow because the alternative was to share a four-bunk coupé with complete strangers. This was fine if you were with a friend, but females on their own sometimes had to contend with the undivided attentions of three males for the duration of the journey.

The reason railway employees gave me for refusing platzkart tickets to foreigners was, 'The conditions are not those you are used to at home.' I wondered if anyone from the October Railway Company had ever been on the overnight train from Reading to Edinburgh. I had a seat on it opposite a drunken Scotsman, who sang loudly and waved his beer bottles for several hours before his greasy head slumped onto the table in front of me. The floor of the carriage was full of people stretched out on top of each other because they'd booked seats in a carriage which hadn't been attached to the train.

There was nothing wrong with the Russian platzkart: when I finally did travel that way, the people around me settled down quietly on their bunks and the night passed uneventfully. The real reason why foreigners were barred from having these tickets was of course that the railway company wanted more money from them. In the grand old tradition of Western free market economics, which we export so enthusiastically.

In Foggy Albion

'How's life in foggy Albion?', I've often been asked by Russian friends in their letters and telephone calls. I try to convince them that Moscow is a foggier place than London town, but if they've never been to Britain, they don't believe me. Russians who were educated under the Soviet system are justifiably proud of their knowledge of English literature: they can quote reams of Dickens, Byron and Jerome K. Jerome from memory, and are appalled when their British visitors are unable to do the same. But the mythical image of Britain which has been instilled in them since childhood is stuck in the past. Millions of Russians are fascinated by a country which is long gone, which they know only through the minds of dead fiction writers, poets and the makers of Ealing comedies. When freedom came, thousands of them rushed to Britain to try and find it.

After I came back from my last trip to Russia, in the summer of 1996, I wanted to meet some of those people. Not Russians who were here on holiday for a few days or weeks, not New Russians who had moved to Knightsbridge to be nearer to Harrods, but Russians who lived and worked in Britain as I had lived and worked in their country. I wondered how far reality had matched their dreams. I began my investigation as many Russians begin their adventure here - at the Russian Refugees Aid Society.

The large house in a well-to-do suburb of west London was a far cry from the kind of place Russian refugees could expect to live in. The interior was even more incongruous. While I waited to see April Zinovieff, who ran the society, I sat in a reception room adorned by portraits of the tsars Nicholas II and Alexander II with their wives. A sign on the door read, 'In devoted memory of Princess Natasha Bagration of Mukhrani 1914-1984. Wife of Charles Johnston.' It was remarkable to think that this charity was set up by White Russians to support their fellow refugees fleeing from the Bolshevik revolution, and yet those same people had been compelled to provide a sanctuary for those who could not bear the economic and social injustices of the democratic revolution.

Zinovieff, a well-spoken, intelligent woman in her seventies, smoked constantly as she talked to me. She was British, married to a Russian from an aristocratic St Petersburg family. She used to write books on the history of opera, but in recent years she'd had to look after her husband, who was nearly blind. Nevertheless, she still found the time to advise refugees and review books on Russia. Her son was a chartered surveyor and had gone to work in St Petersburg. He moved into the flat overlooking the Moika canal which his father left in 1918.

'The Refugees Aid Society was founded in 1920 to help anyone from what was formerly the Russian empire,' Zinovieff told me. 'That also includes Finland and Poland, but the Finns are happy and the Poles have organisations of their own. There are a lot of very unhappy Russians here. I used to just let them come, but about a month ago it became completely out of control, there was a crowd of 25 people on the street at six in the morning. Now it's by appointment - I see between ten and twelve people in a morning, and I'm booked up for the next month. I'm the only person here who speaks Russian. I can't handle it and our money is running out.'

Things were very different before 1991. Hardly any Russians came to Britain, and the society owned four houses which formed an old people's home for some of the refugees. 'Those who spoke some English who came after 1917 helped those who didn't,' said Zinovieff. 'It's a great myth that only aristocrats came over. We had no money, we had to raise money with functions and bazaars and jumble sales, like any charity. The society was started by my husband's uncle, who worked as a taxi-driver during the day and here at night.' When most of the old people died, the society sold three of the four houses for a good price, as they were built by the famous architect Norman Shaw.

Britain's Conservative government hadn't made things easier for charities which attempted to help people seeking political asylum - instead, it tightened up the rules. 'Kind Mr Howard [Home Secretary] and kind Mr Lilley [Secretary of State for Social Security] decided that everyone arriving after February 5, 1996, would get no benefits, so a lot of people here are getting no benefits, they have nothing to eat and nowhere to live. This law has made life impossible for everyone. In the past we bought violins for people, but now it's food and lodging. The old, the young, women, girls. The Home Secretary thought this law would stop people coming, but it hasn't. People say they were told it would be lovely, they'd have lots of food and work. It's changed our thing completely, we used to help people to learn English and bought things for them.

'I had a girl in yesterday, she's 19, doesn't speak a word of English, and isn't very clued-up. She's thick. She doesn't even try to understand English. She's on the streets. I sent her to the homeless persons bureau in Hounslow. She's got no money. She's Ukrainian, a student from Kiev. She said she was threatened there, didn't say who by. In fact, she has a right to benefits because she applied for asylum at Gatwick and if you apply at the airport you get benefits. I sent her to Hounslow because we're in Hounslow and the council know us. It's a matter of luck which borough you end up in - some are helpful and some aren't. To be fair to the Home Office, who annoy me beyond belief, a lot did come because they wanted a better life. But they let them in and will send them out, in two or three years. They should decide much more quickly.'

Asylum-seekers from the former Soviet Union stood virtually no chance of being allowed to stay permanently, if Home Office statistics were anything to go by. In 1995, Britain recognised 570 people from Iraq as refugees, 285 from former Yugoslavia, 165 from Iran, 50 from Turkey, 50 from other Middle Eastern countries and 175 from the rest of the world. There were 1675 applications pending from citizens of the former Soviet Union. Four cases were decided. The Ukrainian and the Russian were rejected; the Azerbaijani and the Georgian were granted asylum.

Refugees qualify for asylum if they have a genuine fear of persecution for political, religious or racist reasons. Very few Russians could prove that, Zinovieff told me, although before 1991 they got asylum quite easily. It was a catch-22 situation: when they couldn't get out, they could stay, and when they could get out, they couldn't stay. I asked her if men who didn't want to be conscripted to fight in Chechnya had a case, and she said she doubted it. 'It seems to me that if the law in your country is conscription, you have to do it. I have seen quite a lot of people from Chechnya, mainly Russians. The Chechens wanted them to fight the Russians. There's been one Chechen woman, too.'

Leafing through a pile of case files, Zinovieff read out some of her notes. 'A man came for a better life - he's from Moldova. A man came with his wife, he found life difficult in Ukraine because he's Russian. It's a constant problem - Russians in the wrong place. A woman from near Chechnya, her husband was killed in Chechnya, he was Russian, she's keen to get out. A woman who is Lithuanian, her husband disappeared, she found out he'd been killed, she went to the police and they said she'd be killed if she asked questions - it was the mafia. Is that a reason for asylum? If you're mugged in London, you don't go to Paris. A very young man was sent to fight in Chechnya, his grandmother lived across the border and she got him out. A few months ago we had masses of Georgians and now it's people from the Baltic states.'

After six months of waiting for a decision from the Home Office, the refugees are allowed to work. Zinovieff said she usually didn't find out what happened to the people who come to see her. 'They either set themselves up or the Home Office sends them off. One family was sent back after three or four years here, they had two children and they'd bought a house - it seems grotesque. Nothing seems to deter people from coming. I ask them if they're sorry they came because they're destitute, and most say no. It's no joke to leave your own country and the English are not tremendously friendly. They're unfriendly by nature.'

'I often ask them to write home and tell people not to come,' Zinovieff continued. 'Particularly in Ukraine and the Baltic states there are cowboy organisations which say if you pay us a certain sum of money which includes the fare but is more than the fare, you'll get a job in England. This is grossly dishonest. I've thought of talking to the Foreign Office about it, they should put up a notice in the visa section of the consulate saying what happens if you come, but I don't think they'd agree to that. The irony is that if you leave voluntarily you have to pay your own fare.'

The Refugees Aid Society was doing as much as it could to alleviate people's poverty while they were in Britain. Zinovieff sometimes referred people to the British Refugee Council, which gave advice and provided lawyers. She also wrote official letters in English for refugees who didn't know the language. 'We could open some centre if they were concentrated in one area of London, but they're not,' she said. 'Even getting to me is a problem - they can't pay the fare. Then there's the problem of children. They have to go to school, which they get for free, but they can't afford the uniforms. They don't get school meals. I managed to get £40 a week for a couple with two children. Every borough is different - some boroughs agree that a child who has no food is at risk, some don't. I know a family with twin girls of ten who will have to get uniforms. And boys have all sorts of dreadful sports clothes.

'Before, we could sometimes pay a deposit on a flat. We were particularly interested in education. We have helped people at university - we can't do that any more - there are some very bright people who'd be an asset to this country if they got their degrees. One boy got a scholarship to Oxford. Refugees from all countries have brought talent. There are doctors, architects, a professor of philosophy - a Tajik - it's not just a load of yobbos. I don't know what they're going to do - winter's coming. It has never been a popular cause, especially when we were raising money for old people; it's easy to raise money for puppies and babies. Hostels for the homeless are full of drug addicts and people get their things stolen. They say they'd rather sleep on the streets. Then there's the terrible prisons problem,' she concluded.

'The, er...?' I prompted. I thought prisons were supposed to be terrible.

'The terrible presents problem.'

'Ah!' I said.

'You know what Russians are like, they feel obliged to give you a present. I gave some money to an unmarried pregnant woman and she went out and bought me flowers.'

As I was leaving, the phone rang. The man on the other end was shouting so loudly that I could hear everything he said. He was Lithuanian and he wanted Zinovieff to give him the money for a ticket home. She dismissed him perfunctorily, as if she'd heard it all a thousand times before, which she probably had. 'I can't do anything for you. Make an appointment. You can have one in a month's time, if you want. Goodbye.'

A rather different kind of help was offered by the Russian Immigrant Aid Society in Stamford Hill, north London. I stepped out of the tube station straight into a scene from *Fiddler on the Roof*. The district was teeming with Hasidic Jews in black overcoats and black bowler hats, indifferent to the blazing temperature. Little boys in yarmulkes with locks of curly hair hanging down by their cheeks played football against a wall. The shops sold bagels with every kind of filling; one even had a special offer for the more liberal Jews, or gentiles with a craving - bacon bagels for 50 pence.

The society's office was a tiny room in a council building which housed several different Jewish charities, including a newspaper, *Jewish Tribune*, 'Organ of Anglo-Jewish Orthodoxy'. The representative of the society who I talked to (not quite a Topol lookalike, but well on the way), didn't want me to use his real name, so I'll call him Goldstein. He told me that the Russian Immigrant Aid Society was set up in the early 1970s, when the first Russians were allowed to go to Israel. It was run by Orthodox Jews belonging to the Agudas Israel organisation, which attempted to off-set the influence of secular Jews. The society helped Russian Jews who emigrated to Israel, but since the collapse of the Soviet Union it had also been dealing with Russians in Britain.

'The main purpose of our organisation is to teach Russians about the religion,' Goldstein said. 'We bring children over for a few weeks' holiday, from Moscow, St Petersburg, Gomel, Tbilisi and Alma-Ata. All these places have little groups of Orthodox Jews working there.' Gomel, Tbilisi and Alma-Ata are in other former Soviet republics, but Goldstein didn't differentiate. 'The children, who are aged between 16 and 18, have had a taste of the religion, but I wouldn't say they're committed. We have a building in Epping, where they live within a Jewish environment, have outings, recreation, a swimming pool, and there's lots of grass to kick a ball about. The idea is that it's an opportunity to try Orthodox Jewish life, but we leave it up to them whether they want to continue with it or not. We've had about five or six hundred children over here since we started. Their parents often just know they're Jewish, but don't know what it is. They feel something has been denied to them and they get interested, but they often think it's too restrictive.'

Orthodoxy demands not only a complete abandonment of activity on the Sabbath (you must not turn on a light or any other electrical appliance), a new wardrobe and hairstyle, and separate kitchen utensils for meat and milk dishes, but also - for men - a painful separation from a useless but cherished bodily part, the foreskin. 'None of the Russian males have been circumcised,' Goldstein told me. 'We try to encourage it and often send people over to Russia to do it - they can do 30 to 40 in a day, from 8-day-old babies to adults of any age. As it happens, we have a group of Russians here at the moment who do not particularly wish to have the operation.'

I asked Goldstein whether this reluctance would exclude the men from the faith altogether. 'We're not Mormons, who brainwash you and cut you off from everything you've had before. But they will come to a point when they'll have a conflict within themselves because they're not circumcised. Nobody would know, but it would be very hypocritical.'

In addition to circumcision, there was yet another obstacle to Orthodoxy which no operation could remove. 'There are two or three million Jews in Russia, but we don't really know the numbers,' Goldstein said. 'To us, only people born of a Jewish mother are Jewish, or anyone who has been converted. Some of the Russian Jews are illegitimate. It's not their fault, but we consider a child to be illegitimate if it is born when a man has a relationship with a married woman, and as a Rabbinical bill of divorce is not the same as a divorce in court, many second civil marriages in Russia cannot be recognised by us, so the children of them are illegitimate. Illegitimate children can only marry amongst themselves, and most of the people who get the illegitimate stigma leave the religion.'

Despite all that, Goldstein had had some success with his campaign. 'A couple of the young Russian men have become too Orthodox, I've told them they've gone too far, but they won't listen. It's funny, a few years ago they were living with girls, getting up to all kinds of things, and now they walk down the street with their heads bowed, not looking at anyone.' I wondered if I could meet them. 'They won't talk to you,' Goldstein said, 'because you're a woman and they are unmarried men.'

Those few Russians who decided to embrace Orthodoxy were assisted by Goldstein's organisation in their applications for asylum. Their religion gave them grounds to claim that they would be persecuted in Russia, according to Goldstein. 'They do have an argument, because they look different, and there is anti-Semitism in Russia. There is a breakdown of authority there, it's a new country building itself; in Moscow, gangs of hooligans will beat up Orthodox Jews. Here, we have our own schools. Yes, we get taunted in some areas of London, if we go to Brixton, for instance, but it's not usual to experience actual bodily violence. There are about 5000 Orthodox Jews in Stamford Hill and another 4000 in northwest London. If one of us was attacked, he'd just have to shout, 'Help!' and 30 or 40 comrades would come running.

'The British authorities deal very kindly with Jewish immigrants. We have about ten asylum applications pending and about ten people already leave to stay here. I haven't heard of anyone being turned down. They can always go to Israel if they can't stay here.' I again asked Goldstein if I could meet a Russian Jewish immigrant, and he said he would see what he could do. I didn't hear from him again. Zinovieff wouldn't give me the telephone number of any refugee who had come to her, but she said encouragingly, 'You'll find some. They're everywhere.' I was dubious, but she turned out to be right.

I didn't have to advertise - the Rozhdyestvenye family advertised themselves. The parents, Lev and Irina, and one of their daughters had formed a musical trio called the Moscow Dawn Ensemble. They lived in east London, a few minutes from West Ham football ground. As I walked to their house I passed a laundry with a large sign on the roof, 'DON'T KILL YOUR WIFE - LET US DO IT FOR YOU', and a group of black people in traditional African clothes who were standing outside a funeral parlour. The Rozhdyestvenye family's house was small and spartan, undecorated, apart from Lev's abstract paintings, a poster for one of the trio's concerts and an old poster with a picture of Lev on it from a gig he did with the Moscow Saxophone Quintet - he played bass guitar.

I sat down at the kitchen table and had a cup of tea with Lev and Irina. The bare table and chairs could have come from a school dining hall; they probably did. The family came to London from Moscow in February 1994 and in that time Irina had got a Cambridge Advanced Certificate in English and an NVQ in Business Administration. Lev apologised to me for speaking Russian. He was clearly deeply into his music - towards the end of our discussion he left to go and practise the violin. This was how the conversation went.

IRINA: At first we were in a council house in this area and then we moved here. Some people think this is a terrible district, but I don't think it's so bad - I've heard that White City is worse, for instance. Anyway, the children were at school here, so we didn't want to move away. We have two daughters here, 13 and 14 years old, and another daughter in Moscow. She's 24. There aren't special Russian societies in London. Ukrainians and Poles have their own communities, but Russians don't. Russians are separate here.
SARAH: Is that because they have to live so close together in Russia?
IRINA: No, they're not close together, you can imagine that they're close, but that's just on the surface. Even when there was communism, on the surface we were all together but you couldn't say what everyone was thinking inside. Anyway, I've lived in a separate flat all my life. In the kitchens in Russia, only very, very close friends discuss their problems with each other.
LEV: People don't change. If you read Dostoyevsky, he says that a simple person doesn't mind being in prison. He's still a simple person. It depends on the level of development. I like talking to artists - I'm used to it. I can't talk to ordinary workers, I can't find anything in common with them. Maybe in church there's some kind of Russian community -
IRINA: I went to the Russian Orthodox church in Kensington once, I think fifty percent of the people there were British.

LEV: What I really like is the libraries here. It's hard to get into the Lenin Library. Even books on 20th-century art are hard to find in Moscow. I'm amazed at how much they collect here, even books on how to paint Russian icons.

IRINA: He enjoys the libraries here very much because they're easy to get into. You can use them all, not just the ones in your area. There's the Britain-Russia Centre, that's very good. Although concerts are expensive, we can listen to Classic FM. And we find out what's going on from Golos Rossii [the Russian overseas radio station]. You can get good Russian films from libraries. The Nikita Mikhalkov film *Black Eyes* was on television here and in the newspaper it was given a low rating, one or two stars. The critic said it was a rather boring comedy. I watched it and thought - where is the comedy? It's not comedy, it's sarcasm. But it's probably boring compared with American films. It's not as fast-moving. There is time to think as you watch.

SARAH: Why did you leave Russia?

LEV: Because of political problems. We had to leave urgently, in three days. Each Russian has his own problems, it's not like the war in Yugoslavia. For some people there are economic advantages.

IRINA: We gave up everything when we left. We didn't want to become New Russians, to start our own company.

LEV: We wanted to play music.

IRINA: We had to leave our instruments behind, because it's illegal to take valuables out of the country. We left two pianos, a flute, a violin... But people helped us straight away. We thought of the children first of all. Our daughter was studying at a specialist music school in Moscow. Materially, we were well-off.

LEV: Maybe we can go back now, things have changed.

IRINA: There's no future here - we live out of suitcases. A letter of refusal could come from the Home Office any day. We can't plan our lives, although in the last months in Russia we couldn't plan our lives, either. It was unstable. When Lev saw Britain, he said, 'It's a country for pensioners!'

LEV: When people ask me why I left, I say because of political problems with my government. I don't want to be reminded of it. There was a power struggle going on all the time. When there's a power struggle, Russians lose control, become wild. As they say, 'When you cut wood, chips will fly.' My life was under threat. If I'd been alone, if I hadn't had a family, I could have gone to the KGB man downstairs and bought a pistol and a hand grenade from him. I could have defended myself. I'd have fought. But I'm not going to go into it. It's another story. You could write a thriller.

IRINA: I didn't work, I was a housewife. He was earning enough money to support me. But when one of my children wanted to go for a walk, I couldn't let her go out on her own, I had to hold her hand.

LEV: For the last ten years I was an artist, not a musician. I don't know why I am here. I don't do anything, I just think.

IRINA: When we got here, I went to the Purcell School to ask about our daughter, because it was linked with the school where she studied in Moscow. But it was £12,000 per year. They couldn't take her. They advised us to go to the Guildhall at the Barbican. It accepted her. A fund for Russian refugees gave us £200 for a flute. The Guildhall, where she studies on Saturdays, costs £450 per term. The local comprehensive, Brompton Manor School, sponsors her to go there. It also gave us a keyboard and a ¾-size violin for our youngest daughter. For fun we tried to play together, Lev on the small violin, me on the keyboard, and Marina on the flute. Our neighbours, who are Americans, invited us to play in a Methodist church where he is a priest. We played on Sundays. Classical music - Bach and Tchaikovsky.

We have friends in Wimbledon, a Russian woman called Galina and her English husband. She worked in the Central House of Art Workers in Moscow. She's a very good organiser, and we played at her barbecue. She said we should organise a concert. She got us in touch with the Starlight Enterprise Agency. We've done between ten and fifteen concerts, in London and outside London.

SARAH: If you don't want to tell me why you left Russia, will you tell me why you chose Britain?

IRINA: In 1992 Lev and his brother had an exhibition of their paintings in Chelsea. His brother had a contract with the gallery, he was supposed to live in England, he said it was great for artists here. Lev came and had a look and said no, everyone counts money here. For the Russian intelligentsia, it's embarrassing to say they can't afford something. It's strange if you can't afford to visit someone because of the cost of the tube fare. Even if it's expensive for me, I'll go, buy flowers, chocolates, cake -

LEV: It's a Russian characteristic.

IRINA: Yes, it's a Russian characteristic. Even if I have to live on bread for three days afterwards. It's strange for us when a middle-class person tells everyone that yesterday they bought something at a sale. Even if they did buy something at a sale, they wouldn't tell people about it in Russia.

LEV: I have an acquaintance here, an English man who was a teacher at Moscow State University. So we knew people here. Although my brother's back in Russia now.

SARAH: How did the children react when you left?

LEV: We didn't tell them anything. We just said we were going on an outing. For a few months.

SARAH: Were you interviewed by the British authorities when you came here?

LEV: Well, you can't say at the consulate in Moscow that you're going to claim asylum. Irina bought a package tour for her and the children and they got their visas automatically. I bought a business-class ticket. I'd already been abroad and come back several times, so it wasn't a problem.

IRINA: Our eldest daughter is there. She came to visit us last year, but now she can't get a visa. They tell her she's not earning enough. They give visas to rich people. This is a closed country. I'm very disappointed.

SARAH: How do British people generally react to you?

IRINA: We've been to parties, and we're always asked the same questions - 'When did you come here?' and 'How do you like it?' They think it's always cold in Russia. They all love Gorby - he's sacred. When I start to criticise him, they say, 'no, no, no.' A lot of people say they're meeting a Russian for the first time in their life.

SARAH: Do you have a place to live in Russia if you're sent back?

IRINA: We had a dacha in Ukraine, but we sold it to buy the tickets. We have a flat in Moscow where our daughter lives, and we'll go there if we are sent back. She doesn't talk about us - the neighbours think we're in Ukraine.

SARAH (to Lev): Are you a member of a political party?

212

LEV: No, my party is art.

IRINA: Under communism you knew what was forbidden. Now you don't know who you'll offend.

LEV: But there's no material for me here. Chechnya is a subject, for instance, if I went back I could do something on Chechnya, but then a Chechen might want to kill me. Here everything's fine, it's quiet. I know a Russian here who wants to work in an office, have a house and a car - but I want things to be happening, to be stormy. Growing roses is boring.

IRINA: I have to find work here, but it's not worth earning £150 a week and losing my benefits. We buy our clothes in the charity shop, we count every kopeck. We pay £125 every three months for Lev's violin. We have to phone Russia sometimes. We economise very strictly here - we didn't in Russia. The house costs £150 a week and we get £120 housing benefit, so we have to make it up somehow. If I'm going to have a career here, it's a very long path. But in Russia most of the jobs are offered only to people under 35. We live day by day. As my mum says, another day has passed, praise God. We live in eternal expectancy of the refusal letter. We've thought about Canada, but we need £10,000 for that - it's not realistic. We have to wait for the refusal and to be sent home for free.

I don't regret coming here, we were under great stress in Russia, it was a difficult time for us. At least the children don't cry at night now. We're more relaxed. I've always remembered what my dad said, even though he'd never been anywhere - people are the same everywhere, they have the same problems.

I went to see Natasha Chouvaeva to talk about her Russian-language newspaper, the *London Courier*, and discovered that she and her husband were amongst the lucky few to have been granted 'exceptional leave to remain in the UK' after the collapse of the Soviet Union. Natasha and Yevgeny arrived in Britain a few months before the 1991 coup attempt. 'We were granted asylum quite quickly because we weren't bogus,' Chouvaeva told me. 'But getting citizenship is a long process, seven years, I think, and we haven't got it yet.'

Yevgeny came from a Russian family which lived in Azerbaijan, and he was due to serve in the Azerbaijani army and fight in the war with Armenia. So he and Natasha left, when they were both aged 25. They were both graduates of the Lenin State Pedagogical Institute in Moscow, which had strong links with Surrey University. That was how they made contacts in Britain. They moved to Redhill in Surrey and in 1995 Natasha had a baby daughter, Marie. 'You couldn't get a proper job in Azerbaijan if you were Russian,' Chouvaeva explained. 'A white girl [i.e. not from the Caucasus] couldn't walk on her own in the street - there was so much harassment, as in every eastern country.'

Chouvaeva never expected to become the founder editor of the newspaper for Russians in London. She had no experience in journalism until she came here - she trained as an interpreter and translator. 'When I came here I was looking for a job and I found one with the magazine *Russian Business International*, which was based in Redhill and has now ceased to exist,' she said. 'It was one of the first Russian-language publications in Britain. I started there as a translator and then I did some writing, but very little. I don't write very much now, although it's fun. I don't pretend to be a journalist - I'm more of an organiser. I keep track of what's going on in London, send people out to cover events.'

In its two years of existence the paper's circulation had increased from 2000 to 15,000. It was distributed free by five airlines and about 1000 people in Britain and Russia subscribed. The style of the paper was mixed - there was serious news and commentary on events in Russia, but also humorous features about life in Britain from the well-known journalist Vitali Vitaliev (a regular guest on the Clive James show) and English Corner by a jovial chap called Brian Lockett, who explained the meanings of anachronistic phrases such as 'What the Dickens?' and 'Job's comforter'. To help Russians with their visa problems, there was a Legal Advice column written by solicitors. 'But I think the British rules are fair,' Chouvaeva said. 'There are too many economic immigrants. The country isn't that big and it can't fit everyone in.'

Before the birth of the *London Courier*, there was no source of information for Russians in Britain. Chouvaeva always asked people to bring Russian papers when they came over. The *London*

Courier had four contributors in Russia, including Yevgenia from *The St Petersburg Press*, who provided a digest of the Russian press in each issue. The paper appeared monthly at first, then went twice-monthly in its second year. 'When I started I didn't think I could make a living from it - but I do. I was on my own at first. Yevgeny had a job with a Ukrainian bank, but now he's full-time here. The biggest problem at the beginning was distribution. Companies like WH Smith and the *International Herald Tribune* would laugh at me. I collected addresses from all sorts of sources and sent the paper out to them.'

Chouvaeva didn't know the precise number of Russians in London, but estimated that there were 70,000 at any one time. 'It's a very controversial figure, I don't have anything to prove it, but if you use immigration statistics, our mailing lists and common sense, you get that figure.' I asked her why Russians were so reluctant to make contact with each other. 'One of the reasons why Russians are here is because they were not happy with the way they were treated in Russia. When I first arrived, I was so glad to hear Russian in the street that I would approach the person, but now - no way. Safety's not the reason. It's a waste of time. There aren't many interesting Russians shopping. If I was at a business meeting I would want to talk to them, but for a commercial reason. I'm commercially motivated. Every Russian is a potential subscriber, a source of information or a source for an interview.

'I think Russians don't socialise much with each other because there is some kind of jealousy,' she continued. 'If a person who's middle class sees a rich Russian, there's a certain inferiority complex because he hasn't done so well, he can't afford to shop in Knightsbridge. Anyway, these New Russians are so vulgar, swearing too loud, you don't want to know those people, it's a shame they're from the same country as you. There are a few Russian restaurants in London, but I wouldn't call them meeting places. I go there once a year, when I'm nostalgic and want to speak Russian. There were a few concerts of Russian bands which attracted large numbers of people.'

I was intrigued by the selection of advertisements which the *London Courier* carried. There was one for a traditional Russian

215

dumplings delivery service (minimum order 150 for £15), a job ad for investment officers in Ukraine, several English-language schools and translation agencies, Lyuba's Bistro, the Al Basha Lebanese restaurant, the Russian Art Studio and a 'famous fortune-teller'. In the issue I looked at there was also a personal announcement: 'MY NEW NAME. I, a dissident from Russia, Nikolai Ivanovich BARANOV, declare that from now my name Nikolai has been changed to ADOLPH.'

I asked Chouvaeva whether the Russian companies which advertised in her paper were successful. 'Russian companies in London haven't made millions of pounds, but they're growing and the number of them is increasing. It's quite easy to set up a company here. Quite a few are just cheating, they have a very short life. We ran an ad for the International Financial Fund, which wanted people to invest a minimum of $10,000. It was absolutely fake. They didn't pay for their ad and their phones were disconnected. Telesales companies are very famous for not organising exhibitions and conferences the way they promise, they just rip people off and disappear with the money. Russian Pelmeni (dumplings delivery) is a good company. Everybody who has used it orders again and again. I've tried them - they're quite delicious.'

Some British companies were also becoming aware that targeting Russians could be lucrative. One which advertised in the *London Courier* was Philip Hockley of Mayfair, 'because not many English people are interested in fur.' The paper was going strong, but Chouvaeva had her regrets. 'I had lots of friends in Russia who I don't see now,' she said. When she left, she had no idea that communism was about to disappear. 'If I look back, I would have stayed if I could. But I didn't. And in spite of all the changes, I don't want to go back there now.'

Whilst everyone I had talked to insisted that Russians in London generally avoided each other, there were one or two places where they could be found. For instance, there was the Britain-Russia Centre in Grosvenor Place. Admittedly, from the outside it didn't look particularly welcoming to the public, as it was one of a row of elegant mansion houses with a gold plate on the door and an intercom for visitors to speak through. But membership was a reasonable £20 per year, and for that price you received a journal three times a year, use of the library and information about the talks on all subjects which were held at the centre.

I spoke to Helen O'Connor, the centre's information officer and journal editor. She studied Russian at Leeds University in the 1970s, but for years hardly used the language at all. 'There were very few opportunities. I went into the information business, I drifted there by default - mainly database production - and I eventually ended up in the electricity industry for seven years. I used languages and worked in overseas relations, but mainly German and French. I never went to Russia at all during my previous career. I started here in 1990.'

The Britain-Russia Centre was set up in 1959 in opposition to Dom Druzhbi (House of Friendship) and the British-Soviet Friendship Society, which were 'front organisations for Soviet propaganda', according to O'Connor. 'MPs and members of the government felt there should be a counterbalance to this, a medium for information and a forum for mutual relations. We are funded by the Foreign Office. Our work has changed radically in the last few years. It used to be mainly cultural, now it encompasses everything. In those days you couldn't just invite whoever you wanted, the Soviet government had the final say. It is now the main body in the UK for providing information on Russia and fostering contacts with other republics, apart from the Baltics. We call it the British East-West Centre if we send a letter to Kyrgyzstan, for instance.'

The noticeboard and the talks at the centre were an excellent way of finding Russians in London, although only about 180 of the centre's 1500 members were Russian. 'That's gone up enormously since 1991,' said O'Connor. 'The proportion seems to be going up all the time. Our non-Russian members are a mixture of business people, people who use Russian in their jobs, teachers, students, people with Russian friends and people learning Russian for recreation. A lot of students can get books which aren't in their university libraries, or are often out of their libraries. Our library is very small and quite manageable.'

More people were getting interested in Russia, O'Connor added. 'Now that it is so much easier to travel independently, people are planning their own journeys. But sometimes I have to tell them their plans are going to fail. A couple came in here recently who wanted to go on a motorcycle trip all round Russia and the Caucasus, but they didn't even know there were wars going on there. They just drew a line on the map. A large proportion of our researchers are in the arts - costume designers, set designers, photographers, people in the media and film world.'

Diplomacy was crucial in the work of the Britain-Russia Centre, O'Connor stressed. 'The Russian ambassador has given a talk here and we can't express disapproval of the Russian government's policies, we have to keep on good terms with them.' Nevertheless, O'Connor herself had strong views on matters such as Chechnya. 'Britain is doing nothing,' she said. 'The government wants to be on good terms with Yeltsin and doesn't want to rock the boat. The official line is that it's an internal affair of Russia. I feel that the whole thing was a tragic mistake, Russia should never have invaded. They should have put a frontier around Chechnya and made all Chechens have visas to come to Russia. I see young men here, aged 19 or 20, who are probably evading military service. I think individuals in Britain are sympathetic to them, but the British government isn't.'

I pointed out that the British expatriate community in Russia didn't always promote harmonious relations between the two countries. 'Yes, but in the business community we're not as bad as the Americans who have a very arrogant attitude and go over to make a quick buck, they think everything ought to be done their way. We let people see for themselves. Russians are aware that there are companies trying to foist sub-standard products on them.'

Our conversation was interrupted by a telephone call. Apparently someone wanted to know how to say 'hello' in Russian, as O'Connor replied, 'You can say dobriy dyen. That's d-o-b...'

'You must get some interesting queries,' I said.

'Yes, we've had people ringing because they wanted to give their racehorses Russian names - spelt the French way - and because they wanted to give their child a Russian name. Whenever someone phones the Russian embassy and asks a question which isn't to do with visas, they are referred to us.'

Another way to meet Russians in London was through one of the two Russian Orthodox churches. Apparently (I found this out later), there was a mainstream church and a fringe church. The mainstream church was in Kensington. I went to the one in Gunnersbury. The services were advertised in the *London Courier*, so I phoned the priest, Father Vadim Zakrevsky, and asked him if I could come and talk to him. He suggested meeting after a Wednesday morning service. The incense was in full swing when I arrived at the large, white-painted house. I'd brought a jacket with a hood, anticipating that I'd have to cover my head, but I was halted at the door by a sign, 'Women with uncovered heads or wearing trousers should not enter!!!' I was wearing trousers, but in any case there was hardly any room inside and the entrance hall was packed, too.

I could see enough to know that the interior of an Orthodox church had been replicated in every detail, from the icons, candles and ornate swing doors to the choir of babushkas. The church had an honoured guest that day - Mark, archbishop of Germany and Britain. I gathered from a notice outside the church that this was a stern patriarch. 'On the ground of the calumny against fellow Christians spread in the August issue of Orthodox News, Andrew Bond is forbidden to fulfil any of his duties as a reader until complete repentance. Hereby all his rights and privileges as a reader are suspended. Mark, Erzbischof von Berlin und Deutschland.' Next to that there was an advertisement posted by Dr Marina Chernova, gastroenterologist with private clinic, offering hydrotherapy sessions.

The other people with me in the entrance hall included a Serbian woman with her baby, a dishevelled man with a long, grey beard and a young man who looked like a deserter from the Russian army, but disappointingly turned out to have a London accent. I went away to a café for a couple of hours. When I came back, no one had moved, apart from a few parents who had taken their babies to the front to be blessed. Things seemed to be drawing to a close, finally, when the entire congregation filed out behind the priests with their banners. To my dismay, they shuffled all around the house and stopped in the garden when they'd done a full circuit, while the priests sprinkled incense everywhere. Then they filed back into the church. Eventually, the service did end and I was invited in with them for lunch.

The walls of the room where we ate were graced by pictures of Nicholas II, Cossacks on horseback, and double-headed eagle banners. Apparently I had stumbled on the headquarters of the Russian monarchists. The young man opposite me, a second-generation immigrant, was chairman of the Society of Russian Monarchists. Also present was the 84-year-old, one-eyed Ataman of the Cossacks in London. Most of the congregation were nearer to his age than mine, although at my left arm I had Adrian, in his twenties, who said he had become Orthodox in Greece and thought that people who wore black ties were agents of the Antichrist. He told me the church had an icon which wept tears of myrrh. He took a plastic bag out of his pocket which had something white in it that looked like cotton and said that this was weeped myrrh.

After the lunch (they do say, there's no such thing as a free lunch - and they're right), I talked to Father Zakrevsky, who was in his thirties and had a black beard which was attractive as it was priestly. Having noted the average age of the congregation, I asked him whether any new immigrants ever came to the church. 'New immigrants don't know what the church is, they don't need the church,' he said. 'Many of them are like a small child taking its first steps, learning to go to church. They're drawn to God - that's normal - but they need lessons. You have to find the way to the person's soul. In Australia, an Orthodox church used a jazz band to attract young people there. I don't think that's the right way of doing it - those people who went didn't get what they were supposed to get in church. The right path is through belief and love. But it's also the most complicated path. You have to explain the point and significance of the church.'

Father Zakrevsky explained what the difference was between his church and the one in Kensington. 'There's the Russian Church of the Moscow Patriarch, and there's ours, the Russian Church in Exile. It was founded by people who left Russia after 1917 with the White emigration. They didn't want to stay in a country which was destroying the church. The church which remained in the Soviet Union changed so much - there were some negative aspects. We're not in the world council of churches; the Moscow church is. I think it leads to the destruction of belief. Churches lose their traditions. We want to preserve the religion as it is. We believe in the Second Coming and the Day of Judgement.'

Apart from the services, the church held a Sunday school where children learnt Russian, music and religious studies. It was trying to raise £600,000 (of which £144,000 had already been donated), to build a new church which would look like a church rather than a house. 'We have a British architect consulting with Russian specialists on the plans,' Father Zakrevsky said. 'We've asked for a donation from Prince Charles and he promised us one in a letter, but we haven't got it yet. Count Andrei Tolstoy, the brother of [historian] Count Nikolai Tolstoy, is the chairman of the fund-raising committee.'

Father Zakrevsky came to England in 1992. I was curious about why he left, just when religion became legal again. 'People who were communists in Russia yesterday are democrats today, what does it matter, they have the same principles. I became a priest under Gorbachev, in Ukraine, and I saw incorrect things in church, but I couldn't understand what they were. I wrote a letter to Mark and then saw a different life in the Church in Exile.' Did he miss Russia? 'Well, it's my country, it's where I was born, I have my brother, sister and parents there. But only here I have the freedom to correctly and openly practise religion, so when I think about that, I don't want to go back. A lot has changed in Russia, but it's not all for the best.'

The picture of Nicholas II was in the church because he and his family had been canonised as saints, Father Zakrevsky told me. He himself wasn't a monarchist. 'We have the pictures so that the old émigrés can remember the imperial family, remember the traditions before communism. The Church doesn't involve itself in politics. Personally, I think that politics isn't a completely clean thing, it's better to pray.' But the next person I talked to at the church had left Russia because of his monarchist beliefs. Mikhail, 36, also came to Britain in 1992.

'Lots of people leave because they don't accept the changes,' he said. 'I had my own problems, being in the monarchist movement. I worked for Intourist. When I travelled, I distributed monarchist literature, and in the summer of 1992 I had conversations about this with the KGB. They told me they would take my foreign passport away. So on my next trip abroad for Intourist I stayed and claimed asylum. Now I constantly listen to Radio Liberty and Golos Rossii and I've noticed a decline, not just in the economy, but in morals. Young people are becoming criminals. In Britain a person can work and exist honestly. It's very hard, or even impossible to do that in Russia outside Moscow and St Petersburg.'

Mikhail was from Rostov-on-Don. In London he worked for a company which helped Russian businessmen. 'A lot of people start to miss Russia after they've been here for a year or so, and they go back, or to America or Canada. But compared to Germany or Belgium there are no bad feelings towards Russians here, I've never felt any hostility. Maybe because Russia and Britain fought together twice against the Germans. Most Russians here are law-abiding, they don't try to do anything criminal.' I asked him if he was still a monarchist. He was pragmatic. 'A return to the past hasn't found support in Russia. Russia has gone down a third path. There are attributes of monarchy, such as the flag, but unfortunately we won't see a monarchy in Russia this century.'

The last Russian who I interviewed about life in foggy Albion divided her time between London and Birmingham. Masha, a 28-year-old post-graduate student from Moscow, was the daughter of a diplomat and an English-language linguist. She had an extraordinary childhood: she was born in Vienna and spent her first five years there, then the family moved back to Moscow, and in 1976 they moved to New York, where Masha's father was working at the United Nations. 'I loved New York,' Masha told me. 'I wanted to try all those disgusting things like cornflakes, cereals and candies. If my mother hadn't stopped me, I would have eaten all this junk and probably wouldn't have survived.'

Masha and her parents lived in a flat on the 17th floor, in a compound for Soviet families surrounded by a high fence. 'It was a kind of Soviet Union implanted in New York. I probably would have done the same things if I'd been in the Soviet Union at the time, except that we had gadgets from the outside, frozen pizzas, cartoons on television that we watched.' There was even a Soviet-style pioneer camp. When Masha returned to Moscow, in 1980, she 'didn't want to create unnecessary fuss,' so she didn't tell her classmates that she'd been to America. 'Then I told my friends and they were flabbergasted. That was much later. I was fourteen. I timed it right, it didn't matter, they were already my friends.'

Masha studied political economy at Moscow State University, hoping to specialise and study the US economy. 'After I'd been in the States I had this bug in me, I wanted to study America and go there.' To enter the department, she had to be recommended by the local Communist Party committee. 'I told the guy I wanted to study the economies of foreign countries to take the best bits and apply them to our socialist economy. He thought I was mad. He didn't think I should look for good things in a capitalist society. But he did recommend me.' She studied French and Italian as well as political economy and graduated a few months before the 1991 coup attempt.

'We were at the family dacha outside Moscow when the coup happened. A woman, one of the neighbours, came rushing in and told us that this thing had happened. At first we didn't believe it. We thought we were living in a stable society. I had predicted that by autumn the Soviet Union would collapse, but not in that way, you don't expect it to happen when you're doing mushroom-hunting. It makes things more acute. I had to go to the university for something. I was on Kutuzovsky Prospekt waiting for a bus and tanks were passing by me - then it really hit me. A woman grabbed me and began to cry on my shoulder, and said it was like the war again. I rushed back to the dacha to be with my mother and we stayed there for the rest of the coup. We did think of taking some sandwiches to the barricades, but we didn't do it, so I won't say I was a hero.'

Masha came to Britain in 1992 and did a Masters degree at University College, London. Then she began her PhD at the University of Birmingham, on 'Restructuring, privatisation and conversion of Russian enterprises during Russian economic transition.' I thought it ironic that she decided to study a Russian topic. 'When you're in the Soviet Union, the rest of the world seems more interesting. Once you are abroad, it's more interesting to study your own country.' She considered Britain the most tolerant towards foreigners out of all European countries, although there were some drawbacks. 'Deep inside, the English think they're superior - they're category 1, people from the EU are category 2 and Russians are category 3, maybe before the blacks. It does exist, not in all people, but as a system of society. But they don't openly make you feel uncomfortable. They can make it felt in other ways, the reserved English sarcastic way of saying things, but usually people refrain from that.'

Academic resources here were very good, Masha said. 'The level of library provision and funding is much greater here than in Russia. I kind of look down on my economics department now, because I think it was all a waste of time. Languages there were on a very high level, though. In science the standard was also very high. Russian university education is quite different from university education here, it's more encompassing, there are lots of subjects, you can go to different departments and listen to lectures. Here, people have four courses in a term. It's nothing - we had about twenty at a time - not that a lot of it's left in my head. The bad thing about it was that most of the subjects were obligatory. We took on the German system.'

When she was at university in Moscow, Masha lived with her parents, so she enjoyed the freedom of student life here. 'Students' residence was a revelation for me. The hall of residence at Birmingham was brilliant, we had parties, there was a Franco-Russian mutual admiration society.' I asked her if the British were as she'd imagined them to be. 'I've found worse things in them than their stereotypes,' she said. 'The perverse nature of the English, their eerie fascination with animal copulation and scenes of animal violence that they seem to like to watch on television nature programmes. But for a foreigner this is the best place, although it can be boring. English people don't know how to have fun. Like getting together and having a nice talk and getting deep into things - they don't do that, people just get pissed.'

Russia in 2020

This was my entry for a 1995 essay-writing competition limited only by the title and a maximum of 2000 words. It won the competition, organised by the Centre for Russian and East European Studies (CREES) at the University of Birmingham, and a copy of it is in the CREES archive, to be opened in 2020. In the original, former general Alexander Rutskoi was elected president in 1996 and Boris Yeltsin tried to make a speech on a Mercedes. As the 1996 election is now in the past, I have updated the story a little. Former general Alexander Lebed uncannily fits in to Rutskoi's role.

We have caught up at last. The bright future is in our grasp - that is - the day when Russia takes her rightful leading place in the superstrata of international communications. We are in the final stages of the electronification of every single word published here since words could be printed, and as the Virtual President (the ViP) inspirationally declared in his annual CD-ROM address downloaded to each citizen personally in their own cubicles, 'Millennialism is the free market economy plus the electronification of the whole country.'

I am so proud to be a vital node in the organism which is giving birth to this marvel, gestating and blossoming faster than similar, smaller projects in the Southeast Asian Confederation, and, of course, way ahead of the United States of Europe, Britain, or America.

All that remains to do is to finish photo-inputting the Zs. We use the Roman alphabet for filing, for the benefit of the world cybercommunity. When native users type in Cyrillic their cubicle information centre instantaneously translates each word or letter into international English (IN-GLISH), so that anyone in the world can read their message. The receiving modem translates it into the foreign language. The same happens with our new electrolibrary: we photo-input the original Russian text and the computer automatically stores it in IN-GLISH. I supervise the photo-inputting of fictional works.

The work programme for completing the Zs is preset to terminate in 120 days. We rarely pause - two-point-five minutes is the stipulated hourly break for expulsion of unwanted fluids or ingestion of nutrition - but as I scan the constellation of words which glows and hums on my monitor, my eye occasionally alights upon something so beautiful that I cannot fail to be distracted by it. Or so significant - as has happened this minute. A passage from Zamyatin's *We*, a novel which is a century old this year: 'We have succeeded in constructing a temporary wall of high voltage waves on the transversal 40th Prospect.' How prophetic... If it weren't for our cocooning cone of steel shields curving up into the clouds, narrowing to a distant, shimmering spire which mockingly points to the moon like a rocket, we'd all be sheltering in bombed-out buildings and teaching our fur-clad children to spear wild horses.

We are enclosed in a prison of our own making. That was the cost of preserving the democratic Russia which our parents won on the White House barricades. After Alexander Lebed won the snap presidential election of 1998 which followed Boris Yeltsin's long-anticipated demise, promising to 'restore order and dignity to the Russian nation,' he declared martial law and announced that Russia needed no more foreign loans. It seemed that we were about to experience 'capitalism in one country'.

A law was passed banning any 'non-Russian products which we already manufacture ourselves', including cigarettes, vodka, dumplings, condoms, shoes, pistols, tractors and souvenir paperweight busts of famous writers. McDonald's, Mars bars and Mexican soap operas survived the rout because the government feared a popular uprising if they were to go. All homeless people were dragged off the streets and put into uniform; if they weren't fit for the army (most were), they became hospital orderlies or ticket collectors on trams and buses. In these cases they could be put in prison for ten days if they didn't turn up for work. Harsher punishments were introduced for all crimes, especially hooliganism, which included dropping litter and being drunk in public - the penalty for these offences was a five-year spell of working with nuclear waste. Juveniles were sent to assist with the rebuilding of Grozny, which was renamed Grachev (Grozny was a terrible name, anyway), after the new governor of Rossiskaya Chechnya.

Disgruntled millionaires began to form secret societies and send faxes attacking Lebed. There was a month's private vehicle amnesty in which BMWs and Toyotas were supposed to be exchanged for Ladas and Volgas, but the government was astounded to discover that in the whole of Moscow apparently only eleven people owned foreign cars, and all of them were Africans who did not wish to be deported. Figures were even lower for the rest of the country. Around this time, sales of grey spray-paint soared to an unprecedented level. Car-owners lay low for a while, but they were already plotting their revenge. Communicating by mobile phone and e-mail, they set the date for the Great April Manezh Square Park-in, as we now know it.

Subsisting only on cognac and Big Macs for six days and nights, with nothing but their car stereos and the rousing speeches of company directors to keep their spirits up, these heroes of the Russian investing class brought Moscow to a standstill and the country to the brink of a new era. Lebed ordered the army to disperse the demonstrators and seize their vehicles, but the rebels had already prepared for this contingency. Each approaching soldier was handed a wad of banknotes, $100 for ordinary conscripts and up to $10,000 for colonels and generals. There were few moral dilemmas: tanks and guns were turned around to face in the direction of the Kremlin.

This would have been a bloodless revolution, except that Gennady Zyuganov, sensing the last chance for his embittered Communist Party to regain power, attempted to emulate Boris Yeltsin's actions of August 1991 by climbing onto the polished roof of a Mercedes estate and addressing the crowd. Just as he was about to open his mouth, a gust of wind caused him to lose his balance and he toppled over, hitting his head on the protruding manufacturer's emblem. He never regained consciousness.

Lebed fled the capital, but he was not alone. Doctors, teachers, post office workers and indeed most state employees quickly realised that there was no place for them in a city now dedicated to the free market in its purest form. Non-profitable schools and hospitals were to be closed down. The Coca-Cola Pushkin Museum was one of the first galleries to be ceremonially renamed.

The construction of the shields began almost immediately, because the hordes of poor people clamouring to be allowed into the city had become unmanageable; shields were needed to protect Moscow from the army of unwealthy elements, conscious-stricken students, Djugashvili junkies, cassocks and Cossacks who were marching towards it. A single nuclear missile fired into the Urals was enough to keep them at bay while the shields were completed, as the inhabitants of cities realised they ought to behave themselves or be reduced to very fine particles of radioactive dust, and in the countryside Lebed's army could not get enough supplies together to mount a serious attack. Even so, it was deemed prudent to drop some conventional bombs on random sections of the population to demonstrate the strength of the dollar.

So we have two Russias, the Inner and the Outer. Our Inner state has become self-sufficient, generating the precious light and electricity which the Outer Russia has lacked ever since radioactivity made most of Siberia uninhabitable. Outside, the masses of Ineligibles who cannot afford to enter our shining bastion of freedom live off what is left of the land. Towns and cities, squalid and unhygienic, were abandoned as flat-dwellers transmuted into nomads. Crumbling churches, palaces and monuments remind the wretched travellers of the lost civilisation which was once theirs. There is no law out there. We watch them on our giant public monitors, installed on every square metre of the shields - not only so that we can instantly identify and repel attackers with our deadly lasers - but also to save us from mental instability by showing us that we are not all alone in a vacuum; on the contrary, we live on a paradise island in the midst of madness.

'Naked, they took to the forests. There they learned from the trees, beasts, birds, colours, sun. They became hirsute, but to make up for that they had preserved warm, red blood under their hirsuteness.' I approach the full introsorbation of the text. With regret I shall have to move on to the Zamyenkins and the Zamyudovskys, relentlessly pursuing the triumphant Goal: letting our words fly to foreign lands, where we ourselves will never go. For if we leave, they will kill us, there is no doubt of that. We shut them out, for the greater happiness of the smallest number. If only they could understand the astronomical necessity factor of doing what we did; but they cannot, of course, they have no perspective. The international currency markets have passed them by and they have no respect for global multimedia networks. Their values are different to ours, we could not live with each other, so we opted for separate development.

The worst season for them is winter, of course, when they huddle together in derailed trams, dragged hundreds of miles across the ice to the edges of lakes and rivers so that they can have some shelter while they sink their hooks and pray that a meal will bite. They live in tribes, and fight bitterly amongst themselves, just as they always did, ethnic origin being the only criterion for judging friend or foe. The Muslims are the luckiest, welcomed with open arms by Azerbaijan, Turkey and Iran, and some of the Jews make their way to Israel, but the Slavs, as ever, are unwanted. Sometimes the nightmare visions that cross our screens are so depressing that the ViP blanks them out with a classic favourite, *Forrest Gump* or *It's a Wonderful Life*, or a tranquil rainbow montage to soothe us in these longest hours.

Glancing at my holographic time auditor, it has been indicated to me that my daily workspan is at an end and I must vacate my operational unit so that it can be occupied by a night controller. What an array of choices presents itself to me on my digital activitycard to fill my leisurespace this evening. This week's virtual reality travelmenu offers Chicago, Birmingham, the Costa del Sol and the moons of Jupiter, but I am saving my travel credits for a three-day trip to 19th-century St Petersburg with my virtual lover.

I am a romantic by nature, you see, and the work I did photo-inputting Gogol moved me deeply, bringing back memories of my mother's bedtime stories about her life in the city of White Nights. I would be Outside myself if she and my father had not moved to Moscow in 1990 when he was appointed director of a television factory, so that she gave birth to me not on the banks of the Neva but within sight of the Bolshoi Theatre seven years later. The shields bisected the suburbs, of course - physics would not permit the diameter of the base to be longer than two kilometres - so Inner residence rights were available primarily to people who lived in the centre, although those Outside with salaries of more than $5000 per month were easily accommodated, and certain persistent law infringers and insolvents were removed.

No, I shall not strap myself in to my virtuasuit tonight, not even for the exhilaration of the Mineralniye Vodi Helicopter Chase, nor for the Infection-Free Sexual Experience of a Lifetime with my personally configured Dream Lover. I am in a more contemplative mood just now and feel a need for some old-fashioned actual human interaction. I shall take the monorail to Ulitsa Proktorend Gamblskaya, where the historic Irish House still stands, and the bar still serves that burning liquid which has sustained generation after generation of Russians, through war and revolution, and war, and war, and revolution, and which I depend on as much as my ancestors toiling in the fields for Ivan the Terrible did.

There'll be real laughing there, and real singing, and real crying, because that's what the magic spirit does to you, brings it all out. They serve the Absolut in bottles there, not radiation-proof plastipacks. I'll take one, look out for my circle of non-hostile co-communicators (friends, we used to call them), pour them each a drink and propose a toast to the motherland, to all who live here, Inside or Outside, and to peace and harmony the world over. It only takes a few of those, and then I reach blissful oblivion...

NEW RUSSIAN WRITING

*He suddenly realized what it was that had been nagging him about
the fighter he had captured. The boy was very beautiful.*
A Russian soldier falls in love with his Chechen captive. Will beauty
save the world as Dostoevsky promised? Russian Booker Prize
winner Vladimir Makanin blasts this latest inhumanity of war.
Also stories by Victor Pelevin, Vasily Aksyonov, and Zinovy Zinik,
and an excerpt from Georgy Vladimov's Booker winner
A General and His Army,

ISBN 5-7172-0027-7   £8.99

"Glas **has become almost disturbingly indispensable. The texts
and voices out of Russia come through with formidable insistence.***"*
George Steiner

Obtainable from good bookshops and from Glas, Dept of Russian
Literature, University of Birmingham, B15 2TT. UK. Cheques
payable to "Birmingham University". Add £1.50 for handling.
Tel and fax 0121 414 6047. Email a.l.tait@bham.ac.uk.
World wide web: http://www.bham.ac.uk/russian/glascover

Funded by
THE
**ARTS
COUNCIL**
OF ENGLAND